CONGRESSMEN IN COMMITTEES

RICHARD F. FENNO, JR.
The University of Rochester

LITTLE, BROWN AND COMPANY · BOSTON

CONGRESSMEN IN COMMITTEES

The
Study of
Congress
Series

Foreword

The Study of Congress is sponsored by the American Political Science Association with the support of a generous grant from the Carnegie Corporation. The project was first conceived by a small group of scholars and congressmen (the latter led by Chet Holifield, D-Calif., and Thomas B. Curtis, R-Mo.) who held a series of discussion meetings on Congress with financial aid from the Philip Stern Family Fund. These discussions led to an agreement to seek support for a comprehensive study of Congress. A formal proposal was prepared by Evron M. Kirkpatrick, Executive Director of the American Political Science Association, and Donald G. Tacheron, Associate Director, which resulted in the grant by the Carnegie Corporation.

The Study of Congress gave political scientists an opportunity to cover ground in one concerted thrust which they might individually inch over in a decade. Such an opportunity was unprecedented, and it increased the urgency and importance of the basic questions: What should be the target of the study? Who should do it? How should it be done?

Reform of Congress is always in the air. Congress is criticized, even by its own members, because, as a representative body, it mirrors the weaknesses as well as the strengths of the represented. Moreover, it is powerful; almost alone among the national legislatures, it has withstood domination by the Executive and has remained the coordinate branch the Founding Fathers meant it to be. What Congress does matters very much, here and abroad, and for that reason one is tempted to try to change it, to alter some procedure or structural arrangement in order to increase one's influence on the legislative product.

Nevertheless, reform is not the target of this research project. Congress does change, but slowly, adaptively in things that matter, and seldom according to blueprint. Structure and procedure are not neutral; they are used to work the will of those who control them. Moreover, alterations in them often have unforeseen consequences. This is more likely to be true when structure and rules, and to whose benefit they work, are imperfectly understood. The Study of Congress began, therefore, with a modest admission and an appropriate resolution: there are large gaps in what political scientists know about Congress and the Study would try to fill in as many as it could.

Each of the studies which make up the Study of Congress has been undertaken by a scholar already deeply immersed in the subject. The research in each case promises to produce a book, a monograph, or one or more scholarly articles. Each man is free to recommend changes in the organization and procedures of Congress, but there will be no "official" list of recommendations by the Study of Congress itself. The purpose of the Study is to produce original research studies of Congress. Like other research enterprises, the usefulness of this one will be determined by the people who use it.

The Study of Congress Series presents associated studies designed to tell interested people as much as possible about how Congress works. It provides analytical descriptions of Congress, its subsystems, and its relations with its environment. The series fills in research blanks and suggests relevant variables for future research. It provides some basis for stating the functions performed by Congress for the political system, evaluating the performance, and pointing out alternative structural arrangements and modes of action which realistically seem to be open to Congress. Until these tasks are completed, our lists of congressional reforms are little more than statements of personal preference.

In this sixth volume of the series, Richard F. Fenno, Jr., builds upon his own pioneering study of the appropriations process, *The Power of the Purse* (1966), John F. Manley's companion volume in this series, *The Politics of Finance* (1970), and other committee-centered literature. The end product is a major breakthrough in this stream of research, the first truly *comparative* analysis of how congressional committees make decisions.

Fenno begins with the deceptively simple assumption "that congressional committees matter" and develops a basic theme as to how congressional committees differ. Similarities and differences are examined with respect to five variables — "member goals, environmental constraints, strategic premises, decision-making processes, and decisions." The author applies his carefully developed and clearly articulated analytical framework to six sets of committees — the House Committees on Appropriations, Education and Labor, Foreign Affairs, Interior and Insular Affairs, Post Office and Civil Service, Ways and Means, and their six Senate counterparts. The principal time frame of the study is twelve years, the 84th through the 89th Congresses. Fenno also attempts a "pre-test" of the viability of the theory in an epilogue which highlights events in Congress from 1967 to 1972.

Whether one wishes to understand change, engineer it, or both, Fenno succeeds in his quest for a framework for differentiating among committees and the ways in which they operate in the two houses. In the current climate for congressional reform, inclined to be global and prescriptive in tone, his arguments for a selective reform strategy are highly persuasive.

Ralph K. Huitt
Robert L. Peabody

Acknowledgments

My largest debt is to John Manley, who did a great deal of the interviewing for this study, and on whom I have leaned as research assistant, critic, and friend throughout. He generously granted me unrestricted access to and use of his own 1964–65 series of interviews on the Ways and Means Committee. All the quotations from Ways and Means Committee members are taken from these interviews or from his excellent book, *The Politics of Finance;* but with his permission, I have not footnoted them individually.

For their research assistance, I should also like to thank James Murphy, Steven Maser, Dennis Parazino, Bennett Steinhauer, Mark Stern, and Lisa Walker. And for their helpful comments at various stages of the manuscript, I am grateful to Peter Aranson, Gerald Cullinan, Morris Fiorina, John Kessel, Nelson Polsby, H. Douglas Price, Steven Rhoads, David Rohde, Robert Samberg, and Lisa Walker. I am grateful to Janice Brown for her cheerful, professional typing of the manuscript. Finally, for their special kinds of encouragement and support, I thank Ralph Huitt and William Riker.

Table of Contents

ix

List of Tables and Figures

Introduction

This book rests on a simple assumption and conveys a simple theme. The assumption is that congressional committees matter. The theme is that congressional committees differ. Both are commonplace. But the book has been written because those who think committees matter and those who think committees differ have not yet fully accommodated one to the other — not intellectually and not in practice.

Generalizations about congressional committees are numerous and familiar. The oldest and most familiar is Woodrow Wilson's book-length assertion that committees dominate congressional decision making. A corollary states that committees are autonomous units, which operate quite independently of such external influences as legislative party leaders, chamber majorities, and the President of the United States. Other staples of committee commentary hold: that members specialize in their committee's subject matter, and hence that each committee is the repository of legislative expertise within its jurisdiction; that committee decisions are usually accepted and ratified by the other members of the chamber; that committee chairmen can (and usually do) wield a great deal of influence over their committees. A broader generalization holds that Congress, and by extension its committees, is gradually losing policy-making influence to the executive branch.

Most of our empirical generalizations are of the same order. Each one is uttered as if it were equally applicable to all committees. And taken together, they convey the message that committees are similar. Our recent studies of individual committees have taught us, to the contrary, however, that committees are markedly different from one another. Indeed, as we shall show, committees differ in all the respects previously mentioned — their influence in congressional decision making, their autonomy, their success on the chamber floor, their expertise, the control exercised by their chairmen, and their domination by the executive branch. If such is — even partially — the case, the need for a new set of generalizations is obvious. One immediate temptation, of course, is to scrap all our familiar generalizations in favor of a single statement asserting the uniqueness of each committee. But that is a counsel of despair; political scientists ought not to eschew the possibility of making limited comparisons before they have tried. This book should be read as one such effort — to describe and generalize about committee similarities and differences at a level somewhere between that which assumes committee uniformity and that which assumes committee uniqueness.

The need for a middle range of generalizations is not purely academic. Reform-minded members of Congress and citizen groups have also viewed committee operations from the perspectives of uniformity and/or uniqueness, and they have been as ill served by this outlook as the scholar. Every congressman knows that committees are dissimilar. Assertions to that effect are hard currency on Capitol Hill. "Committee behavior all depends on the chairman and every chairman, of course, is different." Or, "Committee behavior all depends on the subject matter and every committee, of course, handles a different policy area." Why, then, when they prescribe committee reform, do congressmen abandon their own wisdom and insist on applying every reform in equal dosages to every committee? The answer may be partly intellectual in nature — that they cannot conceive of committee similarities and differences in such a way as to formulate a mixed strategy of reform. It is as if the practitioner were waiting for the student to equip him with a middle range of categories in which to think and make his prescriptions. Thus, the political scientist's search for explanation may be related to the reformer's search for change.

Our theme is, then, that committees differ from one another. And, we shall argue, they differ systematically. We shall examine their similarities and differences with respect to five variables — *member goals, environmental constraints, strategic premises, decision-making processes,* and *decisions.* We shall pursue the following line of argument. The members of each congressional committee have certain

Figure 1
Analytic Scheme for Comparing Committees

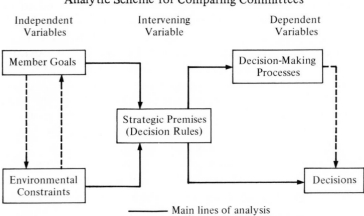

Independent   Intervening   Dependent
Variables   Variable   Variables

——— Main lines of analysis
- - - - Secondary lines of analysis

goals that they want to achieve through membership on a committee. If there is a high level of consensus on goals, they will organize
their committee internally in ways that seem likely to aid them in
achieving these individual goals. However, each committee operates
within a distinctive set of environmental constraints — most particularly the expectations of influential external groups. Committee
members will, therefore, also organize their committee internally in
ways that seem likely to satisfy the expectations of these groups that
make up their environment. The members of each committee will
develop strategies for accommodating the achievement of their individual goals to the satisfaction of key environmental expectations.
These strategies become the proximate premises on which each committee's internal decision-making processes are based. From these
strategies, operationalized as decision rules, flow committee decisions.
In our explanatory scheme, then, member goals and environmental
constraints are the independent variables; strategic premises (or, decision rules) are an intervening variable; and decision-making processes and decisions are dependent variables.

We shall use this scheme to analyze six committees of the House
of Representatives as they functioned in the period from 1955 to
1966, from the 84th through the 89th Congresses. They are the

Committees on Appropriations, Education and Labor, Foreign Affairs, Interior and Insular Affairs (hereafter referred to as the Interior Committee), Post Office and Civil Service (hereafter referred to as the Post Office Committee), and Ways and Means. We shall consider, a good deal more briefly, their Senate counterparts, i.e., the Committees on Appropriations, Finance, Foreign Relations, Interior and Insular Affairs, Labor and Public Welfare, and Post Office and Civil Service. Both houses of Congress and, hence, all committees were controlled by Democratic majorities throughout the period. No claim is made for the representativeness of the time span or the sample. But we would argue that in both respects our data are sufficient to support an initial foray into comparative analysis.

For the most part, this book is a description of committee activity based upon what committee members and interested outsiders say it is like. I have not, save for an occasional glimpse, been able to observe these committees in action. Hence, the heavy reliance on interviews. Throughout the book, I have included noninterview data to confirm or modify the descriptions derived from the interviews. I have also relied, as later footnotes will amply indicate, on previous studies of these and other committees. But the interviews have provided the leading edge of the description. Therefore, it is of particular interest to note briefly how, when, and with whom the interviews were held.

All were semistructured interviews, the contents of which were reproduced immediately following the interview. The interviewing was done by the author and by John Manley. Appendix A displays the number and type of individuals interviewed on a year-by-year basis for the six House and six Senate committees. Interviewing proceeded, as Appendix A indicates, from 1959 to 1968. The broadest interviewing occurred, however, in 1965, toward the end of the period we have formally designated for this study. All interviews are, to some degree, time-bound. And the reader should remain sensitive to the problem of generalizing from such interviews to a twelve-year period. We have tried to minimize the problem by encouraging interviewees to differentiate between past and present, by utilizing noninterview data that can be surveyed over time, and by taking care to distinguish subperiods when the importance of doing so is readily apparent. We think the book does present a fairly accurate picture of the six committees in the period 1955–1966. But the reader should be aware that we did not interview throughout this period. Consequently, it is probably more accurate for 1966 than for 1955. In the concluding section, we shall return to this problem, as we take a brief look at our committees in the period 1967–1972.[1]

[1] Readers of the literature on committees may wonder why this study does not utilize the same conceptualization as the author's earlier study of the two Appropriations committees. Since my aims are primarily descriptive and secondarily explanatory, I have used, in both studies, those ideas that seemed most appropriate to the phenomenon I was trying to describe. What struck me most forcefully in observing the House Appropriations Committee was the degree to which it was a self-contained social system. And, seeking to describe it, I turned to the literature created by people studying social systems. The functionalist literature helped identify focal points for analysis, i.e., adaptation, integration; the literature on roles helped in analyzing the committee's elaborate internal structure; and the literature on political systems oriented me toward an "input-internal structure-output" view of the committee. I hope that that conceptualization has helped people to understand the two Appropriations Committees. Having observed six committees, however, I find the conceptualization of the social-systems literature less appealing as a framework for description. All committees are not pre-eminently social systems. All committees do not have an easily differentiable set of roles. In both respects, Appropriations lies at one end of a spectrum — or so it now appears. And finally, the clumsy idea of "withinputs" used by the political-system theorists hardly conveys the magnitude of the contribution which the individual members of a "system" make to its "internal structure" and to its "output." In comparative perspective, the member contribution seems both large and distinctive. The point comes through very strongly in my interviews; and I have made goal seeking by the members a keystone of this analysis. The resulting conceptual framework is, therefore, somewhat more individualistic than the previous one. But both are similar in their concentration on the expectations and perceptions of the participants and in their effort to view the world from the perspectives of the participants themselves. This explains why — despite the fact that one will not find "adaptation" or "integration" or "roles" mentioned in the book — my earlier description of the two Appropriations Committees can easily be accommodated within this framework.

CHAPTER ONE

Member Goals

A member of the House is a congressman first and a committee member second. As a congressman he holds certain personal political goals. As a committee member he will work to further these same goals through committee activity. Committee membership, in other words, is not an end in itself for the individuals. Each member of each committee wants his committee service to bring him some benefit in terms of goals he holds as an individual congressman. And he will act on his committee in ways calculated to achieve such goals. We think it useful to begin our comparative analysis of committees here, by asking each member of each committee what it is he wants committee activity to do for him as a congressman.

Of all the goals espoused by members of the House, three are basic. They are: *re-election, influence within the House, and good public policy.* There are others. A fourth one, *a career beyond the House,* will be treated peripherally. (A fifth one, *private gain,* will not be treated at all.) The first three are the most widely held and the most consequential for committee activity. All congressmen probably hold all three goals. But each congressman has his own mix of priorities and intensities — a mix which may, of course, change over time. If every House committee provided an equal opportunity to pursue re-election, influence, and policy, congressmen holding various mixes would appear randomly distributed across all committees. Such is definitely not the case. The opportunity to achieve the three goals varies widely among committees. House members, therefore, match their individual patterns of aspiration to the diverse patterns of opportunity presented by House committees. The matching process usually takes place as a congressman seeks an original assignment or a transfer to a committee he believes well suited to his goals. But it may occur when a congressman adjusts his personal aspirations, temporarily or permanently, to fit the opportunities offered by the committee where he happens to be. By a combination of processes, then, House committees come to be characterized, at any point in time, by distinctive, nonrandom distributions of individual member goals.

We asked the members of our six committees: "Why did you want to get on the —————————— committee in the first place?" And our description of member goals resulted primarily from their answers. Our willingness to rely on their responses was strengthened by knowing that in 81 per cent (145 out of 179) of the cases, the members interviewed had deliberately sought and actively worked for assignments to the committees on which they sat.[1] Presumably the chosen committees held some positive attraction for them. Presumably, too, they knew what they wanted for themselves from their memberships. Insofar as the decision to join a specific group is conscious, voluntary, and motivated, the goals of individual members become crucial for explaining the group's behavior.[2]

APPROPRIATIONS AND WAYS AND MEANS

Members of the *Appropriations* and *Ways and Means* Committees voiced strikingly similar personal goals. When asked why they sought membership on these two committees, an overwhelming majority replied that they sought "power," "prestige," or "importance." And in overwhelming numbers they viewed one or the other committee as "the most powerful," "the one with the most prestige," or "the most important" in the House. They used these words almost interchangeably to connote that the two committees exercise the purse power so vital to the House as an institution, that the members of the two committees possess special capacities to affect the political fortunes of their House colleagues, and that, consequently, assignment to the two committees is highly prized by House members. We, too, connote all this when we say that these men wanted to become influential men in the House by becoming members of the committees they perceived to be most influential. This desire *to have more influence*

---

[1] For the breakdown by committee, see Table 2.4.

[2] Some respondents may, of course, have confused the present attractiveness of their committees with the initial attraction. But there was no apparent difference in the responses (to this question) of members just appointed to committees and members with long seniority.

inside the House than other Congressmen is the distinctive, dominant goal of Appropriations and Ways and Means members.

Two newcomers, the first to Ways and Means and the second to
Appropriations — both after six years of prior House service — discussed their goals in these terms:

> Ways and Means is powerful around here because it's inter-
> preted as being powerful. Power is interpretation around
> here; it's all interpretation. . . . The only way I can describe
> what I want to be is power. I don't know what I'd do with it
> when I got it, but I want to have it where I can reach out
> and use it when I want to.

> I thought the power would be important. Like Kennedy said
> about the Presidency — "That's where the power is." . . .
> The process here is one where consent must be obtained be-
> fore anything gets done. If you are one of those from whom
> consent must be obtained, then you are a more important
> person in the House. When you are on the Appropriations
> Committee you are that kind of person. That's all. It's a
> question of power.

Similar sentiments, viewing influence as reputation and/or as a larger-
than-average share in House decision making, were expressed by
75 to 80 percent of the members of both Committees.

The primary source of their influence lies in their dual control
over "the money power" of the House of Representatives. A veteran
Republican, speaking for a majority of his Appropriations colleagues,
declared: "The Appropriations Committee is the most powerful
committee in the House. It's the most powerful committee in the
Congress. This is where all the money starts rolling." As far as inside
influence is concerned, a position on the purse-string committee guar-
antees you the ear and deference of your fellow congressmen. Another Appropriations man said: "They are very polite to us. They've
all got projects in over here and they know what we can do to them."
Ways and Means members talk similarly — with extra emphasis being
given by Democrats to their Committee on Committees function.
As one said: "It's the top committee in the House of Representatives. The entire revenue system is locked into the Committee. . . .
And if that isn't enough, there's the added power of appointing
other members to committees." Committee Democrats relish their
special source of internal influence. "They call you 'Mr.' and 'Sir'

when you are on the Committee on Committees. . . . We are leaders." But Republican aspirants do not see the Committee as any less
advantageous to them because they do not make committee assignments. "I think we have almost 25 people interested in it," said one
veteran Republican member, referring to the single Republican vacancy in 1964. And he explained, "Boy, it's because of this power.
Every year, year in and year out, it's the most powerful committee."
Subject matter — taxes, trade, social security — would seem to be a
sufficient source of influence on both sides of the aisle.

Without question, the subject matter of the two committees has
its own independent appeal. But only a handful of members — one
or two on Appropriations and two or three on Ways and Means —
gave topmost priority to the pursuit of policy goals when they sought
membership. All of them were conservative Republicans, whose desire
to balance the budget, hold down expenditures, limit taxes, or preserve free enterprise impelled them toward the committees best positioned to help them achieve such goals. This is not to say that the
other members of these committees do not hold or will not fight for
certain policy preferences. They do and they will — especially on
Ways and Means. The point is, however, that their main goal as
committee members, does not concern policy. If the men presently
on the Appropriations and Ways and Means Committees believed
that the District of Columbia Committee was the most powerful
committee in the House, they would seek membership on it. These
congressmen are attracted, in other words, more by the putative
"importance" of their subject matter than by its content.

In addition, members of the two committees are concerned about
serving their constituents and winning re-election. But, here again,
the goal of re-election gets subordinated to the goal of power in
the House. The vast majority of Appropriations and Ways and
Means members hold relatively safe seats. And they can nurse their
ambitions inside the House partly because they have to expend less
energy than some other congressmen on insuring their re-election. A
few members, however — one or two on Ways and Means and three
or four on Appropriations — did seek membership primarily for the
goals of serving their constituencies and getting re-elected. The attraction is stronger on Appropriations, since nearly everything going
to a district funnels through that Committee. Most Appropriations
members believe that there is no better committee from which
to "do more for the people back home"; they surely do not feel as

though they are sacrificing their ambitions for re-election by serving on the Committee. Ways and Means members, on the other hand, are likely to express the feeling that they could serve their constituents better on other committees — frequently on the committees from which they transferred. And, as Manley concludes, "the overwhelming response of those who were asked if the Committee helps them get re-elected was that the Committee is of little value in their districts." [3]

To sum up, the vast majority of Appropriations and Ways and Means Committee members come to these committees seeking influence in the House. Though dwarfed, in both committees, by the emphasis on House influence, a secondary concern for furthering their policy and their re-election is displayed. Here, priorities differ. Ways and Means members emphasize policy more than re-election. Appropriations members give second priority to re-election and least concern to policy.

INTERIOR AND POST OFFICE

Congressmen who ask for membership on the *Interior* and *Post Office* Committees have the primary goal of *helping their constituents and thereby insuring their re-election*. In place of talk about "power," "prestige," and "importance," one hears almost exclusively about "district interests" to be served, "projects" to be authorized, and "political help" to be gained. The close correspondence between the Interior Committee's jurisdiction and the most pressing constituency problems of Western congressmen make the Committee uniquely attractive to them. A Westerner can serve such a high proportion of his district's special interests from this one committee that he may be hard put to think of reasons why he should *not* seek membership on it, at least until his tenure is secure. The Post Office Committee has no such imperative attraction for any group of members. But some congressmen find their constituency includes a sufficient number of civil servants (especially the politically active postal employees) to make it useful to give them special attention. Most members of Post Office serve on another committee as well, so that any political dividends accruing from helping employee interests represent a welcome increment to their re-election capital.

[3] John Manley, *The Politics of Finance* (Boston: Little, Brown, 1970), p. 82.

When Interior members voice their personal goals, they leave no doubt about what led them to the Committee. Two Far Western Representatives explained:

> I was attracted to it, very frankly, because it's a bread and butter committee for my state. I guess about the only thing about it that is not of great interest to my state is insular affairs. I was able to get two or three bills of great importance to my state through last year. I had vested interests I wanted to protect, to be frank.

> You take a look at the problems of Interior and you have a list of the problems of my district: Indians, water, mines, parks. I have to stay on at least until I get that water bill through.

Such comments could be multiplied endlessly — from committee members from other regions and from both sides of the aisle. Thus a southeastern Democrat emphasized his interest in Great Smoky Mountains National Park, the Cherokee Indians, and the Blue Ridge Highway. And a northeastern Republican exclaimed, "The biggest industry in my state is mining, so Interior is perfect."

Congressmen who sought membership on the Post Office Committee did so, too, for reasons of constituencies and re-election. A small-state Democrat and a suburban Republican explained:

> We have over 10,000 civil service and postal employees in my state. While we are here first and foremost to represent the national interest, and while I'm a firm believer in that, nevertheless you have to look out for the interests of your people. . . . Politics is a great way to promote your ideals, but first you have to help your constituents.

> Post Office was entirely a defense mechanism for me. I have a growing suburban area with a need for increased postal facilities. When the Kennedy Administration came in, I felt I would be shafted, so I picked up and left my old committee. . . . By being on the Committee, I thought I'd increase my leverage.

Here, also, as with Interior members, the constituency interests of Post Office members are the same for Democrats as they are for Republicans.

For a member of either committee, the making of good public policy is a distinctly secondary consideration. He first asks himself what his constituents want or what actions on behalf of his constituents will help to re-elect him. He then pursues the policies dictated by the answers to his question — by seeking membership on the relevant committee. Whereas the member of Appropriations or Ways and Means wants membership on any committee whose subject matter will bring him power in the House, the member of Interior or Post Office wants membership on any committee that will enable him to help his constituents and further his re-election. The subordinate place of policy in the hierarchy of goals is the same for the members of all four groups.

One member of Interior included among his reasons for going on that committee a desire to prevent the admission of Hawaii and Alaska to the Union. But he was the only one to voice a policy goal that was not, first of all, a re-election goal. Though the Committee sometimes becomes seized by the controversy over public power versus private power, not one Committee member (of those interviewed) said he sought membership because of an interest in this policy problem. Conservation policy may, in the future, draw some ardent preservationists to the Committee; but such was not the case in the period we studied.[4] The same can be said for the Post Office Committee. It is conceivable that a House member might have an interest in government-employee problems or in the postal service, such that he would seek membership because of the subject matter. But no such instances were discovered in the interviewing. Certainly, the members of these two committees have ideas about desirable public policy that they want to promote in Congress. The point is, simply, that they have other reasons for joining the Interior and Post Office Committees and will pursue other goals more strongly as committee members.

Similarly, these men may want influence in the House. But they are not attracted to Interior or Post Office for that reason. Neither they nor anyone else in the House perceives these two committees as providing a source of power and prestige inside the House. Members of Interior and Post Office who cherish influence in the chamber will ordinarily seek it by transferring to committees like Ways and Means and Appropriations — as twenty-seven of them actually did in the 1947–1967 period.[5] A minority of Interior members prob-

[4] See Epilogue.
[5] See Table 2.2.

ably do, however, have *career ambitions beyond the House*. More members — thirteen — left Interior to run for the Senate than left any of the six committees for that purpose from 1947 to 1967.[6] Coming as they do from the less populous states, many Far Western congressmen have constituencies that cover a large portion, if not all of the state. The ease with which they can cultivate the senatorial constituency makes them the natural challengers to incumbent Senators and the logical successors of retiring ones. Eleven of the thirteen who pursued this "progressive ambition" were from the Far West.[7]

Membership on Interior or Post Office can bring power and prestige to a few members, those who remain long enough to reap the rewards of seniority. And the time it takes to gain committee seniority varies directly with the prestige of the committee. Here is one of the ways in which continued membership on a committee can alter an individual's pattern of personal goals. An Eastern Democrat explained:

> I was elected in a special election. They didn't know what to do with me so they put me on the first one with a vacancy — Interior. I was a little horror-stricken at first. I mean, my God, Interior had nothing to do with my district. I have no irrigation, reclamation, mines or parks. But they just put me on it because there was no place else. But then I started thinking it over. I looked around and saw everyone was leaving and that this might be a good place to stay and move up. And I was right. Within two and a half years I was a subcommittee chairman and in six years I was ranking majority member . . . I'm glad I stayed. (Later) I had a chance to go on Appropriations but I wouldn't take it.

A few members of the Post Office Committee also found that seniority brought enough influence in the chamber to inhibit desire for further movement.

But the difference between the two pairs of committees remains. Whereas a few members of Interior and Post Office may, *in time,* give top priority to the goal of "inside power," all members of Ways

---

[6] The figures from 1947 to 1967 are: Interior, thirteen; Foreign Affairs, eleven; Appropriations, nine; Ways and Means, eight; Education and Labor, six; Post Office, zero. See Table 6.5.

[7] The concept is that of Joseph Schlesinger, *Ambition and Politics* (Chicago: Rand McNally, 1966), p. 10.

and Means and Appropriations emphasize "inside power" from the moment they arrive on these committees. For Interior and Post Office members the distinctive, dominant personal goal is re-election through constituency service.

EDUCATION AND LABOR AND FOREIGN AFFAIRS

Members of the *Education and Labor* and *Foreign Affairs* Committees express a set of individual goals different from any thus far discussed. They emphasize a strong personal interest in and a concern for the content of public policy in their committee's subject matter; in short, they want *to help make good public policy.* Congressmen who seek membership on these two committees do so, they say, because these committees deal with "interesting," "exciting," "controversial," and "important" subjects. A large proportion of the most controversial items in the President's program come to Education and Labor, they say. And Foreign Affairs, obviously, deals with matters of national and international significance. Some members on each committee see membership as positively helpful to them in their districts; more view membership as having either no effect (mostly Foreign Affairs) or an adverse effect (mostly Education and Labor) on their re-election. And none cites influence in the House as a relevant reason for seeking membership.

Corroborative evidence for this somewhat unexpected affinity comes from the pattern of committee-assignment requests among freshman Democrats in the 86th, 87th, 88th, and 90th Congresses. These records show a marked overlap of members attracted to the two committees. Congressmen, in other words, who seek assignment to Foreign Affairs also tend to seek assignment to Education and Labor and vice versa. As Table 1.1 shows, the committee demonstrating the greatest overlap with both committees was Banking and Currency — a committee which, according to our impressions, shares many characteristics with Education and Labor.[8] From our interview materials we find additional, unsystematic evidence for the proposition that this affinity also exists among Republicans. Eight of the fifteen Republican members of Education and Labor interviewed

---

[8] An excellent confirming treatment of Banking and Currency is Bruce F. Norton, *The Committee on Banking and Currency as a Legislative Subsystem of the House of Representatives* (Syracuse University, 1970), unpublished manuscript.

Table 1.1

Other Committee-Assignment Requests of Freshman Democrats
Requesting Foreign Affairs or Education and Labor:
86th, 88th, 90th Congresses[9]

Other Committees Requested	By Those Requesting Foreign Affairs	By Those Requesting Education and Labor
Education and Labor	9	–
Foreign Affairs	–	9
Banking and Currency	7	7
Judiciary	7	3
Interstate and Foreign Commerce	6	6
Public Works	4	6
Armed Services	4	3
All others	three or less	three or less

volunteered that both committees were among their committee preferences.[10] There are, it appears, some Congressmen who want to serve on whatever committees happen to be dealing with the most pressing, controversial, national problems of the time. They want to be "where the action is." In the 1950's and 1960's, Foreign Affairs and Education and Labor were two such committees.

Education and Labor members emphasize their subject-matter interest, their desire to make policy, and their commitment to certain broad policy orientations. In the language of a liberal freshman Democrat:

> I'm the most issue-oriented guy you'd ever want to meet. I know there won't be a Wagner Act with my name on it during my first term. But if I can get a few of my ideas in I'll be satisfied. Legislating in Washington, for the district and in the public interest. That's what interests me the most. Serving your constituency — that's a noble effort, too. But, frankly, I consider any time spent in Washington with a constituent as time wasted that I could have spent doing more important things.

[9] The data were gathered from the working documents of the Ways and Means Committee by John Manley and Robert Salisbury. Some of the calculations were done by David Rohde.

[10] Two had given up Education and Labor to go on Foreign Affairs; one had dual membership on the two committees; one wanted to add Foreign Affairs as his second committee; three had originally wanted Foreign Affairs but settled for Education and Labor as a lesser preference; and one had tried but failed to leave Education and Labor for Foreign Affairs.

A conservative freshman Republican explained his choice thus:

> I've had some experience in both fields. My first position in
> politics was as a member of the city school board. And I own
> a business; so I understand the management point of view.
> I'm the kind of person who jumps right into these hot spots.
> So I figured if this was the most controversial committee in
> the House, I'd like to get on it. And I thought the manage-
> ment point of view would be good for the Committee.

Many of those seeking membership punctuate their statements of
policy aspirations with statements about their precongressional involvement in the two fields. A number of them served on similar
committees in their state legislatures; several are former school teachers; a few have practiced labor law.

Foreign Affairs members voice a similar combination of personal
interest, prior experience, and policy commitment in explaining their
attraction, albeit with a somewhat different emphasis. Interest in an
important policy area is the dominant theme. "I had an interest in
world problems and wanted to make some contribution. Subject
matter — there wasn't anything more to it than that." "I think foreign policy is the most important problem there is. So why fool
around with anything less?" Previous experience is a corollary theme.
But the substance of that experience (study and travel) is far more
remote from actual policy content than is the work experience of
Education and Labor members.

> There were two things. One, my interest in it. Secondly, I
> felt my background experience qualified me for it more than
> some others. After college, I spent a year in England, trav-
> elled around Europe and Africa.

> I had an interest in foreign affairs even before coming to
> Congress. I majored in Political Science and took a lot of
> foreign governments, diplomatic maneuvers, that sort of
> thing.

Policy commitments from Foreign Affairs members, accordingly, remain more amorphous than those from members of Education and
Labor. Still, there are some clear ones, such as: "I've always been
something of a one-worlder, strengthen the U.N., that sort of thing."
"I always thought we should have more men on that Committee
who oppose foreign aid." Interest in policy is equally strong on both
committees, but Foreign Affairs members are less specific about the

ingredients of good public policy than are their colleagues on Education and Labor.

An Interior Committee congressman captured the contrast between his committee's appeal and that of the two committees more concerned with policy. He said: "I would have liked Foreign Affairs or Education and Labor because they deal with such exciting topics. But . . . water is the lifeblood of my district; to do my district some good, I knew I had to get on Interior." On neither Foreign Affairs nor Education and Labor is reelection through constituency service the major attraction. Northern urban Democrats on Education and Labor are the only people on either committee to give reelection goals top priority. And only three of the fifteen interviewed did so. One said, "I had 30,000 members of the United Mine Workers in my district and I wanted to help them all I can — knowing that this would help me get re-elected." Until very recently, service on the Committee has been thought to be positively harmful to the re-election chances of Republican congressmen; freshman Republicans were admonished throughout the period under discussion not to apply.

In no case did a Foreign Affairs member of either party give top priority to constituency-related goals. Majority opinion was expressed by one member who said: "Politically, it's not a good committee for me. My constituents are interested in bread and butter, and there's no bread and butter on Foreign Affairs." An urban Democrat recalled:

> The first few weeks I was here I would go home on the weekend to see constituents. One night, there must have been 45 people waiting to see me, this big ward leader came in, big fat guy, a head taller than me. He said, "What's the big idea keeping me waiting?" I tried to explain to him that, gee whiz, we had a committee meeting. Berlin was falling apart, the Secretary of State was briefing the Committee on Berlin, and I didn't feel that I, as a new member, should be rude to him by walking out. I said, "John Foster Dulles appeared before the committee, the meeting went a little overtime, and I missed the plane." He said, "John Foster Dulles. Hell, he wasn't even with us last time out!" There's no relation between your committee work and back home.

A few members see some home-front advantages to be gained by pushing pro-Israeli or anti-Communist amendments on the foreign aid bill or merely by associating with the Secretary of State. But the theme is a minor one.

The goal of influence in the House is even more minor. Not one member of either committee used the word "influential" or "powerful" to describe his committee. While they frequently used the word "important," the significant thing is that they used it only to describe the subject matter and not the committee. Aspirants to Ways and Means and Appropriations want to be on powerful committees, not merely "interesting" or "exciting" committees. Two or three Foreign Affairs members did see "prestige" associated with membership, probably because a place on the Committee is moderately difficult to obtain. But this "prestige" does not translate into internal influence in the manner of Appropriations or Ways and Means. If the prestige of Foreign Affairs furthers any member's goal, it is more likely to be the one involving *a career beyond the House*. The Committee provides an obvious platform where members can talk knowingly about matters of war and peace, thus increasing their visibility, acquiring statesmanlike reputations, and enlarging their geopolitical boundaries. From 1947 to 1967, eleven members left Foreign Affairs to run for the Senate — a number second only to the Interior Committee among the six committees. Even so their "progressive ambition" is a secondary goal. The distinctive, dominant member goal on Education and Labor and Foreign Affairs is to help make good policy in an area of substantial personal interest.

We have begun our committee analysis by trying to find out what the individual members of each committee want for themselves from their present committee service. And we have found three quite different patterns, each of which gives special prominence to one of the three basic goals of House members. Furthermore, we found a remarkable consensus on goals among each committee's membership, a discovery that has persuaded us to ground our analysis here. Moreover, each of the three goals (and this was more fortuitous than planned) is the consensual one for two of our six committees. Appropriations and Ways and Means are populated mostly by influence-oriented members; Interior and Post Office are populated mostly by re-election-oriented members; Education and Labor and Foreign Affairs are populated mostly by policy-oriented members. Such modal characterizations are admittedly oversimplifica-tions. But they do have sufficient validity to serve as a basis for predicting gross similarities and differences in committee behavior. Assuming that members will work in committee to achieve their stated goals, committees with similar goal patterns should display im-portant similarities in behavior, and committees with different goal patterns should display important differences in behavior. More specifically, these similarities and differences should appear with respect to decision-making processes and decisions. But even such rudimentary predictions as these will hold only when "all other things are equal." And we know enough about committees to know that such a condition does not obtain. Most important, perhaps, we know that each committee works in a somewhat different environ-ment. We need, therefore, to add this key variable to the analysis.

CHAPTER TWO

Environmental Constraints

Every House committee inhabits an environment in which committee nonmembers seek to persuade committee members to act in ways
the nonmembers deem necessary or desirable. Of the various clusters
of outsiders, the four most prominent are: members of the *parent
House,* members of the *executive branch,* members of *clientele
groups,* and members of the two major *political parties* — or, more
operationally, the leaders of each. These four elements make up the
environment of every House committee. Each has an interest in
committee behavior coupled with a capacity to influence such behavior. But their interests and their capacities are not the same for
all committees; all committees are not, therefore, affected by the
same outside influences in the same degree. From the viewpoint of
the committee member, the likelihood is that not all the elements of
his environment will have an equal effect on his ability to achieve his
personal goals. And he will be constrained to take into greater account those outsiders who are more likely to affect his goals than
those who are less likely to do so. We begin our analysis of committee environments from this latter perspective, by examining the
environments of each of our three pairs of committees.

APPROPRIATIONS AND WAYS AND MEANS

For an *Appropriations* or *Ways and Means* Committee member, the
critical question posed by the environment is: which outsiders have
the greatest capacity for affecting my acquisition of influence in the
House? And the answer would seem to be, first and foremost, *the
other members of the House.* For no individual or committee can
be influential in the chamber unless the other members — better

perhaps, the other leaders of the House — accept their influence. "Inside power" is bestowed by insiders and can be taken away by insiders. If the opportunity to achieve prestige or importance exists on Appropriations and Ways and Means, it is because House leaders and members have decided that these committees shall be the most prestigeful and the most important within the institution.

This collective judgment has been registered, for example, in the provision of the Legislative Reorganization Act of 1946 designating Appropriations, Ways and Means, and Rules as the only "exclusive" committees in the House. A ranking of our six committees according to the percentage of their members holding more than one commit- tee assignment provides a crude indicator of House judgments con- cerning relative committee importance. Our assumption is that gradations of this sort tell us something about the opportunity for gaining inside influence — that the opportunities are far greater on Appropriations than they are, for example, on Interior.

Table 2.1

Average Percentage of Members Holding More Than One
Committee Assignment: 84th-89th Congresses[1]

	Democrats	Republicans	Total
Appropriations	0%	2%	1%
Ways and Means	0%	3%	2%
Foreign Affairs	37%	35%	36%
Education and Labor	43%	66%	51%
Interior	81%	46%	66%
Post Office	76%	81%	77%

Congressmen, of course, know this — which is why so many of them leave Interior and transfer to Appropriations. By charting the flow of House members to and from our six committees, we view the collective judgment on committees as the product of individual choices. Tables 2.1 and 2.2 portray the same patterned prestige hier- archy among our six committees. The pattern depicts the committee- based opportunity structure for influence-oriented Congressmen. The importance of the parent House to members of Ways and Means and Appropriations is conveyed by the fact that it is the members of

---

[1] This table has been adapted from Lewis Gawthrop, "Changing Member- ship Patterns in House Committees," *American Political Science Review* (June, 1966).

Table 2.2
Transfers Among Six Committees:
80th–89th Congresses[2]

From	To						
	W.&M.	*App.*	*F.A.*	*E.&L.*	*Int.*	*P.O.*	*Total From*
W.&M.	--	0	0	0	0	0	0
App.	1	–	0	0	0	0	1
F.A.	1	1	–	0	0	0	2
E.&L.	4	5	1	–	0	0	10
Int.	3	16	3	1	–	0	23
P.O.	3	5	8	3	1	–	20
Total to	12	27	12	4	1	0	56

the House — not the members of the two committees — whose judgments produce this opportunity structure.

Ways and Means and Appropriations are especially important committees in the eyes of House members. Why? The answer lies in the policies they handle and in the vital connection between these policies and the power of the House of Representatives within the American political system. The two-sided power of the purse — taxing and spending — is generally believed to be the most fundamental legislative power in representative democracies. Defending the American Constitution, James Madison generalized:

> This power of the purse may, in fact, be regarded as the most complete and effectual weapon with which any country can arm the immediate representatives of the people for obtaining a redress of every grievance and for carrying into effect every just and salutary measure.[3]

In the United States, the House has been given special institutional prerogatives in this area. By constitutional provision, all taxing measures originate in the House and by cognate "immemorial custom" all appropriations measures do, too.[4] House members view their money power as the core of their institutional power. They, therefore, view the two committees entrusted with taxing and spending

[2] Data for 80th–85th Congresses were compiled by Warren Miller and Donald Stokes.
[3] *The Federalist Papers*, Everymans Edition (New York: E. P. Dutton, 1934), pp. 298–299.
[4] The phrase is the Appropriations Committee's. *History of the Committee on Appropriations*, House Document 299, 77th Congress, 1st Session (Washington: U.S. Government Printing Office, 1941).

policies with a degree of interest and concern qualitatively different
from that directed to any of the other four. And they hold, not
surprisingly, a fairly well-developed set of prescriptions concerning
their behavior.

Basically, House members want their two money committees to
be *influential* committees — that is, to make independent policy
judgments (particularly vis-à-vis the executive branch) and have
those judgments supported in the parent chamber. To this end, the
House prescribes and/or acquiesces in rules and customs allowing
the two committees a special degree of procedural autonomy. Ways
and Means is the primary beneficiary of the closed rule — bringing
all its major bills to the floor protected against amendments. And
Appropriations is the only committee to hold all of its hearings in
secret executive sessions.[5] To further buttress their policy-making
influence, the House has treated the two committees more generously in regard to staffing than it has other House committees. Appropriations is the only committee without statutory or budgetary
limit to the size of its staff, the largest in the House. For its taxing
committee, the House maintains the Joint Committee on Internal
Revenue Taxation, a committee which is merely a holding company
for a staff of tax experts who work for the Ways and Means and
Senate Finance Committees. Provisions of these sorts reflect the
House member's belief that powerful, autonomous, expert committees are a necessary condition of the House's own institutional influence in money matters.

At the same time, however, House members prescribe for the two
committees a special degree of *responsiveness*. If they are going to
assert policy leadership on behalf of the House, so goes the reasoning, then the two committees should remain all the more sensitive to the wishes and sentiments of their House colleagues. Many
methods are available with which to promote committee responsiveness to House desires. They range from the maintenance of informal
channels of communication to the formal reversal of committee
recommendations on the floor. But the most distinctive and most

---

[5] From 1966–1968, for example, the percentage of closed hearings for each
of our six committees was: Appropriations, 100%; Ways and Means, 63%;
Foreign Affairs, 60%; Post Office, 33%; Education and Labor, 30%; Interior,
25%. See *Congressional Quarterly*, November 8, 1968, p. 3104. Since the
Legislative Reorganization Act of 1970, however, some subcommittees have been
holding some of their hearings in open session.

important for the two money committees is the special care taken in choosing their members. One indicator of such care (see Table 2.3) is that congressmen wait longest for assignment to these two committees. The longer a member serves in the House before being assigned to a committee, the greater the opportunity for committee makers to assess his legislative performance and the less likely they are to make a mistake in judging his responsiveness to his colleagues.[6]

Table 2.3
Prior House Service at Time of Appointment
to Six Committees 1955–1966

Committee	Average Years Prior House Service per Member
Ways and Means	6.6 (52 members)
Appropriations	3.7 (100 members)
Foreign Affairs	3.1 (69 members)
Post Office and Civil Service	1.2 (78 members)
Interior and Insular Affairs	.80 (88 members)
Education and Labor	.78 (75 Members)

As another indication of care in selecting Ways and Means and Appropriations members, party leaders play a more active part in recruitment and selection for these two committees than for the other four. They are instrumental (according to our interview results) in the appointment of about 40 per cent of the Ways and Means members and 30 percent of the Appropriations members, while they have a comparable impact on no more than 15 per cent of the appointments for the other four groups. One particular recruitment method, co-optation, is sometimes used to pick money-committee members. It is a method *never* used in the case of the other four committees. Table 2.4 displays the recruitment patterns for the six committees. *Self-starters* decide on their own to seek a committee assignment. *Inner-circle choices* have the idea suggested to them by someone else. *Co-opted* members are taken off the committee on which they sit, without their request, and assigned to an-

[6] Committee makers, especially within state delegations, may choose to use pure seniority as the criterion. In such cases Table 2.3 reflects the use of that criterion and not carefulness in selection. But seniority is only one of a number of criteria used; and that fact leaves plenty of room for discretion in the selection process.

Table 2.4

Recruitment Patterns

	Self-starter		Inner-Circle Choice		Co-opted		Assigned		Total	
	%	No.	%	No.	%	No.	%	No.	%	No.
Ways and Means	71	(15)	5	(1)	24	(5)	0		100	(21)
Appropriations	65	(33)	23	(12)	12	(7)	0		100	(52)
Foreign Affairs	93	(26)	7	(2)	0		0		100	(28)
Education and Labor	58	(19)	21	(7)	0		21	(7)	100	(33)
Interior	61	(17)	21	(5)	0		18	(6)	100	(28)
Post Office	29	(5)	18	(3)	0		53	(9)	100	(17)
Total	64%	(115)	17%	(30)	7%	(12)	12%	(22)	100	(179)*

*Ten congressmen were members of two of the six committees when interviewed. They were counted twice.

other committee. *Assigned* members are placed on a committee they did not request; if nonfreshmen, they do not lose any other assignment they may already hold. Approximately one-quarter of Ways and Means members and one-tenth of Appropriations members were taken off the committee on which they had sat, without their request, and were given the more prestigious assignment — *not* because there were no applicants for the position, but because none of the applicants was deemed acceptable.[7]

More often than not the measure of acceptability involves a criterion that committee makers apply to prospective members of Ways and Means and Appropriations but not to *any* of the other four committees. That criterion is "a responsible legislative style." [8] It is a uniquely House-oriented criterion, and is applied similarly by both parties. Its main elements are good interpersonal relations and institutional loyalty. When money-committee members and their selectors discuss the reasons for their appointments, they typically mention personal attributes such as "cooperative," "popular," "reasonable," "sober," "easy to work with." Conversely they were

[7] The greater number of inner-circle choices on Appropriations results from the concern of state delegations that someone be on the committee handling money for state concerns. Hence, the numbers are an indication of the greater constituency orientation of Appropriations members, described in Chapter I.

[8] See Nicholas Masters, "Committee Assignments in the House of Representatives," *American Political Science Review* (June, 1961).

not (as their competitors sometimes were) "screwballs," "running around kicking everyone in the teeth," "shooting their mouths off," "going off half-cocked." By attending to legislative style, House leaders screen in (or, in the case of co-optation, invite in) Congressmen who value good working relationships with their colleagues, and they screen out Congressmen whose working style seems egregiously outside established House modes. The idea, of course, is to insure a responsive committee by selecting responsive members.

Another House-oriented criterion — geographical representativeness — is applied more often to these two committees than to the other four. And the rationale of enhancing responsiveness to the chamber is the same.[9] Since the two committees are granted so much working autonomy, careful selection may be the most effective guarantor of amenability available to the House.

To this point in our analysis, we would predict very similar patterns of behavior for the Appropriations and Ways and Means Committees. Their members hold similar personal goals and confront similar environmental constraints. But we have examined only the parent chamber, i.e., the *institutional environment*. And we have examined only one set of constraints — institutional constraints. We consider the parent chamber and the institutional constraints it purveys (i.e., procedural autonomy and responsiveness) to be the most distinctive and differentiating external influence on the two money committees. But we cannot ignore the impact of the other three environmental elements. Theirs, briefly, is an impact on policy. The executive branch, clientele groups, and political parties are important to committees as purveyors of policy interest and policy preferences. They, along with House members, of course, fix the policy constraints or the *policy environment*, within which committee members seek their personal goals. With respect to the policy aspects of their environments, Appropriations and Ways and Means members face somewhat different constellations of interest. And these differences point toward divergences in their behavior. Before discussing these environments specifically, we might clarify the terms in which we propose to examine the policy environments of all our committees.

Prescriptions for public policy are shaped and carried to every

---

[9] Ways and Means and Appropriations are the most geographically representative of the six committees. See Table 3.3.

House committee by coalitions in which all four environmental elements (plus entrepreneurial committee members themselves) participate. Our voluminous case studies of national policy making have taught us that no two policy coalitions are exactly alike. Yet our need to categorize and generalize, for comparative purposes, is obvious. We shall attempt to do so by characterizing *environmental policy coalitions* in terms of the relative prominence of the four environmental elements in the coalition. Viewed from this angle, it appears that some fairly distinct patterns of coalition leadership can be observed. We can distinguish *executive-led, party-led, clientele-led,* and *House-led* coalitions, and we can see certain of these types appear more regularly and influentially in the environments of some committees than in others. Admittedly, once again, our categories are oversimplifications. Much as in the case of members' goals, we shall be talking in gross terms about modal patterns. But we think they have sufficient empirical validity and explanatory power to be useful in this exploratory essay.

Policy coalitions concerned with appropriations are usually *executive-led.* Decisions allocating federal money to agencies and programs are of lifeblood concern to every executive official. The requests made of the Appropriations Committee originate in the executive branch, are aggregated in the executive branch, and come to the Committee via the Chief Executive's budget. All the Committee's working documents are products of the executive branch. Clientele groups typically enter the budgetary process through the relevant executive agencies and have relatively little direct contact with the Appropriations Committee. A veteran staff man noted: "A few lobbyists may be influential with Appropriations, but not many. With most of our subcommittees, I'd say the registered lobbyist's influence is zero." And most clientele leaders agree. Said one, "Appropriations is an in-House process, and there isn't much anyone on the outside can do to influence it." When members of the House press specific claims on the Committee they, too, usually act indirectly, as supporters or opponents of a budget request being tendered by executive officials.

Of course, the very makeup of the parent chamber stands as a constraint on the activities of every committee. The changing size, for example, of "the conservative coalition" places outer limits on all committees whose work has liberal-conservative dimensions. When the chamber speaks to a committee in terms of policy, it does so, we think, by way of an amorphous and evanescent policy mood, e.g., "We must do something about such-and-such a problem this session," or, "Do more/less of this/that faster/slower than you have been." Once in a while, for example, an "economy mood" in the House will affect Appropriations Committee behavior.[10] Committee members should always apprise themselves of "the mood" or "the temper" or, in Sam Rayburn's phrase, "the rolling waves of sentiment" in the chamber. But House-led coalitions as the prime shapers and movers of external policy coalitions are strictly a sometime thing.

The executive branch and the House together impose one consequential policy constraint on the Appropriations Committee. It is their permanent injunction that appropriations bills must be passed each year. The Committee does not have, as almost all other committees have, the potent option of doing nothing. As we might expect, Appropriations Committee activity is strongly affected thereby. For it means, among other things, that one of the alternatives most committees argue about has been foreclosed to Appropriations.

It is more difficult to characterize the coalitions in the policy environment of Ways and Means. House members are no more the active purveyors of specific policy here than they are in Appropriations. John Manley does, however, emphasize the parameters set by the chamber's conservative coalition. Clientele groups, on the other hand, deal much more continually and directly with Ways and Means than they do with Appropriations. "Few committees draw their attention like Ways and Means," says Manley.[11] But, he says, clientele groups ordinarily carry their demands first and foremost to executive officials. And they make direct requests of the Congress only on appeal from policy proposals aggregated in the executive branch. The basic, formative decisions on legislative program — to impose, extend, or alter a tax, to liberalize or contract trade policy, to change social security, welfare, or medical care policy — remain executive branch decisions. The policy proposals that structure the work of Ways and Means come from the executive branch. Accordingly, the policy coalitions facing Ways and Means are more aptly described as *executive-led* than as clientele-led. When we examine

[10] See Richard Fenno, *The Power of the Purse: Appropriations Politics in Congress* (Boston: Little, Brown, 1966), pp. 10–16; 472–487.
[11] John Manley, *The Politics of Finance* (Boston: Little, Brown, 1970), p. 324.

the Senate counterpart of Ways and Means, we shall find confirmation for this judgment; the case of the Senate Finance Committee gives us a measure of what clientele dominance of a committee in this very policy area really looks like.

If, then, policy coalitions in the Ways and Means environment have a strong element of executive leadership, they also contain an equally strong element of *party leadership*. And herein lies the major *difference* in the policy environments of the two money committees. Party leaders — the leaders of both parties in House and Senate and the President — are primarily concerned with winning elections. Their interest in any House committee, therefore, will be a function of the perceived electoral relevance of that committee's policy output. On Capitol Hill and in the White House, Ways and Means decisions are believed to have much greater nationwide electoral consequences than those of Appropriations. A Ways and Means member commented, "We deal with things on which Republicans and Democrats are in fundamental disagreement." And these policy disagreements have traditionally provided much of the policy content for party identification and national partisan controversy. Party stands on trade, social security, taxation, medicare — such are believed to help influence voters and win elections.

To be sure, Republicans and Democrats have long contested, also, over the level of federal expenditures. And from time to time, Republicans mount an attack on the federal budget. But in terms of voter interest, Appropriations decisions lack the visibility and the salience of Ways and Means decisions. An increase or decrease in taxes, an extension of social security, a new medical care policy — these decisions have a recognizable, tangible, direct effect on voters. An increase or reduction in the budget of an agency or a cluster of agencies — these decisions have no such effect. Each is a fragment of spending policy, easily blurred by compromise and hard to measure for effect — quite unlikely to sustain the interest of party leaders or attract the attention of the voter. If ever Appropriations debates became general debates over spending and balanced budgets, partisanship would surely blossom. But so long as the executive branch and Congress deal in budgetary fragments, partisanship will remain a secondary theme.[12] When the President argues, now, for his full

---

[12] Conversely, should any of the oft-proposed reforms bringing greater centralization to the appropriations process be enacted, we would predict an increase in partisanship on appropriations decisions.

budget request, he does so primarily as the head of a nonpartisan bureaucracy. But when he presses for tax, social security, trade, or medical care legislation, he speaks much more as the leader of his party.

When party leaders make appointments to Ways and Means, they make policy orthodoxy a test of membership. Candidates from both parties are checked to make sure they adhere to the party position on such matters as trade and medicare and to ascertain whether they will follow the party leaders, especially the one in the White House.[13] "To get on Ways and Means" said a Democratic member, "you have to be pretty much in favor of the Administration, what the Administration wants." And a Republican committee maker explained, "We screen members very closely and make sure they are OK on major issues — conservative on taxes and business, against medicare." Republicans do a similar screening for Appropriations. "We don't want anybody who will just spend and spend and spend." But Democrats, the majority party from 1955 to 1966, did not make policy orthodoxy a stringent criterion. As a top party leader said:

> We don't ask them whether they are spenders or not. That doesn't enter into it. It isn't an ideological matter. We don't care about his stand on policy. *It's not like Ways and Means* where if a man is opposed to reciprocal trade we can't afford to put him on.[14]

Furthermore, the same veteran Democratic leader distinguished basic party interest and influence in selecting members of the two committees:

> The leadership has a great deal of influence on (choosing members of) Rules and Ways and Means. But on the other

---

[13] In Sam Rayburn's day, oil was another such subject. A Northern Democrat recalled this colloquy with the Speaker: *Rayburn:* You are going on the Ways and Means Committee. *Member:* No, Mr. Speaker. *Rayburn:* What? *Member:* No, Mr. Speaker. *Rayburn:* Why not? *Member:* Oil depletion — I'd have to argue against it. You know that. *Rayburn:* You've got something there. What do you want? *Member:* Rules. *Rayburn:* Go tell McCormack that I say you are going on Rules.

[14] In 1963 the Democrats deliberately added five policy liberals to the Committee. One Ways and Means member noted that "we put some people on who would support the administration and the party position." So policy orthodoxy does come into play. But not as regularly or as pervasively as on Ways and Means. Support for this distinction can be found in Table 3–2.

committees, not so much. . . . The Ways and Means Committee has the most intimate connection with the leadership
. . . only once in my 38 years has the (party) caucus failed
to go along with the wishes of the leadership.

Party pressures, we believe, are more important in the environment
of Ways and Means than of Appropriations. Should one party control both White House and Congress, the President or "the Administration" would clearly be the dominant force in the Ways and
Means policy environment. We think of policy coalitions, then, as
executive-plus-party-led, or *Administration-led* in Ways and Means
and *executive-led* in Appropriations. With both committees, however, the distinctive features of their total environment remain the
interest and influence of the parent House. In their decision-making
processes and in the characteristics of their decisions, therefore, we
should expect to find Appropriations and Ways and Means more
like than unlike each other and, probably, more like one another
than either is like any of the other four committees.

EDUCATION AND LABOR AND FOREIGN AFFAIRS

For a *Foreign Affairs* or *Education and Labor* Committee member,
the question posed by the environment is: which outside groups
have the greatest capacity for affecting my ability to make public
policy contributions? And the answer would seem to be: *whatever
groups dominate the policy coalitions confronting the committee.*
When committee members seek House influence, the most important environmental constraints come from the House itself, and
policy coalitions are of secondary importance. But when committee
members seek to make good public policy, it is the policy coalitions
that produce the primary environmental constraints. A congressman
who wants to use his committee membership to achieve policy goals
must operate within the confines of policy coalitions in which he
and his committee play only a part. The more prominent any given
environmental element in those coalitions, the more will committee
members be constrained to take it into account and the greater its
impact on committee behavior will be. The makeup and influence
of policy coalitions may, of course, vary a good deal from one committee to another, as we suggest they do with our two money committees. Such would also seem to be the situation — indeed much
more so — with Foreign Affairs and Education and Labor. Thus,

while the members' goals in these latter two committees are similar, the environments in which they must pursue their goals are quite different — a blend which we will expect to cause divergencies in their patterns of behavior.

Policy coalitions in the realm of the *Foreign Affairs Committee* are *executive-led*. About this generalization, there is no dispute in the literature on foreign policy making. The foreign policy prerogatives of the Chief Executive are grounded in the Constitution and nourished by imperatives of decisiveness, speed, unity, information, and secrecy in the conduct of international relations. All the Presidents in our period have spent more of their time and energy on foreign policy than on domestic policy. And all have fought strenuously to protect their institutional supremacy in this area — from Eisenhower's fight against the Bricker Amendment to Johnson's defense of the Tonkin Resolution.

The primacy of presidential leadership in relation to the political parties or to clientele groups is so evident as to warrant little discussion. The Committee's most important decisions, by far, pertain to the foreign aid program, an issue believed to have little electoral sex appeal. In 1963, House Republican leaders acted to stem the natural flow of pro-aid members to the Committee by allocating five of the six vacancies to anti-aid applicants. This was the most serious expression of party interest in the period.[15] But it only affected a "minority of the minority" on the Committee. As for clientele groups, their relative lack of influence in foreign affairs is well known; and Michael O'Leary referred to their influence in foreign aid policy coalitions as "so small that it would scarcely be considered at all in other areas of policy." [16]

The Chief Executive's only serious rival for policy leadership has been the Congress itself, which raises for us the question of the impact of the parent House on the environment of the Foreign Affairs Committee. A general answer would be simply that Congress on the whole has not mounted a very potent challenge. For the 1955–1966 period, Holbert Carroll concluded, "Viewing the

[15] The high prior-service average for Foreign Affairs, in Table 2.3, is accounted for by the Republicans, whose average prior service is 4.5 years compared to a Democratic figure of 1.9. The appointments of 1963 do help explain this high Republican figure. The five anti-aid men, chosen with great care, averaged eight years of prior House service.

[16] Michael K. O'Leary, *The Politics of American Foreign Aid* (New York: Atherton, 1967), p. 58.

environmental changes since the mid 1950's upon the President, the
Senate and the House, the President has gained additional initiative,
discretion and authority in foreign affairs relative to the Congress." [17] A specific answer would be that the congressional challenge, such as it is, has come from the Senate, which has its own
constitutional prerogatives in this field, and not from the House,
which has none. Committee on Committees Democrats, for instance, were at a total loss to expound any agreed criteria for selection. "That's the most amazing thing I've seen since I've been in
Congress," said one. "I don't know why we put men on Foreign
Affairs — those who like to visit embassies, I guess. Seriously, I
just don't know how to answer that question." House members have
no institutional concern in the field of foreign affairs, no special interest in their Foreign Affairs Committee, and make no special
effort to influence the behavior of its members.

All key prescriptions come, instead, from the President and his
executive branch subordinates. Their prescriptions for behavior emphasize *legitimation* as the basic task of the Foreign Affairs Committee. That is, they want the Committee to place a legislative
stamp of approval on recommendations that they believe have been
thoroughly and expertly worked out in the executive branch. They
also may want the Committee's judgment on matters of *legislative
feasibility* or acceptability. But they do not designate for Foreign
Affairs anything approaching the independent policy-making influence which House members ordain for Ways and Means and Appropriations. Executive officials do ask that the Committee members be
knowledgeable about foreign policy subjects. But what they want is
the capacity to consume and comprehend executive-transmitted information. They do not — in contrast, again, to the House prescriptions we described for the two purse-string committees — urge Foreign
Affairs to develop an independent subject-matter expertise. Executives
want the Committee, furthermore, to accept the executive frame of
reference, i.e. its definition of the problem, and its statement of the alternatives. Requests for legitimating resolutions in the Formosa Straits
(1955), the Middle East (1957), and the Gulf of Tonkin (1964)
are excellent examples of this executive prescription. And, of course,
there is the corollary request for executive branch "discretion" and

[17] Holbert N. Carroll, *The House of Representatives and Foreign Affairs,*
Revised Edition (Boston: Little, Brown, 1966), p. 351.

"flexibility" in implementing any Committee decision unencumbered by legislative "handcuffs," "strings," or "restrictions." Whenever Foreign Affairs makes foreign aid decisions on a country-by-country basis, for example, executive officials react strongly, as the Secretary of State did in 1963. "I must say that I am very concerned about the tendency in Congress to legislate foreign policy as it may apply to specific situations and specific countries," said Dean Rusk. "These are the responsibilities carried by the President of the United States." [18] A final executive branch desire is that Committee legitimation be done — as President Kennedy said of the foreign aid program — "from a bipartisan point of view . . . completely removed from the Democratic-Republican dialogue." [19] The President seeks consensus support in foreign policy. Executive officials place great emphasis on nonpartisanship in day-to-day dealings with the Committee on the theory that procedural nonpartisanship will stimulate substantive bipartisanship.

The capacity of the President and the executive branch to enforce these prescriptions and, hence, to influence Foreign Affairs Committee members comes first of all from their control of the policy initiative — great in any case but greater in foreign than domestic policy. Speaking of the foreign aid program, O'Leary summarized:

> The primary initiator and organizer of opinions about foreign aid is the executive branch of the government, The history of foreign aid is principally the history of policy initiatives taken by the President and his advisers.[20]

The President's negotiating prerogatives and his Commander-in-Chief prerogatives give him the ability to initiate actions and create commitments that the Foreign Affairs Committee is virtually powerless to alter. Eisenhower's action in Lebanon, Kennedy's action in the missile crisis, and Johnson's action in the Dominican Republic are cases in point. We can expect, further, that once a presidential commitment is made, the President will summon up whatever personal and institutional resources are necessary to gain committee acceptance.

The executive's second source of influence is its possession of

[18] *New York Times*, November 9, 1963, p. 10.
[19] Harold W. Chase and Allen Lerman (eds.) *Kennedy and the Press* (New York: Crowell, 1965), p. 313.
[20] O'Leary, *op. cit.*, p. 89.

superior information. One reason why the Committee finds it difficult to assert initiative with policy is that, as Roger Hilsman writes, "This power over information and this plethora of expertise give to the Executive . . . the intellectual initiative in foreign policy." [21] A Foreign Affairs member explained:

> There's no real hot line to let you know what is really going on. . . . Sure, if you sat down in Mac Bundy's basement all the time, you'd know as much as he does. But information is lacking. What do you do when they say the Dominican Republic is being taken over by Communists? I looked at the 58 names, too, but they meant nothing to me.

A State Department official concurred, "The executive has all the advantages. We have the menu and we can pick and choose. I don't know how we can get the Committee to play a more positive role." A "positive role" is, of course, the very goal that Foreign Affairs members want most to achieve through their Committee activity. They must seek their personal goals, it appears, in an environment that is a good deal more monolithic and forbidding than that constraining the Committees on Ways and Means or Appropriations. The difference was captured by a Republican who recalled being faced with a choice of committee assignments between Foreign Affairs and Ways and Means. "I talked it over with my dear friend General Eisenhower, when he was President. He told me to take Ways and Means. He said that on taxes Ways and Means was king but that on foreign relations, he was."

If "monolithic" accurately describes the policy coalitions facing Foreign Affairs, then "pluralistic" is probably most descriptive of the policy coalitions facing *Education and Labor*. And herein lies the main difference in the environments of this pair of committees. In one negative respect, it bears repeating, the external worlds of Foreign Affairs and Education and Labor are similar. The parent chamber has little institutional interest in either social welfare policy or foreign policy. That is, House members do not relate the performance of either committee to the influence of the House of Representatives within the American political system. Neither committee, therefore, gets the kind of special attention accorded Ways and

---

[21] Roger Hilsman, "Congressional-Executive Relations and the Foreign Policy Consensus," *American Political Science Review* (September, 1958), pp. 729–730.

Means and Appropriations; and neither is constrained by such distinctive House prescriptions as policy independence, procedural autonomy, and responsible legislative style. Otherwise, the striking characteristic of Education and Labor's policy environment is the extent to which, unlike Foreign Affairs, all elements — executive, clientele, parties, and allied House members — are involved. This means, of course, that the policy-oriented members of the Committee must contend with all of them.

The interest of the executive branch reflects the pivotal character of the Committee's work for the domestic program of the President. When President Kennedy took office in 1961, he announced his "must" domestic program of five bills, two of which, minimum wage and federal aid to education, came to the Education and Labor Committee. When President Johnson assumed office, the first distinctive Johnsonian policy was the poverty program, also within the bailiwick of Education and Labor. Still, policy coalitions were not dominated by the executive in the manner of Foreign Affairs. The interest of the clientele group was equally strong. Consider the following expression of concern by an AFL-CIO official:

> We watch the Education and Labor Committee very carefully; but it's the only one we're interested in. Otherwise, you would spread yourself too thin. We have to control the labor committee. It's our lifeblood.

Such a comment implies a level of clientele involvement totally without equal in the environment of Foreign Affairs. And the interest, if not the influence, of the labor organizations has come to be matched by that of education-oriented groups, such as the National Education Association. Educational policy has become an increasingly important activity of the Committee, and it has become an ever greater source of attractiveness for the Committee's newer members.[22] Finally, the subjects of labor, education, and poverty pose issues over which Democrats and Republicans have tended to divide and which have often been the major points of domestic disagree-

---

[22] Education and Labor recruitment patterns appear to have undergone a marked secular change. Of the 22 interviewees who came to the Committee prior to 1965, 9 (41%) were self-starters and 7 (32%) were assigned. Of the 11 interviewees who came to the Committee between 1965 and 1968, 10 (91%) were self-starters and none had to be assigned. The interviews led me to attribute the increased attractiveness of the Committee to the increased importance of educational policy.

ment in Presidential and congressional campaigns. Each subject propounds ideologically inflammable questions of government involvement in the society. In the 1950's and 1960's Democrats tended to give liberal (more involvement) answers and Republicans tended to give conservative (less involvement) answers. We all know the exceptions to this generalization, but speaking in terms of a central tendency, there has been a high degree of partisan-ideological congruence in these areas of policy. This partisan-ideological dimension also differentiates the environment of Education and Labor from that of Foreign Affairs.

Given the variety of interested groups making up the environment and the variety of policy subjects which concern them, it is impossible to make any single satisfactory characterization of policy coalition leadership. The closest approximation, we think, is to emphasize the prominence of the two political parties and to think of the policy coalitions facing Education and Labor as distinctively *party-led*. More often than not, the parties have provided a rubric under which all other environmental elements have organized to influence the Committee. And the more nationally controversial the subject — in terms of the personal goals of the Committee's members — the more prominent the parties have been as the aggregators of executive, clientele, and House member policy preferences. Or put conversely, the executive branch, clientele groups, and House members have been especially quick to use party resources to fight their battles in nationally controversial policy areas. The parties do not disagree on all policies coming to the Committee. Higher education, manpower retraining, vocational education, vocational rehabilitation, and library aid are nonpartisan, nonideological matters. But they were not always noncontroversial. The Committee confronts policy demands in geological layers: some are long-settled, cold, and solidified; some are unresolved, hot, and volatile. It is the *latter* type which, at any point in time, give the Committee environment its distinctive characteristics. In its partisan-ideological character, the environment of Education and Labor resembles that of Ways and Means more than it does that of Foreign Affairs. But Ways and Means members confront a complicating, attenuating institutional interest on the part of the House. Education and Labor members face partisan-ideological constraints to a degree unmatched by any of the other five committees.

The policy prescriptions of party-led coalitions are very much a function of electoral politics. Each coalition will wish the Committee to act in ways that will bring it *advantages at the polls*. In this sense each coalition looks to the next election. But from another perspective, each policy coalition is a prisoner of the last election. Factors such as the control of the Presidency and the size of the Democratic House majority set limits on what policies are possible and determine the makeup and strength of policy coalitions. As Table 2.5 indicates, the years 1955–1966 produced four quite different permutations of partisanship in the Education and Labor environment. And the prescriptions of the coalitions depended very much on the permutations of party control. In the 89th Congress, for example, the prescriptions coming to the Committee were strongly Democratic and liberal. In the 84th and 85th Congresses, on the other hand, policy prescriptions were compromises of various sorts. In the 86th Congress the Committee faced two contrasting sets of prescriptions — liberal from an outsized Democratic party in the House and conservative from a Republican President. And in the 87th and 88th Congresses the policy demands of a Democratic President had to be modified to meet the problems of slim House majorities. An important characteristic of Education and Labor's environment is this party-related instability — the most unstable environment of the six committees.

Table 2.5
Patterns of Partisanship 1955-1956

Size of Democratic House Majority	Control of Presidency	
	Democratic	*Republican*
Large	89th Congress, 1965–1966	86th Congress, 1959–1960
Small	87th Congress, 1961–1962 88th Congress, 1963–1964	84th Congress, 1955–1956 85th Congress, 1957–1958

The capacity of party-led coalitions to influence Committee members is considerable, as a few examples will attest. In the wake of the Democratic sweep of 1958, liberal House Democrats persuaded Speaker Sam Rayburn to exercise his influence and change the party ratio on the Committee from 17–13 to 20–10. When the party committee makers subsequently stacked the Democratic side with policy liberals, a blocking coalition of Republicans and Southern Democrats was permanently broken. On the Democratic side of the Committee, party leaders shared their committee-making prerogatives with coalition allies from organized labor. An AFL-CIO official explained, in 1965:

> With one exception in the last few years, John McCormack and Andy Biemiller (Director of AFL-CIO Legislative Department) have decided who gets on that Committee. Last year, for example, they picked all six members. A year ago in January, Adam Powell got up at our legislative conference and said, "Here are the names of the six new members of the Education and Labor Committee." Then he read the names from a slip of paper and said, "I got this slip from Andy Biemiller, so they are all right." That wasn't too bright, saying that with so many newspapermen around. But we do that. The only exception was ————. John came to us and said, "I've got to put one southerner on. You've already got a good working majority." So we said, "OK, give us one that won't do anything." And he did.

In return, of course, the AFL-CIO devotes enormous resources of manpower, money, and organization to help elect liberal Democratic Presidents and Congressmen — including members of the Education and Labor Committee.

Republican committee makers operate without help from clientele groups. A U.S. Chamber of Commerce official pointed out:

> We don't have anything to do with choosing members. That's not our province. We don't interfere in any matter of internal organization. There are a lot of things the unions do that business can't do. We don't have any COPE either.

But selectors do try to choose an orthodox Republican group. One said, "Our Committees will put the most conservative people on this Committee." "Charlie Halleck put me on," said a Committee member, "for his purposes, not mine. He knew I was a conservative and he saw me as a safe vote." In 1964 the Committee on Committees accepted no one who would not first agree to oppose the repeal of 14B of the Taft-Hartley Act, thereby sustaining state right-to-work laws. But increasingly, Republican policy orthodoxy includes a disposition to construct policy alternatives and not (as earlier) merely opposition to Democratic programs.

More remote partisan influences come from the President when he acts as party leader in pushing his policy preferences. Describing the poverty bill as "a prime example of executive legislation," John Donovan emphasized the partisan caste and the partisan strategy imparted to the Powell-Landrum bill by the President:

> Northern liberal loyalists would obviously vote for a bill so close to the President's heart. Landrum was to help line up a sufficient number of southern votes to make this a Democratic program. If ambitious young Republicans wanted to oppose a war on poverty in an election year, so be it. This was the strategic pattern within which the Economic Opportunity Act was sent to the Congress. It is hard to imagine that such a daring strategy was set by anyone other than the President himself.[23]

Committee Republicans accepted the strategy in kind. Throughout the poverty bill debate, said one, "They were trying to make a record and we were trying to knock their record and make one of our own." Another said, "On OEO, we had 87 amendments, and they didn't accept a single one." In one sense, since political parties are aggregators of the environmental groups, party leaders can command the resources of a combination of groups. And their capacity for influencing Education and Labor members is proportionately wide ranging.

INTERIOR AND POST OFFICE

For an *Interior* or *Post Office* Committee member, the question posed by his environment is: which outside groups have the greatest capacity for affecting my ability to secure re-election? And the answer is, obviously, *my constituents*. In this study we are concerned only with those constituents who are actively interested in a member's committee activity. Most such constituents will be organized, whether their organizations be single-interest or multi-interest, temporary or permanent, strictly local or local outposts of regional and national groups. We speak of all these organizations as clientele groups. And they are the dominant force in the environment of the Interior and Post Office Committees. They all seek favorable deci-

---

[23] John C. Donovan, *The Politics of Poverty* (New York: Pegasus, 1967), p. 34; also p. xv.

sions at the hands of the committees and they all have some capacity for influencing voter opinion at home. No other environmental element takes so great an interest or poses so credible a threat at the polls.

The uniformly low prestige ranking of both committees in the House provides an accurate measure of parent chamber interest. Similarly, natural resource and federal pay policies are hardly the stuff that attracts the concern of party leaders — not like the policy subjects of Ways and Means or Education and Labor. Partisan conflict over policy is strong on one Interior Committee issue — public versus private power — but the issue rarely comes to the Committee in sufficiently undiluted terms to draw party concern. Interest from the executive branch is, of course, present — witness the Interior and Post Office Departments. And the executive branch is of secondary importance to both committees. But none of the Presidents studied gave as high a priority to the programs of these departments as to programs coming to the other four committees. Two members, who combined service on Education and Labor and Interior, volunteered that "the Administration has much more of a say in Education and Labor matters than in Interior matters" and that "Education and Labor is more responsive to the Administration than Interior." The growing salience of ecological problems may alter these generalizations. But as late as 1968, an official of the Citizens Committee on Natural Resources summed up interest in Interior Committee politics this way:

> Much as I hate to admit this, because conservation is so dear to my heart, most of our bills are minor bills—nationally speaking. We aren't the space program, we aren't programs for the cities, we aren't Viet Nam, we aren't foreign aid. We have to work very hard to get public attention and we have to keep pressure on for a long time before we get results. . . . Usually our bills are way down on the priority list.

For clientele groups, however, the priority, the stakes, and the involvement are consistently high.

Policy coalitions facing Interior and Post Office are, then, *clientele-led*. And, given the similarity in members' goals, we would expect this environmental similarity to lead to very similar patterns of behavior. The structures of the two sets of clientele groups are, however, vastly different — a fact which introduces a note of complexity.

The Post Office Committee deals (or did, during the period under study) [24] with two main policy subjects — the working conditions of federal employees and postal rates. Each subject attracts a relatively small, easily identifiable, stable, nationally organized set of clientele groups. One set wants better working conditions, especially pay. Its most important standard bearers are the postal employee unions — most prominently the National Association of Letter Carriers, less prominently the National Federation of Post Office Clerks and, least prominently, the American Federation of Government Employees. The other set wants the lowest possible postal rates on second, third, and fourth class mail. Its leading spokesman is the Associated Third Class Mail Users, backed by various magazine publishers' associations and large mail order houses. There is no necessary policy conflict between these two clusters of groups. Throughout most of the period, indeed, the same man served as lobbyist for a powerful magazine group (Time Inc.) and remained a paid consultant for the National Association of Letter Carriers.[25] In their typical operations, the employee groups are on the offense, constantly seeking better working conditions, whereas the mail users stay on the defense, lying low until someone proposes rate increases. For both groups, the adversary is not other clientele groups, but the executive branch, which normally advocates smaller pay raises than employee groups want and higher postal rates than user groups want. Post Office Committee members, then, face an extremely concentrated, one-sided clientele barrage. To the degree that their environment is clientele dominated, to that extent it is monolithic — much more akin to that of Foreign Affairs than to that of Interior.

The Interior Committee, for its part, deals with a variegated array of policy subjects — national parks, irrigation and reclamation, public lands, mining, Indian affairs, territories. Many of these subjects are further fragmented into numerous independent, discrete "projects" — a dam, a park, a piece of public land, an Indian claim, an historical monument — each requiring a separate Committee decision, and none drawing the same cast of clientele characters as another. The Interior Committee's environment is, therefore, profuse with clientele groups — some national, permanent, and well known, many

[24] See the last chapter of this book for a comment on changes since the postal reorganization.
[25] Jerry Kluttz, "J. Don Kerlin: Letter Carriers Champion," *Washington Post*, July 23, 1967, p. A22.

local, *ad hoc*, and ephemeral. No one or two or three can be said to dominate any one policy area, let alone the total Committee environment. In a great many situations these groups do not conflict; but sometimes they do. Regarding water policy, a leader of the pro–public power National Rural Electrical Cooperatives Association wrote, "Powerful forces are aligned on each side and they clash in fierce lobbying battles over virtually every Federal river basin project which is considered." [26] But such projects always (save, perhaps, the Hells Canyon project) involve more than public-versus-private power issues. They involve conflicts over irrigation, flood control, recreation, and conservation. One important conflict among clientele groups, which infuses several policy areas, pits commercial users of the public lands against preservationist groups. In the classic case of the preservationist-inspired Wilderness Bill, for example, the following groups testified in favor:

> Wilderness Society, Wildlife Management Institute, Sierra Club, National Wildlife Federation, Izaak Walton League, National Audubon Society, American Nature Association, American Youth Hostels, Garden Clubs of America, American Planning and Civic Association, Federation of Women's Clubs, AFL-CIO, National Grange.

User-oriented groups testifying in opposition to the bill included:

> American Forestry Association, National Cattleman's Association, American Mining Congress, American Pulpwood Association, National Lumberman's Association, Rocky Mountain Oil and Gas Association, Independent Petroleum Association of America, U.S. Chamber of Commerce, National Association of Manufacturers, National Reclamation Association, American Farm Bureau Federation.

The Interior Committee member pursues his re-election goals amid a much more pluralistic and much less circumscribing clientele structure than does his Post Office Committee counterpart.

For the clientele groups, existing as they do outside the official government structure, their prescriptions reflect the problem of access. Their basic desire is for *sympathetic committee member-spokesmen* with whom they can maintain intimate and unimpaired communica-

---

[26] Clyde Ellis, *A Giant Step* (New York: Random House, 1966). A good case study is Angus McDonald, *The San Luis Reclamation Bill* (New York: McGraw Hill, 1962), p. 120.

tion. "That's the most important thing — getting committee members who are sympathetic." They want these spokesmen — and the more the better — to advocate the policy position of the clientele and to spearhead that position in legislative combat.

Postal employee groups are the most influential and the most aggressive confronting Post Office members. They want Committee members to advocate the union position in the predictable, biennial labor-management confrontation between federal employees and the executive branch. "Historically," writes a former president of the National Association of Letter Carriers, "each Postmaster General has opposed almost every attempt by postal employees to get a raise in salary." [27] Even though most union leaders are Democrats, the conflict is not usually a partisan one. A National Federation of Post Office Clerks leader explained in 1965:

> The Administration is our chief stumbling block and always has been, under the Republicans as well as the Democrats. Our rapport with the Congress, especially with the committees, is excellent. That's been true under both Republican and Democratic administrations. We're having a lot of trouble with Johnson right now, and we may have to put the arm on him next session.

Clientele prescriptions call for strenuous committee member support at whatever points may be necessary to bring their demands to fruition. When their Committee spokesmen are in a minority, they cheerfully advocate use of the forbiddingly difficult discharge petition, requiring 218 House member signatures. When their Committee spokesmen are in a majority, they push for bills that openly court a presidential veto. And if the veto comes, they may urge their Committee spokesmen to lead a fight to overturn it. Committee members who want clientele help at election time will be asked to commit themselves to battle and to join in mapping battle plans at every stage in the legislative process.

The same prescriptions are directed at Interior Committee members. The difference is that Interior attracts a greater number of substantive requests, most of which have an equal claim on the time, energy, and support of Committee members. Each request is likely

[27] William C. Doherty, *Mailman USA* (New York: David McKay, 1960). An excellent historical account of executive attitudes will be found in Gerald Cullinan, *The Post Office Department* (New York: Praeger, 1968).

to be supported by a different constellation of clientele groups. Each constellation is equally ardent and no one of them is likely to be perceptibly more powerful than another. It is a further characteristic of these separate and equal clientele requests that they benefit one or, perhaps, several congressional districts and that the congressmen involved are as often the leaders as they are the led in their clientele relations. Congressional Quarterly summarized one case this way:

> For the most part the Colorado River Bill was not lobbied in the conventional sense. Large industry organizations and trade associations did not become intimately involved. Rather . . . the Members of Congress from the states in the Colorado River Basin were the primary lobbyists for the Colorado River Bill.[28]

A high proportion of requests coming to Interior are retailed by fellow House members; and many of the policy coalitions facing Interior are tightly knit clientele–House member alliances.

By the same token, members of the Interior Committee will often be found leading such policy coalitions. That is why these members came to the Committee in the first place. Much more than do members of Post Office, therefore, Interior members act as policy entrepreneurs — seeking out projects that benefit their district and bringing them to the Committee, creating clientele pressure rather than reacting to it. Something of this important difference in committee spokesmen can be sensed by comparing the recruitment patterns of the two groups. As Table 2.4 showed, a much higher percentage of Interior members (of those interviewed) actively sought membership — either by initiating the move themselves or at the request of their state delegations. ("Interior was my primary choice, number one. . . . To do my district some good I knew I had to get on Interior. . . . I went in to say hello to every member of the Ways and Means Committee.") Conversely, many more Post Office members were assigned to the Committee without requesting it. ("I don't know how it happened. I didn't want it, didn't ask for it. The Ways and Means boys just put me on.") The point is that more Interior members have specific constituency projects they want to achieve through committee membership and will not, therefore, have to be pressured to act as the point of the clientele lance in legislative combat. Conversely, clientele groups will have to be more aggressive

---

[28] *Congressional Quarterly*, November 1, 1968, p. 3020.

in making policy activists out of a less strongly committed group of Post Office members. Postal groups can probably draw some comfort from the perverse recruitment figures of Table 2.4. Assuming that the unwanted assignments go predominantly to freshman members, these assignees are likely to feel electorally insecure and, hence, susceptible to employee and mailer blandishments.

The distinctive source of clientele influence is their local power base and their consequent capacity to touch members through their constituencies. There are few techniques of influence that have not been perfected by the postal groups; and nearly all of them are rooted in local strengths and abilities. When they act as recruiters to the committee, they do so by working locally. An official of the National Federation of Post Office Clerks explained:

> The membership of the committee . . . that's something most lobbyists don't get into — at least not the ones I talk to. But it's very important. This year we got this fellow ———— to go on. He's against unions, but with us he's been just fine. We contacted our people back in his district. We had started an educational campaign with him before he left home. When he got to town, I went over to see him and we talked about our mutual friends in his city. It was very friendly. The first time I testified before the Committee, you would have thought we were old buddies.

When they try to persuade someone to seek membership on the Committee, what do they tell him? A National Association of Letter Carriers leader answered.

> We tell them quite frankly what the Committee means. You get to meet a lot of people. In some committees, you don't meet people, but on Post Office you do. And it's the people you know who work for you and help you get re-elected. You tell me someone you want to know and I'll get a group of letter carriers together and someone will know him and introduce you. . . . Our people are very active politically. We see that they all register and vote and that their families vote, too.

There are a great many specific ways in which the local strength of the postal workers translates itself into electoral strength for the Committee member. The same NALC official commented:

> Letter carriers are under the Hatch Act, but their wives are not. We have the largest ladies auxiliary of any organization

> I know. When one of our friends is in trouble, these ladies
> will volunteer to help with the typing, the letter writing, the
> envelope stuffing. That's the hardest kind of help to get and
> it is much appreciated. But that's the least we can do for
> people who have helped us. The letter carriers have a tradi-
> tion of being grateful. . . . Another routine thing we do to
> signal our membership is that I may send a letter full of
> praise for the work of a congressman. We don't say "vote for
> him" but the message is clear. . . . We help organize testi-
> monial dinners to raise money for our friends. When there's
> a testimonial dinner, we always take one or two tables at
> least. We are constantly working to find ways of making our-
> selves attractive to our friends.

Postal group executives estimate that they spend 40 to 50 per cent
of their working hours on Capitol Hill talking with members of
Congress — mostly, of course, with Post Office Committee members.
And they have few peers in the art of direct lobbying. But the resources they manipulate are either local, or local in their impact —
that is, they have some ultimate bearing on the electoral fortunes of
Committee members.

The influence of clientele groups concerned with natural resources
comes, likewise, from the local stratum of American politics.[29] Committee members support the policy preferences of clientele groups
because they want to help their constituents and secure constituents'
support at election time. An official of the American Mining Congress struck this note when he said:

> In most instances, the Interior Committee is more sensitive
> to the problems of the (commercial) users than is the In-
> terior Department. That's because they have to get re-elected
> by the citizens every two years. They get a better grasp of
> public attitudes than the people in the agencies, (who) . . .
> don't know what a ballot box or a precinct is.

The fragmentation of Interior-bound policy requests, their equality
before the Committee, and the policy entrepreneurship of Interior
Committee members combine to make clientele activities more subtle
and their descriptions more difficult than those of the postal groups.
Furthermore, the techniques of clientele influence appear to be

---

[29] See Grant McConnell, *Private Power and American Democracy* (New
York: Knopf, 1966), Chapter VII.

more *indirect* with Interior than with Post Office. Sierra Club successes, for example, have been largely the result of the club's efforts to stir up grass roots protest.[30] And with reference to one direct method of clientele pressure — influencing committee assignments — a Sierra Club executive declared: "That's something we would never do. That's not how it works at all. A Congressman's committee assignment is his own business. That's a real no-no for us." Commercial trade associations, too, seem to eschew the corridor-pounding *modus operandi* of the postal unions." I haven't talked to a congressman or a senator in I don't know how long; I'd take an oath on that," exclaimed a top executive of the National Association of Electrical Companies. But, he continued:

> We have a pluralistic power economy. And we rely on the local companies to deal with Congress . . . (On Hell's Canyon) the Idaho Power Company was involved and it was their show. We didn't call a single shot on that one. Idaho Power called all the shots.

Whatever the technique they use, the ultimate source of clientele influence is local, as much with one committee as it is with the other.

We began this chapter by dividing our six committees into three pairs, on the basis of their members' goals. And we have kept the same pairings for the purpose of describing their environments. The question now arises: how far do committee patterns that are based on members' goals correspond to committee patterns based on environmental constraints? That is, do committees whose members have similar goals operate in similar environments? The answer to both questions, we would now have to conclude is: "a little, but not much."

The two committees with distinctively influence-oriented members are also the two committees with the parent chamber as the most prominent environmental element. Similarly, the two committees whose members are re-election-oriented are also the two committees for which clientele groups are the most prominent environ-

[30] *Congressional Quarterly*, November 1, 1968, pp. 3019–3031.

mental element. This is what we mean by "a little." On the other hand, for each of these two pairs of committees, there are some marked dissimilarities in environment. The policy coalitions facing Ways and Means are more complex and more partisan than those facing Appropriations. And the policy coalitions facing Interior are more complex and more pluralistic than those facing Post Office. In terms of their environments, the influence-oriented and re-election-oriented committees are as much unlike as they are like one another.

The environments of the two policy-oriented committees have almost nothing in common. The policy coalitions facing Education and Labor are more complex than those confronting Foreign Affairs. The environment of Foreign Affairs most closely resembles that of Post Office in its monolithic character. And the environment of Education and Labor most nearly resembles that of Ways and Means in its partisan character. Overall, within each pair of committees, one committee seems to confront a distinctly more complex, more pluralistic policy coalition than the other. The policy environment of the Ways and Means is more complex than that of Appropriations, that of Interior more complex than Post Office, and that of Education and Labor more complex than Foreign Affairs. As we move to describe committee behavior, we might expect it to be more difficult to predict the behavior of a committee operating in a complex environment than that of a committee, composed of members with the same goals, subject to a relatively simple set of constraints.

What seems most striking, in answering our earlier question, is the degree to which the environments of our pairs differ from one another. None of our three pairs, alike in member goals, is wholly alike with regard to the environment. We conclude, therefore, that the environmental variable is a largely *independent* one. It is not possible to predict the characteristics of a committee's environment by knowing only its members' goals. Nor is it possible to predict the goals simply by knowing the environment. Each variable can be expected to make an independent contribution in explaining a committee's behavior. And each must be investigated carefully. We do not mean there is no relationship between member goals and environmental constraints. The small degree of interconnection we have noted indicates that there are some linkages. And we would certainly expect that for any given committee, a change in one variable might produce a change in the other. But, clearly, each must be given independent weight throughout the analysis which follows.

In this chapter, we have viewed the committee environment in terms of the influence outsiders have on committee members. But if one is searching for the antecedents of these external constraints, one finds that the subject of the policy and its associated characteristics must be given a central place. We have compared the relative prominence of four categories of interested outsiders. But we have found, again and again, that similarities and, more often, differences in their interest and prominence are related to the policy area itself. Our idea of "policy coalition" is intended to acknowledge the importance of policy subjects, without, at the same time, making them an independent variable of the analysis. Some readers will probably wish we had done just that — developed a classification of policy subjects and/or policy characteristics to serve as major independent variables. Those who feel this way should be encouraged to try.[31] There is nothing in this study to challenge and much to confirm Capitol Hill wisdom that committee differences are related to policy differences. From the foregoing analysis, one might suggest that such policy characteristics as their importance to the parent institution, their salience, and their fragmentation would be useful categories. But we have chosen to compare committees at one level removed from their policy subjects because to do so helps us to advance the argument we have been making. We have given special emphasis to the goals of committee members; it is more in keeping with that emphasis to consider the environment in terms of people actively applying constraints to the members. From this perspective, policy subjects become important primarily because of the outsiders that take an interest in them and, hence, in the committee. It is obviously necessary to know about policy characteristics in order to locate the crucially important outsiders. But it is the outsiders that interest us most in this analysis.

[31] They should first read the stimulating works of: Theodore Lowi, "American Business, Public Policy, Case Studies and Political Theory," *World Politics* (July, 1964) and Robert Salisbury, "The Analysis of Public Policy: A Search for Theories and Roles" in Austin Ranney (ed.), *Political Science and Public Policy* (Chicago: Markham, 1968).

CHAPTER THREE

Strategic Premises

Once we know something about committee members' aspirations and something about the environment in which they must pursue these aspirations, we are almost ready to describe committee decision making. Almost, but not quite. It will help, we think, to understand the processes of decision making and the decisions themselves if we take an intermediary step and ask whether the members of each committee share any underlying guidelines for their decision making. Are there, in each committee, any agreed prescriptions for decision making — particularly any substantive decision rules — which might help us as we move to view the committee less as an aggregate of individuals and more as a working group? Each member of each committee faces this strategic problem: how shall I proceed in the committee to achieve my personal goals, given the environmental context in which my committee operates? It is a problem very difficult to solve on an individualistic, every-man-for-himself basis. For the solution, we can now see, necessitates some fairly complicated accommodations between the desires of individual committee members on the one hand and the desires of the interested and influential groups that comprise the environment on the other. These accommodations require a degree of collective action, action which takes the form, mainly, of committee decision making. Our concern is to describe members' agreements on strategy that help to promote collective action and that, therefore, underlie the pattern of committee decisions. We call these agreements — designed to implement, through committee action, a given set of member goals in a given context of environmental contraints — the *strategic premises* of decision making.

Agreements on strategic premises take operational form as agreements on rules for making substantive decisions. In this chapter, we shall try to explicate these *decision rules* for each committee. The evidence may not always be persuasive. Committee members do not readily or easily articulate such agreements. They come closest when they discuss "the job of the committee," but congressmen are notoriously formalistic and tongue-tied on that topic. Some decision rules are easier to discover than others; the wider the agreement and the more operationalized the rule, the easier to find. Every committee formulates — explicitly or implicitly — a few such rules. Indeed, it must. For if a committee is to make hundreds of substantive decisions, it will need to simplify the task by developing standardized decision contexts and standardized responses to them.[1] As simplifying devices, a committee's decision rules will obviously influence its decision-making processes and its substantive decisions. Precisely what that influence will be depends on the strategic context in which a committee's rules get formulated. Because those contexts, as we have seen in the first two chapters, are different for each committee, we shall proceed, in this chapter, on a committee-by-committee basis.

The decision rules we shall describe are the ones each committee seems to have adopted. We do not say they are the only ones that could be adopted in each strategic situation. Just why these particular rules, rather than some others, have been adopted in each instance is a question we leave unanswered. Perhaps the historical circumstances in which they were originally adopted would contain clues. But there is nothing inexorable or inevitable or permanent about them. They are, simply, the ones we found to be operative at the time we asked how each committee's members normally pursued their goals in their environment.

APPROPRIATIONS

The primary strategic problem for members of the *Appropriations Committee* involves pursuing their goal of House influence in the context of House prescriptions calling for both influence and responsiveness. That question is, how can the committee assert independent policy leadership (thereby remaining influential) while demonstrat-

---

[1] An excellent discussion of this problem will be found in: Robert Samberg, "Conceptualization and Measurement of Political System Output," unpublished manuscript (University of Rochester: Rochester, 1971).

ing a sensitivity to other House members' wishes (thereby remaining responsive)? A second strategic problem involves the pursuit of House influence in the face of executive-led policy coalitions seeking the Committee's acceptance of executive budget requests. The question is, how can the Committee remain influential while acceding to executive budget requests?

An influential committee, as we define it, is one which can make an independent policy judgment and win support for that judgment in the House. For Appropriations members, this means making policy judgments that are independent of the major policy coalitions of its environment — that is, independent of executive-led coalitions pressing for approval of budget estimates. The Committee has adopted as its first strategic premise that it should *reduce executive budget requests*. Members could assert independence by either raising or lowering the budget estimates sent to them. But they believe that only the latter course brings influence. By keeping resources scarce, they magnify their allocative power. By denying, limiting, or withholding funds, they keep environmental groups more mindful of them. So their basic posture is a negative one. In the words of former Chairman Clarence Cannon:

> It has long been an unwritten rule of the Committee on Appropriations that the budget estimate is to be taken as the maximum and the efficiency of the subcommittee has been judged — and the chairman of each subcommittee has prided himself on — the amount he was able to cut below the budget.[2]

Or, as Chairman George Mahon says, the Committee has acted "to veto or diminish the budget requests as often as reasons deemed sufficient to do so could be found." [3]

The Committee is supported in its budget-cutting posture by some members of the parent chamber. For one thing, all House members want to assert an institutional independence of the executive. For another thing, a substantial number of House members — the conservative coalition — support reductions in expenditures as a matter of personal philosophy and/or in response to a persisting pro-economy strain in American public opinion. Committee members work to solidify these existing bases of House support. They argue,

[2] 102 *Congressional Record*, p. 11128.
[3] *Congressional Record*, Daily Edition, March 2, 1965, p. 3866.

first, that a negative posture is essential if the House, in pursuit of its institutional interests, is to keep a close check on executive branch activity. They argue, second, that *some* institution must protect the federal treasury against the excessive claims made upon it by the manifold special interests in American society. The protecting institution is the House and, on behalf of the House, the Appropriations Committee. These arguments — in essence, that an effective purse string is a tight purse string — blend institutional and policy rationales.

The Committee further defends its budget-cutting premise before the House by arguing that its decisions are not really policy decisions at all, but only dollar-and-cents adjustments in funding levels. "A disagreement on money isn't like a legislative program — it's a matter of money rather than a difference in philosophy." The distinction, portraying Appropriations as a "business" and not a "policy" committee, appeals especially to members of substantive legislative committees, worried as they are about the Appropriations Committee's encroachment on their policy domains.

Budget cutting is, or can be made, acceptable to the parent House. Obviously, however, "too much" budget cutting cannot. For most policy coalitions will have at least some — and some will have a great deal of — House member participation. It would hardly be responsive to House wishes if the Committee dealt too unfavorably with House-supported executive requests. In the interests of retaining its influence, therefore, the Committee has adopted a second strategic premise: *to provide adequate funding for executive programs* — the stronger the House member participation in a given policy coalition, the more "adequate" the funding. Thus the Committee remains responsive to House majorities which authorize programs and to the various constituency interests of their colleagues. Thus it responds to the executive-led coalitions dominating its policy environment. These are prudent responses, made out of self-restraint in the pursuit of influence.

Taken together, the committee's two decision rules call for a balance between reduction and funding, in which the internal presumption that the budget should be cut is continuously weighed against the external forces seeking ratification of the budget. And the balance must be one that can win acceptance on the House floor. Beyond these general guidelines, there is no Committee agreement. What is "too much," or "adequate," or "a balance" will be determined on a case-to-case basis. One important guarantee to the House that the Committee will not go "too far" in either direction rests in the responsible legislative style of the members. Beyond this, the accommodation is eased by the way in which Committee members choose to construe the decisions confronting them. Since they are calibrated in dollars and cents and not in ideological terms, compromise is made easier than it otherwise might be. Furthermore, Committee members treat each agency request as independent of every other agency request, thereby avoiding broadly programmatic decisions. Finally, the Committee members view each budget request as composed of a relatively noncontroversial "base" — pretty close to what they got last year — plus an "increment" of new plans. By removing the base from its purview and critically scrutinizing only the increment, the Committee can fund the largest portions of a program and make reductions in a smaller segment, thus pursuing both strategies at once. All these properties serve to mitigate sharp policy conflicts, thereby skirting potential difficulty in the parent chamber.

It would be wrong to claim that there is complete agreement within the Committee on these premises of decision making. But there is a substantial, cross-party consensus together with concurrence by the two men who chaired the Committee from 1955 to 1966. The personnel basis for the consensus is revealed in the ideological and partisan predispositions of the members. For each of the 86th through the 89th Congresses, we have obtained from *Congressional Quarterly* a Conservative Coalition Support Score [4] for each committee member and each noncommittee member in the House. For each Congress and then for the four Congresses we have added and averaged the scores for the two groups. By comparing each committee member with the other House members and each committee with the other committees, we have a crude measure of their general *ideological predispositions*. We have done the same thing from the 84th through the 89th Congresses with the *Congressional Quarterly*'s Party Unity Score,[5] giving us, we think, a crude measure

[4] Conservative coalition votes are those in which a majority of Southern Democrats and a majority of Republicans voted together against a majority of Northern Democrats. A member's Conservative Coalition Support Score is the percentage of times he voted with the coalition.

[5] The Party Unity Score of each congressman is the number of times (in percentage terms) that he voted with a majority of his party when the majority of his party was opposed by the majority of the other party.

of the *partisan predispositions* of each committee. And we shall use these as indicators of the relative ease with which agreement on various strategic premises can be reached in our six committees. It should be remembered, however, that summary figures of this sort do not necessarily reveal anything about committee members' attitudes or their behavior on the specific issues before their own committee or subcommittee.

From Table 3.1, it appears that the Appropriations Committee is, overall, the most conservatively inclined committee of the six, a predisposition that is highly supportive of its budget-cutting premise. Furthermore, the two party contingents lean in the same direction, with the much more marked conservatism of the Republicans reflecting the criteria of selection mentioned earlier. This *ideological convergence* of Democrats and Republicans facilitates a cross-party consensus on budget cutting and would seem to give the minority party a strong stake in existing committee strategy. It should also be noted that the average conservatism score of the Committee chairman during the period [6] was *51* — just about midway between the two party averages. This indicates that chairmen Cannon and Mahon could easily join the consensus — which they did.

The data in Table 3.2 indicate no marked overall tendency either toward or away from partisanship among the members. The strong partisan predisposition of Appropriations Committee Republicans is offset by the lack of a strong tendency of any sort among the more numerous Democrats. The average party unity score of the chairman was *63* — lower than that of his fellow Committee Democrats. A consensus on the Committee's strategic premises would seem to require fairly weak partisan predispositions among a conservatively inclined group, with Committee leaders sharing these characteristics. According to our crude measures, the Appropriations Committee seems to have had a personnel profile that filled this bill.

WAYS AND MEANS

The main strategic problem for *Ways and Means* members involves the same question that faces members of Appropriations — how can they achieve a relationship with their House colleagues that makes

[6] Clarence Cannon was chairman from 1955 to 1963; George Mahon, from 1964 to the present.

Table 3.1
Committee Conservative Predisposition
(Mean Conservative Coalition Scores 86th–89th Congresses)

	Democrats			Republicans			Total		
	Comm. Membs.	Other House Membs.	Diff.	Comm. Membs.	Other House Membs.	Diff.	Comm.	Other	Diff.
App.	33	30	+3	78	69	+9	51	45	+6
W.&M.	26	31	-5	80	70	+10	47	45	+2
P.O.	30	31	-1	73	70	+3	47	45	+2
Int.	30	31	-1	71	70	+1	45	46	-1
F.A.	24	31	-7	57	71	-14	36	46	-10
E.&L.	16	32	-16	71	70	+1	33	47	-14

Table 3.2
Committee Partisan Predisposition
(Mean Party Unity Scores, 84th–89th Congresses)

	Democrats			Republicans			Total		
	Comm. Membs.	Other House Membs.	Diff.	Comm. Membs.	Other House Membs.	Diff.	Comm.	Other House	Diff.
W.&M.	76	70	+6	73	70	+3	75	70	+5
E.&L.	74	70	+4	71	70	+1	74	70	+4
App.	69	70	−1	75	70	+5	71	70	+1
P.O.	67	70	−3	73	70	+3	70	70	0
Int.	69	70	−1	71	70	+1	70	70	0
F.A.	72	70	+2	64	71	−7	69	70	−1

them both influential and responsive? The problem is partially eased, as it is for Appropriations, by the desire of House members for powerful money committees. But the problem here is more difficult than it is for Appropriations because of the variety of policy subjects that come to Ways and Means and the attendant difficulty in arriving at some common decision strategy applicable to all of them.

Before a committee's members can develop strategic premises, they must first, it seems, adopt a standardized view of the context in which they make decisions. For example, Appropriations members see the context of their decisions mostly in terms of whether or not and by how much to reduce executive budget requests. And they define their policy independence in terms of a relationship to the executive branch. When Appropriations members say, "There has never been a budget submitted to Congress that couldn't be cut," or, "There isn't a budget that can't be cut ten per cent immediately," they place their decisions in a common context. And they can operationalize their decision-making task in terms of that context. But how can decisions in the fields of trade, social security, taxes, and medical care be viewed in common context? And how can Ways and Means members define their policy independence in terms of a relationship to any single element in their environment? If they cannot, how can they operationalize their decision-making task except on an issue-to-issue basis? And if they cannot describe their decision-making task, what general guidelines will they follow in producing an independent policy judgment in these matters? The plurality of its issues and the complexity of its policy environment cast a special light on the Ways and Means member's strategic problem.

Committee members have dealt with the problem, we think, by standardizing their decision context at a more abstract level than Appropriations members do. The common characteristics of Ways and Means decisions, members believe, are their substantive complexity, their political delicacy, and, withal, their tremendous impact on the nation's well-being. Invariably, they require special technical skill, special political sensitivity, and, in the words of Chairman Wilbur Mills, "the utmost caution, responsibility, and prudence." [7]

---

[7] *Congressional Record*, Daily Edition, November 21, 1966, p. A5907.

Taken together, these requirements impose on the Committee not a standard substantive context but a standard *procedural* context. In a word, the Committee needs the utmost independence in which to work responsibly toward its own policy judgments.

> We feel . . . that, what the hell, the average Member isn't in a position to judge. We have the benefit of all the testimony, all the disagreements, the statistics, the rationales — it's up to us to use our judgment about what to do.

Ways and Means policy judgments will be carefully constructed, interdependent wholes to be tampered with only at the risk of adverse consequences for the nation. Hence, these decisions will need the protection of the closed rule. In return for its extraordinary independence, the Committee promises to make decisions that are acceptable to the great majority of House members.

For Ways and Means members, the strategy on which they can agree is one in tune with this view of what they are doing. And it is *to write a bill that will pass the House.* So long as they can do this, they can — regardless of the substance of their decisions — retain their influence while at the same time demonstrating their responsiveness to the House. Chairman Mills put the decision rule this way:

> As I see it our job is to work over a bill until our technical staff tells us it is ready and until I have reason to believe that it is going to have enough support to pass. Many of our bills must be brought out under a closed rule and to get and keep a closed rule, you must have a widely acceptable bill. It's as simple as that.[8]

Another Committee veteran declared, "I don't know of anyone on the Committee who wants to report a bill out that can't pass in the House." And Manley writes, "A good bill that cannot pass the House is a contradiction in terms for most members of Ways and Means." [9] To win on the floor is to enhance the influence of the Committee collectively and, hence, of its members individually. To lose on the floor is to severely damage Committee prestige and power. "Writing

---

[8] As quoted in John Manley, "Wilbur D. Mills: A Study in Congressional Influence," *American Political Science Review* (June, 1969), p. 448.

[9] Manley, *The Politics of Finance, op. cit.*

a bill that will pass" is, for Ways and Means members, what "reduce budget estimates" is for Appropriations members — a strategy believed to be directed toward the acquisition and preservation of Committee influence. Each strategy is tailored to a different standardization of the decision context; and each is an operational guide to decision making.

But it is clear that success on the House floor will not necessarily satisfy the partisan-executive, or administration, coalitions that press substantive policy requests upon the Committee. A second strategic premise, fashioned in general response to these environmental demands, is to *prosecute policy partisanship*. That is to say, Committee members agree to act in a partisan fashion — not, in this case, to enhance their individual goal of influence in the House but to meet the strongly held prescriptions of party leaders. We have already seen these prescriptions operate in the selection process. And we see the resulting profile in Tables 3.1 and 3.2. In Table 3.1, Ways and Means Republicans and Democrats are seen to exhibit a sharp *ideological divergence*, in marked contrast to their colleagues on the Appropriations Committee. And, from Table 3.2, it appears that this ideological divergence parallels a strong set of partisan predispositions — the strongest, overall, of any of our six committees. The Committee's chairman is a good deal more conservative than his fellow Democrats, with an average conservatism score of 61. But he seems every bit as predisposed toward partisanship as they, with an average party unity score of 77.[10] It would appear that Ways and Means members are especially well disposed toward the prosecution of partisanship generally. And these indicators point to the existence of a fairly solid consensus in support of the Committee's partisan decision rule.

The two strategic premises are in partial conflict. To the degree that members work to produce a "widely acceptable" bill, they will tone down partisanship. To the extent that they respond to partisan pressures, they will not be making independent policy judgments. The dilemmas of balancing one strategic stance against another are present here as they are for Appropriations members. And in both cases, we would argue, top priority is given to that strategy more directly related to the pursuit of member goals. In the case of Ways

[10] Jere Cooper was chairman from 1955 to 1957; Wilbur Mills from 1958 to the present.

and Means, it works independently to produce a bill that will pass the House. A Committee staff man described the majority party Democrats in the Kennedy-Johnson years in this way:

> I think every member of the Committee has a renegade streak. The majority of them favor the Administration and go along, but still they do have a sense of their own importance, of their position in the House, that they are not just rubber stamps.

As a practical matter they will not have to make a direct choice between the two strategies very often. And, temperamentally, Ways and Means members affect an ameliorative legislative style. Still, their priorities are clear. As John Manley summarizes:

> The kinds of men on Ways and Means are men oriented toward bargaining, accommodation, peaceful settlement of disputes, and *the subordination of specific policy objectives to the maintenance of the power and prestige of their Committee.*[11] (Italics added)

We expect, however, to find both strategic premises reflected in the Committee's decision-making processes and its decisions.

INTERIOR

No fact of group life seems more distinctive to the *Interior Committee* member than the sheer volume of requests confronting him. "Interior handles more pieces of legislation than any other committee in the House." "Twenty per cent of all the bills introduced in the House are referred to the Interior Committee. Did you realize that? Well, I'm telling you — twenty percent!" Most of them (70 percent by member estimates) are congressional in origin, pressed upon the Committee by local clientele groups and their spokesmen in the House. Independent in terms of subject matter, equal in the ardor of their supporters, the bills come to the Committee without any evident standard for determining priorities. For each individual Committee member, the proposals of greatest concern to him are those supported by clientele groups in his district and for which he is both entrepreneur and spokesman. Each member wants, most of

[11] Manley, *op. cit.*

all, for the Committee to pass *his* bills. And in the interests of eas-
ing them through the Committee, he will be predisposed to lend his
support to the bills of his fellow Committee members. But even
more than this, he wants his bills passed in the House. He has come
to the Committee, after all, to "get something for the district" and
thereby to improve his chances for re-election. If he wants a vote-
winning reputation back home, it will not be enough to introduce
proposals and fight for them. He must get his proposals enacted
into law. And this requires cooperation beyond the Committee,
among his House colleagues more generally. So he will be predisposed also to look favorably on proposals being pushed by other
House members.

Lacking any standardized way of distinguishing among the vast
volume of requests, and having incentives, in terms of their individual goals, for being well disposed toward all of them, Committee
members take the view that all requests are, indeed, equal in merit
and support. The Committee takes as its major decision rule a determination to process and pass *all* requests and to do so in such a
way as to maximize the chances of passage in the House. Succinctly,
then, Interior's major strategic premise is: *to secure House passage
of all constituency-supported, Member-sponsored bills.* As members
generalize about this primary mission: "The Committee doesn't get
involved in liberal-conservative issues. It's more a neutral processing
machine than anything else, a traffic cop." By adopting this posture,
Committee members can meet the great bulk of their own personal
goals and the great bulk of the demands emanating from the
environment.

As part of a fully operational decision rule, Committee members
process requests in accordance with some canons of traffic and
quality control. They do not move legislation through precipitately,
but rather within a reasonable time. Whether a bill will pass the
Committee is not a serious question; *when* it will pass remains,
however, within the Committee's control. Once a hearing is granted,
a bill is predictably on its way, but sponsors may have to stand in
line for a while before they can get a hearing. In addition to agenda
control, the Committee makes an imprint on all legislation by scrutinizing it very carefully, no matter how minor the bill. Thus the
Committee emphasizes expertise in areas in which most House
members are nonexpert. By the way in which they process requests,

Committee members believe they enhance the subsequent chance of passage in the House.

> The Committee has a reputation in the House for doing a good job. They know that everything we report has been gone over thoroughly. This isn't true of all committees. The House is suspicious of some committees.

The Committee tries hard to keep a reputation for orderly, careful, thorough legislative workmanship.

A strategy of "House passage for all bills" provides a guideline for most Committee decision making but not for those situations in which members face sharply conflicting policy coalitions. Committee members want all conflicts — particularly intraconstituency or intra-regional ones — to be solved before proposals are made to the Committee. But sometimes conflict outside, and cleavage inside, the Committee cannot be avoided. Quite often, as indicated earlier, such conflicts find Western-oriented clientele groups (such as users of natural resources, beneficiaries of reclamation) plus their Committee spokesmen aligned against Eastern-oriented clientele groups (such as preservationists, nonbeneficiaries of reclamation) plus their Committee spokesmen. Policy conflicts are not, save in rare public-private power confrontations, construed in party terms. A Western Democrat said:

> You're more likely to have geographical partisanship or regional partisanship than party partisanship. I have more in common with a Republican from Montana than with a Democrat from Florida. . . . You might have one issue a year that's partisan, a real red-hot partisan issue — Hells Canyon — but most of the are so non-controversial. It's not like . . . Education and Labor where you have these great national issues with the parties lined up on either side.

Nearly all Committee members see their conflict situations as "more East versus West than Democrats versus Republicans."

For these situations, a majority of Committee members subscribe to a second strategic premise: *to provide in the context of conservation legislation, reasonable protection for the commercial users of land and water resources.* The rule does not deny the importance of conservation; but it calls for particularly sensitive, sympathetic con-

cern for the claims of commercial clientele groups. As one member
put it:

> The Easterners want to turn the West into a vast play-
> ground where they can come to play. That's all right, we
> love to have them; but the West is more than a playland.
> You're talking about our living, our livelihood, our jobs.
> There's more involved than having a playground here.

In conflicts between "Eastern" conservationists and "Western" clientele groups of users, the Committee's overall posture is deliberately
pro-Western and pro-user. As a consequence of this strategic posture, the Committee may find itself in conflict with the more conservationist executive branch. Strongly conservationist measures such
as the Wilderness Bill, the Scenic and Wild Rivers Bill, the Land
and Water Conservation Fund, and proposals for new national
parks come to the Committee via the executive branch and with
strong executive (plus clientele group) support. It is a concomitant
of the Committee's decision rules that it places a high value on its
policy independence from the executive. Committee members say:
"This Committee is pretty independent. I don't think it's an arm of
the executive department." "We make the policy, we are the policy
makers. That's a right that's very jealously guarded by the Committee." An Interior Department executive noted, similarly, that the
Department's greatest problem with the Committee was institutional — "the problem of the legislative and executive branches."
"I've seen (Chairman) Wayne Aspinall dress down a younger Committee member who asked what the policy of the Department was.
Aspinall pounded his fist and said, 'The Congress and this Committee make the policy, *not* the Department.'" From their pro-
Western stance, Interior Committee members have developed a
sense of institutional independence from the executive which is
very similar to that of Appropriations and, though somewhat less
so, to Ways and Means. And they trade on their independence
along with their expertise in soliciting the good opinion of their
House colleagues.

    The Committee displays a personnel profile consistent with both
strategic premises. Table 3.3 compares regional representation in the
House with regional representation on each of the six committees.
This is done by averaging House figures for each of the six Congresses and by calculating for each committee the percentage of total

committee man-years served by representatives for each region. A "representativeness score" — the sum of the differences between House and Committee representation from five regions — shows the Interior Committee to be, geographically, the most unrepresentative of our six committees. And the unrepresentativeness is the product of its lopsided Far Western representation. This finding applies to both party contingents. Committee Democrats from the Far West overrepresent House Democrats from the Far West by 41 percentage points; for Far Western Committee Republicans, the gap is 28 percentage points. Interior Democrats and Interior Republicans are, in fact, the two most unrepresentative of the 60 separate regional contingents on the six committees. Westerners will, naturally, be responsive to the interests of their Western constituencies. And it would seem to be characteristic of these constituencies that they are small enough and economically homogeneous enough to give user groups dominant economic and political strength.

Tables 3.1 and 3.2 display no offsetting ideological or partisan predispositions on the part of Interior members. With a conservatism score of 22 and a party unity score of 75, the average Committee chairman is inclined to be more liberal and more partisan than his fellow Democrats.[12] But the electoral realities of his Western constituency provide the key to his strategic stance.[13] And in this respect, he is solidly within the Committee consensus. A Western Democrat talked about long-time Chairman Wayne Aspinall of Colorado in these terms:

> If you check his record in the House, I think you'll find he's a good Democrat. But when he gets over here in Committee, politics is adjourned and he thinks in terms of what's good for the West — for miners, for cattlemen, for sheep raisers, and farmers. He has to. He has more Republicans in his district than Democrats. The fact that he's re-elected and re-elected and re-elected is a tribute to Wayne Aspinall the man, not to any excess of Democrats. He can't afford to alienate all those Republicans. I'm in the same situation.

The second strategic premise, like the first one, is constituency-oriented. In this sense, little balancing is required between them. By

[12] Clair Engle was chairman from 1955 to 1958; Wayne Aspinall from 1959 to 1972.
[13] See Julius Duscha, "Bonanza in Colorado: Who Gets It?" as reprinted in *Congressional Record*, Daily Edition, March 7, 1966, pp. 4902–4904.

Table 3.3

Regional Representatives of Committees 84th–89th Congresses

Average Percentage House Seats by Region		Percentage of Man-Years Service on Committees By Region											
		Appropriations		Ways and Means		Post Office		Education and Labor		Foreign Affairs		Interior	
		%	Difference	%	Difference	%	Difference	%	Difference	%	Difference	%	Difference
East	26%	27	+1	27	+1	28	+2	37	+11	28	+2	15	-12
South	24%	24	0	28	+4	33	+9	12	-12	19	-5	12	-16
Border	9%	7	-2	10	+1	1	-8	7	-2	4	-5	6	-4
Midwest	27%	28	+1	24	-3	27	0	25	-2	43	+16	18	-6
Far West	14%	13	-1	11	-3	10	-4	19	+5	6	-8	50	+39
		99		100		99		100		100		101	
Representative Score		5		12		23		32		36		77	

East: Conn., Del., Me., Mass., N.H., N.J., N.Y. Pa., R.I., Vt.
South: Ala., Ark., Fla., Ga., La., Miss., N.C., S.C., Tenn., Texas, Va.
Border: Ky., Md., Okla., W. Va.
Midwest: Ill., Ind., Iowa, Kans., Mich., Minn., Neb., N.D., Ohio, S.D., Wisc.
Far West: Alaska, Ariz., Calif., Colo., Hawaii, Idaho, Mont., Nev., N.M., Ore., Utah, Wash., Wyo.

following both, most Interior members can successfully pursue their goal of constituency service and re-election.

The Committee's second decision rule raises a crucial problem, identical to one raised by its first rule — how to secure the passage of its bills in the parent chamber. In the first case, as we noted, the Committee cultivates an image of routinized, expert deliberations. And it relies heavily on this House-oriented image in the second case too. But here the deeper problem involves allaying the suspicions of non-western Members confronting the recommendations of a lop-sidedly Western committee. Westerners are, after all, a tiny minority of the House; Committee Westerners do not sit there as the representatives of large state delegations on whom they can rely for floor support. Most important, the Committee's Westerners deal with the problem internally, by mollifying their non-Western Committee colleagues to the point where they will not foment an East-West controversy on the House floor. These efforts center on the mollification of the Committee's most ardent pro-Eastern conservationist and ranking Republican, John Saylor of Pennsylvania. Externally, the Committee relies on help from non-Western House members wherever they can get it. Some comes from members who need or have received projects from the Committee. "At some time or other, every Congressman is interested in something we handle." "Maybe they needed a project, or a park, in their district a while back. You are aware that they talked to you about their bill a couple of months ago and now you need their support . . ." [14] Other help comes from party leaders predisposed to help any committee and from House Democrats, who are usually predisposed toward helping their fellow Democrats with legislation of special interest to them.[15] The Interior Committee is, in sum, extremely self-conscious about its relations with the parent chamber — a concern which it shares with Ways and Means and Appropriations, but not with the other three committees.

Coming from the West and naturally sympathetic to anything they perceive to be a Western interest, Committee members feel little clientele pressure. They acknowledge talking to clientele groups but comment: "I don't consider this pressure." "Maybe I don't know pressure when I see it . . . but all I ever get from them is information." Members agree that they need the expertise of clientele

[14] *Congressional Quarterly*, November 1, 1968, p. 3031.
[15] On this last proposition, see David Mayhew, *Party Loyalty and Congressmen* (Cambridge: Harvard University Press, 1966).

groups if they are going to help them. "After all, these people are
very well informed on what concerns them and they are very helpful when particular issues come up. They press a little, but we can
handle them." Committee members feel as though they are in complete control of their clientele relations and that they are anything
but subservient to or "tools of" the commercial users with whom they
share a natural community of interest. Such pressure as they do feel
comes, they say, from the most ardent preservationist groups, like
the Sierra Club. Sierra Club lobbying has been, typically, indirect,
as in its successful newspaper campaign to arouse Eastern congressional opposition to the flooding of Dinosaur National Monument
and to the building of two dams in the Grand Canyon. In each case,
the Committee modified its views to the degree necessary to secure
passage of a bill benefiting Westerners in an aroused non-Western
House. A burgeoning conservationist movement may change the
Committee's second strategic premise. More Easterners may be attracted to the Committee or more Western Committee members
may come to define their constituency interests as basically preservationist. For now, however, the Committee remains an arena in which
commercial user groups are likely to obtain their most favorable
governmental treatment.

POST OFFICE

For members of the *Post Office Committee*, seeking re-election help
and inhabiting an environment dominated by a relatively few, single-
minded, and potentially helpful clientele groups, a standard decision
rule is easy to develop. Since employee groups want higher salaries
and better benefits and since mail users want low postal rates, the
responsive posture for Post Office members is to support both sets
of demands. Accordingly, their first strategic premise is: *to support
maximum pay increases and improvements in benefits for employee
groups and to oppose all rate increases for mail users.* A veteran
Committee member summarized succinctly, "Most of the Committee members want to keep postal rates down and salaries up, and
that's all there is to it." And a top Post Office Department executive
agreed, "They always tack a little on the pay bills and shade a little
off the rate bills." It is a working formula well suited to the achievement of re-election goals.

As we suggested earlier, the Post Office member — in sharp contrast to the Interior member — operates under very great pressure from clientele groups. For one thing, the demands of the Post Office clientele tend to be more concentrated and one-sided. For another thing, these clientele demands have much less of a one-to-one impact on a member's district than do those of Interior — thereby reducing the likelihood that a member will act as entrepreneur and accept individual responsibilty for clientele causes. And Post Office members have to absorb clientele pressure directly, with very little of that House member-to-committee member solicitation so common to Interior. An Eastern member of the Interior Committee made this comparison:

> There is not much contact with pressure groups, and I guess this is one reason why the Committee is so enjoyable. Most of the lobbying is done by the members who have introduced bills . . . (With) Post Office, they are on your back every minute there. It must be fierce. I just left a delegation of letter carriers, and I'm not even on the (Post Office) Committee. If I were, they would be pressing me all the time.

This is just how members of the Post Office Committee do feel. "From the first day they were pounding on the door wanting an interview."

> Nobody in the Congress or in the public gives a damn about what we do. Oh, once every few years, we have an orgy on junk mail, but other than that, nobody cares. We are wooed by the whole panoply of outside groups. There's always a dinner somewhere. They come in and fawn over your staff. There isn't a day that goes by that someone doesn't come in here wooing me. . . . This is the dominant fact of life, the distinguishing characteristic of the Committee.

Postal clientele groups may have to work extra hard to woo legislative spokesmen and allies. But many Committee members, in pursuit of their personal goals, gladly serve.

It is not possible to be specific about numbers. A bipartisan minority of Committee members work on the most intimate terms with the postal groups. So close, indeed, is this relationship that members who resent clientele pressure accuse their colleagues of a kind of subservient sellout never remotely suggested by one Interior member about another. "He's a bought man." "He's in the pocket of the unions." "He's in bed with all the groups. They raise money for him and he does their bidding." "They (certain Committee members) run the show as a paid front for various groups." Committee members, it is fair to say, display varying degrees of interest in helping the clientele groups. Those with the greatest interest — perhaps a minority — set decision rules on which a majority willingly agree. On a Committee, three-quarters of whose members serve on another committee and a majority of whose members had no reason for joining it in the first place, it is easy for an "efficient minority" to establish the Committee's strategic posture.

One important countervailing force, the executive branch, does operate in the Committee environment. And the Post Office Department normally seeks modest pay increments and postal rate increases to offset the cost thereof. Most postal bills come from the executive branch, and the Post Office Department is not totally lacking in persuasive power of its own. For one thing it makes district-related decisions on postal facilities and personnel. More important, it can brandish the threat of a Presidential veto in support of its familiar position — "no postal rate increase, no salary increase." To this position, the Post Office Committee finds it necessary to adopt a standard response which operates as a limitation on its basic decision rule. This second strategic premise is: *to accede to executive branch wishes when, in the judgment of Committee members and employee groups, to do otherwise will net employee groups nothing in that Congress.* If the very probable price of undiluted support for both sets of clientele groups appears to be the loss of a pay raise altogether, Committee members will meet executive demands by compromising on the side of the pay increase or accepting a rate increase. Employee groups will say, "It was this or nothing"; mail users will say, "They fought as hard and as long as they reasonably could." Both groups, given their need for continued access and sympathy, will accept the Committee's action. And re-election help will continue.

Postal issues are not *prima facie* partisan issues; postal clientele groups assiduously court both sides of the aisle. When the executive branch, however, comes into head-on conflict with clientele groups, some partisanship does get injected into the picture, as the President looks to his party members for support. Table 3.2, however, shows no overall partisan predisposition. Table 3.1 reveals no marked ideological proclivities — certainly none that could not be neutralized by the kinds of clientele efforts we have described. There is, we think, little evidence in these personnel characteristics to contradict our belief that the strategic premises we have outlined have commanded a substantial cross-party consensus.

What these figures do *not* show, however, is that, unlike any of the three committees thus far discussed, a critical element was missing from the Committee consensus. The man who chaired the Committee for the period under examination did *not* subscribe to either decision rule. With an average party unity score of 50 and an average conservatism score of 76, Chairman Tom Murray was much less partisan and vastly more conservative than his fellow Committee Democrats — more conservative even than Committee Republicans In his words:

> I am proud of the fact that I am conservative. My name is Thomas Jefferson Murray. That was my father's name. That was my grandfather's name. It has been a family name for years, and I am a Jeffersonian, States Rights Democrat." [16]

These differences are indicative of a fundamental disagreement between Chairman Murray and the majority of his Committee on the strategic premises of Committee behavior. This disagreement colored every facet of Committee behavior from 1955 to 1966. The effect was so great that it seems to us that *the most important thing to know about any committee chairman is whether or to what extent he is in agreement with the majority of his Committee on their underlying strategic premises.*

Murray's most favored decision rule was to wait until the executive branch made a proposal and then support it — acting all the while as "the great balance wheel" in resisting clientele-led policy coalitions.

> I am sorry to see the influence that these postal lobbyists exercise upon certain members of the Congress and particularly upon certain members of my Committee. I regret it. . . . I am sick and tired of the tactics of these lobbyists.[17]

Committee members explained his strategic stance thus: "He wouldn't report a bill unless the administration favored it." "Murray would take the administration bill and rubber stamp it through." "The only thing Tom would move on was postal rates. He'd raise

---

[16] 102 *Congressional Record*, p. 11969.
[17] 106 *Congressional Record*, p. 12698.

the rates, but never the pay." Given this chasm in strategy and given the procedural prerogatives available to the Chairman, the Post Office Committee operated as a "house divided" much of the time, with neither side able or willing to impose its position on the other. In 1965, however, a bipartisan majority on the Committee revolted against the Chairman, wrote a new set of internal procedures, and achieved effective decision-making control.

In explaining the 1965 revolt, members agreed that Chairman Murray's passive, pro-administration policy had brought the Committee to virtual impotence — a state in which no member could hope to achieve his personal goals.

> I like to think of Murray as a tackle or guard on a football team. He's the guy who says, brother you'd better run around me because if you don't, I'll flatten you. Everything was over his dead body. If I wanted something, I'd run around him. He was the stumbling block."

"His idea was to pass two or three inconsequential bills a year and then go home. He wouldn't do a damn thing but obstruct." "I had a retirement bill in, to improve retirement benefits. Finally, after months, I get it through the Committee. Tom Murray won't file a report — won't even file a report. God damn, I think I marched up that mountain three times." "No one wanted to hurt his feelings but, my God, you can't be in Congress and do nothing. The Old Man would do just what he had to do and nothing else." Needless to say, the clientele groups were pleased at the outcome. It provided them with sympathetic leadership, a greater number of points of access via subcommittees, potentially greater leverage over the executive, and, withal, an increased likelihood that the Committee would follow its primary rather than its fall-back decision rule. The revolt was a move they had long pressed upon their Committee spokesmen, and they were very active in pushing it along. Said two National Association of Letter Carriers leaders: "We urged that for a long time and did everything we could to further it. We talked to people and got votes for the change." "We quarterbacked the change. . . . I think we supplied a good deal of the impetus." A Committee staffer gave the clientele groups full credit, "It was the pressure from the postal workers and the federal employees union. The members couldn't resist it. That's why we have the new rules." Some Committee members disagree. But it is not necessary to arbitrate the disagreement. For all agree that the clientele groups and their Committee spokesmen worked in close cooperation to effect a basic change in the Committee's decision posture — a change that was beneficial to clientele groups in terms of their policy demands and Committee members in terms of their personal goals.

FOREIGN AFFAIRS

Foreign Affairs Committee members face the problem of achieving their policy goals in a monolithic, executive-dominated environment. In their effort to devise standard, operational decision rules, they begin with only the most general ideas about good foreign policy. Mostly they want to participate in making it; they want to become immersed in this policy area of so much personal interest to them. Surely they do not expect to become the nation's responsible foreign policy makers. But just as surely they look forward to making some contribution. Their strategic problem has both substantive ("what policy?") and procedural ("how much involvement?") dimensions. In both respects, the executive branch prescriptions to which they must accommodate themselves are very clearly defined. The substantive "what" means executive branch requests; and the procedural "how much" means bipartisan legitimation and procedural cooperation. Committee member accommodation to these restricting prescriptions is imperfect and incomplete. And because their original enthusiasm is so great — they have the highest percentage of self-starters according to Table 2.4 — their subsequent disappointments provoke a magnified measure of frustration.

By general agreement, the major executive request is for support of its foreign aid policy, and members give it primacy among their policy subjects.

> Really, we are sort of a committee on foreign aid. We have other bills, and I don't mean to downgrade the importance of the Arms Control and Disarmament Agency or the Peace Corps. But they aren't the kinds of bills you spend six months on.

With regard to this one, central subject, Committee members do agree on a fairly simple decision rule: *to approve and help pass the annual foreign aid program.* Joining in the consensus are an over-whelming number of Committee Democrats, a fluctuating majority of Committee Republicans, and each of the Committee's three chair-men during the period.[18] Tables 3.1 and 3.2 reveal some personnel factors that are, at the least, consistent with the requisite partisan-ideological underpinnings for such a consensus. They show Foreign Affairs to be the least partisan-leaning and the second most liberal-leaning of the six committees. The tables further indicate that it is the Committee's Republicans which make the most difference in both respects, for they are by far the least partisan-leaning and the most liberal-leaning of the six committees' Republicans. Mild parti-sanship and liberalism are indicative, among Republicans, of policy sentiments that favor internationalism, the executive branch, and foreign aid. It was this lopsided Republican support for foreign aid that prompted the countervailing appointment of five conservative, anti-aid members in 1963. The move enlarged "the minority of the minority" but failed to break the cross-party consensus.

Committee members view the foreign aid program as a "contro-versial," "unpopular" program in the country and in the House, a policy orphan supported only by the executive branch and needing all the legislative succor it can get. A Democrat and a Republican convey the feeling of Committee members that House party leaders are of only minimal assistance on foreign aid:

> I never see them do anything. Carl (Albert) might make a speech. (Speaker John) McCormack may get up and say something. But I don't notice any great support of the For-eign Affairs Committee by them. We're sort of a step-child here. . . . They take a whip check. But they have a reluc-tance to support the program.
>
> They don't help us at all. With them, foreign policy is a matter of secondary interest. Les Arends is against it. Gerry (Ford) is for it, I guess. But it's strictly a secondary matter. Foreign aid has a mighty small constituency. And, besides the Republicans are badly split on the subject.

These comments underscore a point made earlier, that the parent chamber manifests a crashing unconcern for the work of its Foreign

----

[18] James Richards was chairman from 1955 to 1956, Thomas Gordon in 1957, and Thomas Morgan from 1958 to the present.

Affairs Committee. Perceptions like these feed the majority view that strong Committee support is essential if the program is to survive in Congress. Thus they become especially well disposed to accept most of the executive's requests.

On the other hand, ratifying foreign aid requests is not sufficiently satisfying in terms of their goal of policy involvement. And so members sometimes talk as if their strategic posture on foreign aid should be more critical than it is. A pro-aid Democrat, while declaring that "I'm a Democrat and I support the Administration," continued:

> I don't think we should give the Administration everything it asks for. . . . I think we ought to act together in caucus and say to the President, "Now, Mr. President, we have been through the bill, and here's what we are going to do." I think I know more about the foreign aid bill than the President does. I've been through the bill country by country; has he?

Anti-aid Committee members would support this kind of posture. But pro-aid members cannot bring themselves to adopt it wholeheartedly. Their feeling is that if the Committee tries to wrest control of the program from the executive branch — with whom they are in substantial agreement on broad policy — the program may suffer. And they may have achieved greater involvement at the price of a tattered policy.

The man who chaired the Committee for most of the period has certainly felt this way. Concerning foreign aid, Chairman Thomas (Doc) Morgan has said, "Under the Constitution, the President is made responsible for the conduct of our foreign relations, and the job of developing a foreign aid program rests with him." [19] Describing himself as "only the quarterback, not the coach of the team," Morgan sees the Committee, in *all* matters, as the subordinate partner in a permanent alliance with the executive branch. And, as far as he is concerned, the group's blanket, all-purpose decision rule should be: support all executive branch proposals. Explained one member:

> I think Doc Morgan feels that the President has primary responsibility over foreign affairs and that he, as Chairman has to do his best to get the Administration's program

[19] 107 *Congressional Record*, p. 15744.

through. And rightly so. The President is the one who has to carry the load.

His fellow Committee members are extremely sympathetic with the Chairman's position. An opponent of foreign aid commented:

> If you talk to Doc Morgan, he'd say "I'm responsible for the Administration's program. I have to get it through, so the other members will have to live with their doubts." I don't know, if I were chairman I might do the same thing.

A solid minority of Committee members agree with Chairman Morgan's stance. They are willing to scale down any greater aspirations they may have had, to treat the foreign aid bill as the essence of their work, and to content themselves with making minor adjustments to it. This is, of course, precisely what the executive branch prescribes. But such a strategy cannot command a consensus on the Committee.

Another solid minority of foreign aid supporters searches for a different strategic premise — one that will bring greater Committee involvement and greater promise of an independent policy contribution.

> Most of the boys think that when the foreign aid bill is passed our job is over. The Chairman thinks the Committee's job is foreign aid and once that's done the job is over. I think it's just a small part.

> I have the feeling that we sit over there like a lot of little birds getting fed, and if you are for the Administration then you are supposed to like the food. But I don't like that. Sure, I'm for foreign aid, but is that all I'm supposed to do?

These members feel they cannot achieve their personal goals in a junior partnership with the executive branch. Their dilemma is, however, that they cannot devise an alternative strategy. They worry about it at great length.

> What is the role of the House in foreign affairs? What do the American people want us to do in foreign affairs? I'm thinking of writing an article on it. The executive says, "Don't rock the boat. We're working behind the scenes." And you don't want to upset the apple cart. But if you're just going to rubber stamp foreign aid, what's the sense of being here? Why bother? The executive says, "We have all

the knowledge, all the information. Don't interfere." I think we should stir things up once in a while.

It is as much a measure of their uncertainty as their unhappiness that they should prescribe such vague alternatives as "writing an article" and "stirring things up once in a while."

A necessary, if not sufficient, condition for pursuing a more activist strategy would be accumulating a degree of Committee-based information and expertise, presently in very short supply. The members do not come to the Committee as policy experts and they do not become noticeably more expert while they are on it. Partly this is the result of executive branch control over information. Committee members complain that they never have adequate information in crisis situations, that their informational briefings are no better than the New York *Times*, and that they are rarely privy to the kinds of intra-executive conflicts that would allow them to get a handle on policy problems. But partly, too, the lack of expertise is related to the subject matter, which is, so much more far-ranging and abstract than an executive budget, a tax problem, or a natural resources project, those subject matters that help our other committees to devise operational decision rules. As Foreign Affairs Committee members see their subject matter: "It's all undefined and amorphous; it's all up in the air." "There's something mystical about the whole area of foreign affairs." They describe themselves as necessarily "broad brush" rather than "technical" in their approach, as policy "generalists" and not "specialists." In a policy world so "global" and "foggy," recognized expertise is hard to come by, let alone in a degree sufficient to gain leverage for dealing with the executive branch.

Foreign Affairs Committee members have, then, achieved only a partial consensus on their strategic posture. They agree to support the foreign aid bill; as for the rest of their activity, they remain divided. And a resolution of their differences seems nowhere in sight. "The thing I've noticed most is a massive disinterest on the Foreign Affairs Committee about what it is the Committee is supposed to do." "Oh, I suppose you could stage a revolution, but what good would it do?" The Committee's members seem to have stabilized their malaise over strategy at a point somewhere between, as one of them put it, "the polarization of being a rubber stamp and Bolshevik Revolution."

EDUCATION AND LABOR

Education and Labor Committee members pursue their policy goals in a more pluralistic environment than do Foreign Affairs members. And they have far less difficulty accommodating to it. They begin with a clearer idea of their substantive policy goals and they end with a more satisfying sense of involvement than do their foreign policy-oriented colleagues. We have argued that the unifying characteristic of Education and Labor's diverse environment is the partisanship of its policy coalitions. And Committee members find it easy to relate to their environment because they so readily accept the policies of and membership in party-led coalitions. Most of them were weaned on the kinds of socioeconomic controversies that have engaged Republicans and Democrats since the 1930's; most of them campaigned in general agreement with their party's viewpoint; most would not have been elected had they adopted the opposing party's position; most came to the Committee as partisans. Familiar ties of policy and party bind the Education and Labor member to his environment and obviate much of the frustration and division felt by Foreign Affairs members as they try to reconcile personal goals and environmental expectations.

Tables 3.1 and 3.2 present a profile of a Committee more deeply divided ideologically than any of the six and more predisposed toward partisanship than any except Ways and Means. In both respects, it is the majority party Democrats which contribute most heavily to the divergence. It is the Democrats, too, who account for the gross underrepresentation of the South depicted in Table 3.3. Control of the selection process by organized labor and party leaders, has produced a markedly unrepresentative committee — a "stacked" committee as its members call it, on the Democratic side. Committee Republicans are a faithful replica of their party colleagues in the House — though it is worth noting how much more conservative and partisan they are than the Republican contingent on Foreign Affairs. It is easy for both sides to standardize their decision context in overlapping ideological and partisan terms.

"We're an ideological committee on Education and Labor and a partisan committee." "This is probably the most partisan committee in the House, because this is where the fundamental philosophical battles are fought." "When you disagree so violently with their philosophy," said a Democrat, "and when you can't have much respect for their views, it's hard to do much business." "It's a polarized situation," agreed a Republican. "Once in a while, there's a feeling of unity with the Democrats, but it's short-lived." An obvious, operational decision rule for both party contingents is to do battle with one another. And they have achieved a consensus on this basic strategic premise: *to prosecute policy partisanship.* By contesting with each other in Committee on behalf of the party-led policy coalitions of which they are members, each side can help achieve personal goals and meet environmental desires.

The pursuit of policy partisanship inside the Committee resonates, as we have said, to the partisan tone of the environment. Typically, each Committee contingent will follow the lead of its own party chieftains in the executive branch (if it controls the Presidency) or in the House (if it does not). Internal policy partisanship changes in intensity with the kinds of external changes in party control portrayed in Table 2.5. In 1961, for example, a Republican described heightened internal partisanship as a result of the Democratic takeover of the Presidency:

> It's the most partisan committee in the House. . . . (But) this year it's worse than ever. The Democrats haven't made a single concession to us on anything. When the Republicans were in control of the administration, the Democrats had to recognize that other ideas had to be considered and there was some compromise. But this year, now that they have the Presidency, they are just ramming the (federal aid to education) bill through. We've dug our heels in. . . . We feel that if they aren't going to do some of the things we think are reasonable, we're just going to have to oppose the whole thing all the way through.

Policy partisanship became even more blatant following the overwhelming 1964 Democratic victory, congressional and presidential — about which a very senior Committee Republican commented in mid–1965.

> Normally, there are many things we can do to affect legislation. But under the conditions that exist, we are helpless. . . . They've got the votes. When you've got a majority of 20–10 in the Committee and 294–141 in the House, there isn't anything the minority can do about it — no amend-

ments, no changes, no nothing. The American people settled that last November.

There is a certain acceptance by the minority that "all we can do is
look forward to the next election." If Republicans could win at the
polls they, too, would prosecute policy partisanship to the limits allowed by electoral constraints — as, of course, they did in pushing
through the Taft-Hartley law in the wake of their electoral triumph
of 1946.

Partisan-ideological warfare is the normal condition of Education
and Labor. But it would be erroneous to depict the Committee as
totally and permanently riven into two monolithic, hostile camps.
For one thing, we know that some policies draw strong bipartisan
support. For another thing we know that profiles of ideological or
partisan predispositions or statements about national party policy
only describe central tendencies. They cannot and do not purport to
demonstrate complete intraparty agreement or complete interparty
disagreement. Neither would square with reality. This fact puts a
different face on the Committee member's strategic problem. What
strategy should he follow when he disagrees strongly with his party?
The answer is that he will pursue his policy goals regardless of partisan constraints. *To pursue one's individual policy preferences regardless of party* thus becomes a second strategic premise for Committee
members. Should the two premises become irreconcilable, the individualistic premise will, we would argue, dominate the partisan one.

From this second perspective, intra-Committee conflict looks sev-
eral-sided. Voting alignments fluctuate; party lines break. Personality, skill, and ideological idiosyncrasy come to the fore. The weakness
of party leaders in the face of conscience and/or constituency becomes evident. A Democrat (in 1961) and a Republican (in 1965)
commented from this angle:

> Usually the Committee splits up into factions. They change
> from issue to issue, but on any one you know who they are.
> . . . Sometimes our side is so fragmented we have to pick up
> some votes on the other side. We go off in six directions at
> once.

> We stretch from John Ashbrook on the far right to Brownie
> Reid on the far left. There's a lot of tension there and it's
> hard to develop teamwork. Brownie Reid is way over on the
> left — so far that he's more liberal than the Democrats. They

say, "What's he doing on your side?" And I feel like suggesting to him, "Why don't you take a chair and go over and sit with the Democrats?" [20]

The basic alignments are still Democratic-Republican, but policy individualism introduces important extrapartisan nuances.

Where policy individualism is an acceptable strategy, the policy goals of the chairman assume particular importance. The Committee had two chairmen during the period — Graham Barden, a white, rural, North Carolina conservative and Adam Clayton Powell, a black, urban, New York City liberal. Barden, a policy individualist *par excellence*, remained in nearly total disagreement with his fellow Democrats throughout his tenure. By working in harmony with the ideologically sympathetic Committee Republicans (and their President), he dampened partisan strategies and kept the Committee relatively inactive for six years. Powell, a liberal activist, operated for most of his six years within his party's consensus. But he did not hesitate to move outside that consensus in order to further his individual policy goals — goals which frequently involved legislation more favorable to black people. And this activity helped bring him, too, into ever increasing conflict with the more orthodox policy coalition of the Democratic party plus organized labor, in Committee and out. Education and Labor shared with Post Office the critical problem of operating with committee chairmen who were out of phase with the strategic premises of their fellow committee members. In all three situations — Murray in 1965, Barden in 1959, Powell in 1966 — the committee majority eventually revolted against its chairman and wrote a new set of circumscribing internal rules.

"Every member his own policy" is hardly a limiting strategic premise. But it is the only common denominator to which every member of a policy-oriented committee can repair. It might be asked, then, why Foreign Affairs members cannot agree upon a similarly individualistic decision rule — "every member his own foreign policy." The very phrasing of the question highlights differences of subject matter and environment that make individualistic policy judgments easier in the one case than the other. Because of the subject matter, Education and Labor members come to their committee equipped with more relevant prior experience. Because of the subject matter, more usable information is available to them

[20] In April 1972, he did!

once they are on the committee. And because of the subject matter, the members of Education and Labor find their individual social philosophies a more appropriate basis for deciding what is good public policy.

Beyond these advantages of experience, information, and ideology, Education and Labor members can find support for almost any extrapartisan policy position somewhere in their more diverse environment. The parties bring some structure to the environment of Education and Labor — indeed most of what there is; but they do not dominate the giving of policy cues and the forming of alliances as the executive branch does for Foreign Affairs. A member of Education and Labor thinks of himself as belonging to a policy coalition, including various environmental allies, with whom there is a constant exchange of policy views. The relationship is permeable and reciprocal. He has absolutely no sense of being dominated by or kept separate from or required to consume the predigested judgments of his external policy allies. Both his environment and his view of it encourage the individual definition of good public policy. Such is simply not the case in the more inhibiting environment of Foreign Affairs.

A final comment about Education and Labor's strategic premises can be made by contrasting them to those of the Interior Committee. The two committees share a common environmental problem: both are widely recognized as unrepresentative of the parent chamber. And unrepresentative committees may have special difficulties in gaining the trust of their House colleagues and in carrying their bills on the House floor. The Interior Committee, we have noted, worries about these problems and incorporates a good deal of sensitivity to the House into its strategic thinking. By comparison, Education and Labor does not. Whatever the explanation may be (and we think the largest part of it is the difference in members' goals), Education and Labor makes no special effort to compensate for its unrepresentativeness. And its strategic premises do not carry, therefore, the same concern as those of Interior for the support or the good opinion of the chamber. "The Committee is extremely liberal. It doesn't take into consideration what the reaction will be to a bill it reports," commented one subcommittee staffer. And another noted, "You can't write bills that appeal to only one-third of the whole House. The Committee is out of whack.[21] Education and

21 *National Journal*, January 8, 1972, p. 74.

Labor remains distinctively oriented toward its external coalition partners rather than toward its House colleagues. And while Interior cultivates an image of independent decision making, which it thinks will help it on the floor, Education and Labor does little to alter the image of a lopsidedly liberal Democratic committee heavily dependent on its liberal Democratic coalition allies. Together with the emphasis on policy partisanship and policy individualism, the de-emphasis on floor success will help explain Education and Labor's decision-making processes and the fate of its decisions in the chamber.

On every committee the members try to accommodate their personal goals to important environmental expectations and to embody this accommodation in broad, underlying guidelines for decision making. No two committees, it appears, will produce the same set of guiding premises. One explanation is, of course, that no two committees share the same set of member goals and the same set of environmental constraints. Another explanation might be that no two committees deal with the same area of policy. For, once again, we find differences among our variables related to differences in policy subject. In this chapter as in the previous one, however, we have conducted our analysis at one level removed from policy subjects. We have been interested, here, in the *perceptions* that each committee's members have of their policy area — on the assumption that members' behavior is based on members' perceptions of policy subjects and not on the objective characteristics of the policies themselves. At least we would argue this way until such time as a satisfactory categorization of policy subjects could be made from which one could deduce members' perceptions. For now, we might simply underscore the value of knowing: that Appropriations members perceive their subject matter to be nonideological, while Education and Labor members perceive their subject matter to be ideological; that Ways and Means members think of their business as freighted with consequences, while Post Office members think of their business as inconsequential; that Interior members view their policy area as specific and detailed, while Foreign Affairs members see theirs as general and vague. These differences in perceptions of subject matter help to account for differences in the decision-making processes of the committees. For example, the perceptions of subject matter held by Appropriations, Ways and Means, and Interior are more conducive to developing and sustaining expertise as a basis for decision making than are the perceptions held by the other three committees.

Despite the uniqueness of each committee's decision rules, two interesting patterns did emerge — interesting because both of them distinguish Appropriations, Ways and Means, and Interior on the one hand from Education and Labor, Foreign Affairs, and Post Office on the other. Each of the first three committees has achieved a consensus on its decision rules; each of the latter three committees has not. Furthermore, the decision rules of the first three committees are all, in one way or another, oriented toward insuring success on the House floor; the decision rules of the latter three are not. By *floor success*, we mean to include *both* House members' reactions to the content of a committee's decisions and House members' reactions to the committee as a decision-making collectivity. Obviously, the explanation for the two patterns — in terms of members' goals, environmental constraints, and strategic problems — differs within and across the two clusters of committees. We have tried to supply committee-by-committee explanations as we went along.

It may be that the two patterns are related. The more a committee concerns itself about floor success, the more likely it is, perhaps, to come to agreement on an operative set of decision rules. Or, perhaps, the greater its agreement on decision rules, the more likely will a committee enjoy success on the floor. Or it may be that the two patterns are not connected at all. Starting with the observation, however, we can ask whether the three high-consensus, House-oriented committees will display different decision-making processes from those of the three low-consensus, non-House-oriented committees. It is an intriguing question to take with us to the next chapter.

Decision-Making Processes

Within certain constraining norms established by the House — norms which act as homogenizing influences — the members of each committee are free to devise whatever internal structure they wish. Accordingly they search for a structure that will help them implement their decision rules — especially as those rules reflect a strategy for achieving their personal goals. A committee will alter its internal structure when a solid majority of members feel that it no longer serves their objectives, provided only that they can agree on an alternative. No decision-making structure will completely satisfy all interested parties. At any point in time, therefore, a committee's structure is only an approximation of an arrangement that would give everyone everything he wants. So long as the members regard it as "good enough" or "satisfactory" or "better than any other practicable possibility," the internal structure displays a certain degree of stability. While the structure is stabilized, we can generalize about it and describe the committee's *normal decision-making process*. We can also describe incremental changes in that process. That is what we shall be doing in this chapter. Our description will focus on three important aspects of committee decision making. They are: *partisanship, participation-specialization*, and *leadership*.

As a prefatory note, however, we should remember that every committee's internal structure is bounded by certain formal and informal norms of the parent chamber. One homogenizing constraint comes indirectly from the congressional electorate, which decides at the polls which party shall control all House committees. Other constraints come directly from House rules. Some internal committee procedures — concerning meeting days, parliamentary practice, record keeping, reporting, for example — are fixed by the House. Committee size and party ratios are set by the House and altered through time by amicable bargaining among the leaders of the two parties. Table 4.1 shows the results of this bargaining for the six committees.

Table 4.1
Committee Membership by Party:
84th–89th Congresses

	App.	*E.&L.*	*F.A.*	*Int.*	*P.O.*	*W.&M.*
84th Cong. 1955–56	30D-20R	17D-13R	17D-15R	18D-14R	15D-11R	15D-10R
85th Cong. 1957–58	30D-20R	17D-13R	18D-15R	20D-14R	14D-11R	15D-10R
86th Cong. 1959–60	30D-20R	20D-13R	21D-11R	21D-12R	16D-9R	15D-10R
87th Cong. 1961–62	30D-20R	19D-12R	20D-13R	19D-13R	14D-11R	15D-10R
88th Cong. 1963–64	30D-20R	19D-12R	20D-13R	20D-14R	14D-11R	15D-10R
89th Cong. 1965–66	34D-16R	21D-10R	24D-12R	22D-11R	17D-8R	17D-8R

For our purposes we need to note the difference in size between Appropriations on the one hand and Ways and Means and Post Office on the other. Size alone forces Appropriations to work through subcommittees, whereas the other two are small enough to have an option. Also we should note the change in party ratios as a result of the elections of 1958 and 1964, especially the critical change in the Education and Labor ratio in 1959. And, by contrast with the number of changes on the other four committees, the paucity of changes on Ways and Means and Appropriations gives further evidence of House interest in stabilizing the activity of its money committees.

Of all the House-imposed constraints, the most consequential is the informal seniority rule for the designation of the committee chairman (and ranking minority member). Because of his prerogatives, prestige, and leadership opportunities, the chairman is normally the most influential member of a committee. It may be that he is, in every respect, cut from the mold of his committee and would be its members' choice for chairman. But the seniority rule brings him to his pre-eminence through a concatenation of electoral and actuarial fates wholly beyond the control of the other committee members. In this sense, the rule stands as a formidable limitation on the ability of a committee's members to shape their internal structure. On the other hand, seniority choices should not be viewed as wholly fortuitous. If a man has chosen membership on a given committee and served on it for a long period of time, the chances are excellent that he will share the goals, the perceptions of the environment, and the strategic premises held by most of his fellow members. Still, there is no guarantee of such agreement. The probabilities, we would guess, are highest on committees having high consensus and House-oriented strategic premises and are lowest on committees with low consensus and non-House-oriented strategic premises. When disagreement exists, as in the case of the three chairmen we have mentioned, Murray, Barden, and Powell, it can have major consequences for committee decision making.

PARTISANSHIP

If a committee's decision rules help to explain internal structure, we would expect to find, obviously, that *partisanship* is greatest inside committees that adopt decision rules calling for it. Two of our six committees, *Ways and Means* and *Education and Labor* prescribe for themselves "the prosecution of policy partisanship." These are the same two committees whose members, according to Tables 3.1 and 3.2, have the strongest partisan leanings and are the most ideologically divergent of the six. By all accounts, Ways and Means and Education and Labor *are* more partisan than the other four. One measure of these differences in internal partisanship is presented in Table 4.2. We have analyzed the committee reports for all bills deemed sufficiently important by *Congressional Quarterly Almanac* to warrant description in its yearly catalogue of "major legislation." [1] We have calculated, first, the number of reports on which there was any recorded disagreement on the committee's final decision and, second, the number of these disagreements on which a majority of one party was found recorded in opposition to a majority of the other party. The latter we call "party disagreements." Whether measured by absolute numbers, percentages, or ratios, Ways and Means

---

[1] The totals in the first column of Table 4.2 are not exactly the same as the twelve-year totals listed under "Major Legislation" in the *Almanacs*. When committee reports could not be located, those bills were omitted from the tabulation.

Table 4.2
Disagreement and Partisanship in Committee Reports—
1955–1966

	Total Major Legislation	Percentage Recorded Disagreements	Percentage Party Disagreements	Party Disagreements As Percentage of All Recorded Disagreements
Ways and Means	114	52% (59)	26% (30)	50%
Education and Labor	96	56% (54)	25% (27)	50%
Interior	78	35% (27)	8% (6)	22%
Post Office	42	38% (16)	7% (3)	19%
Foreign Affairs	66	24% (16)	5% (3)	19%
Appropriations	154*	7% (11)	0% (0)	0%

*original appropriation bills only

and Education and Labor display a much greater degree of partisan-ship, at the decision stage, than any of the other six committees. In both cases, it is a response to the partisan elements in their environments — elements more prominent in these two committees than in the other four.

Though the two committees share a high degree of partisanship at the point of *decision*, the importance of partisanship during the *deliberative* stage of committee work differs radically from one committee to the other. Ways and Means members limit the play of partisanship to the final stages of decision making and do most of their work in a nonpartisan atmosphere. Education and Labor proceeds, at all stages, in an atmosphere charged with partisanship. The two committees are, therefore, as different in their decision-making styles as they are similar in their voting splits. And the difference, we would argue, can be explained wholly on the basis of contrasting member goals and environmental constraints.

Ways and Means members want influence in the House, a goal that forces an internal concern for their reputation in the House and for winning on the House floor. Only if the committee, as a collectivity, retains the confidence, respect, and support of the House will the individual Committee member gain the influence he seeks. To this end, members carefully circumscribe internal partisanship and try to behave in what House members will regard as a responsible, responsive manner. "The House says, here is a bunch of smart guys; we won't tamper too much with what they do." "The House knows we won't pull any fast ones." Education and Labor members, desirous of making good policy, feel no necessity for self-imposed, House-oriented restraints on their partisanship. They acknowledge the practical force of outside partisan constraints (See Table 2.5) and the philosophical right of each member to define "good" public policy for himself. But neither of these limits on partisanship betrays a collective concern for the Committee as an institution — for its reputation or its influence in the House. And both are compatible with heavy dosages of partisanship at every stage of decision making.

Normal decision making in the Ways and Means Committee is described by a staff member:

> I think you will find that Ways and Means is a partisan committee. There are usually minority reports. But partisanship is not that high when they discuss the bill and legislate. About 95 per cent of the time, the members deliberate the bill in a nonpartisan way, discussing the facts calmly. Then toward the end (John) Byrnes (ranking Republican) and the Republicans may go partisan. The things the Committee deals with are big Administration issues, so you are bound to get minority views and partisanship. But Byrnes likes to take a nonpartisan attitude toward things and it gets partisan only toward the end.

The governing rule is what Manley calls the norm of "restrained partisanship" — "that members should not allow partisanship to interfere with a thorough study and complete understanding of the technical complexities of the bills they consider." [2] The "restrained" phase of decision making is a positive response to House demands for responsible behavior. More than any other committee, Ways and Means members see themselves as working *for* the House. "On our Committee, we have a responsibility to the House; we have to do the best we can." The closed rule, of course, provides strong reinforcement for this perception. If Committee bills are to be offered on a take-it-or-leave-it basis, members must make certain that they are "taken" and without unnecessary misgivings. By following the norm of restrained partisanship, Committee members can implement both decision rules — writing a bill that will pass the House and prosecuting policy partisanship. And they can achieve the House influence they seek.

Education and Labor operates under quite a different set of ground rules. Ways and Means members pointed out the contrast. Said one:

[2] Manley, "The House Committee on Ways and Means: Conflict Management in a Congressional Committee," *op. cit.*, p. 929.

"We always try for a consensus. Now you take Education and Labor. They never try for a consensus; they battle it out." And a Ways and Means Republican recalls the behavior of a Democratic newcomer fresh from years of service on Education and Labor, saying:

> In our hearings and in our meetings he was taking up a lot of time making partisan speeches and raising partisan issues. I went to (Chairman) Wilbur (Mills) and asked him, "What's the matter with ————? All this partisanship." Wilbur said, "He'll be all right once he learns the traditions of the Committee. He just doesn't understand yet that we don't fight about those things over here."

"Over there," on Education and Labor, members normally fight about anything at any stage. In the words of one veteran, "You can't get a resolution praising God through this Committee without having a three-day battle over it." When conflicts are not partisan, they are centered on individual ideological preferences, as each member fights for his own version of good public policy. As another senior member put it, "It's a free-for-all; every man for himself." Whether decision making features partisan policy making or policy individualism, there are no informal traditions of restraint, only the formal rules whereby policy victories are won by majority vote.

Within the frame of electoral constraints and individual members' willingness, party majorities will push their advantage to the utmost and at all stages. In the 89th Congress, Republicans were allowed only ritual involvement in subcommittees and less than that in full committee. A Democratic subcommittee chairman described decision making at that level:

> We talk it over. I'll say to him (ranking Republican), "Do you want to fight it out here or in the full committee? You know and I know that I have the votes." He'll say, "I know you have, but let me make my record." I'll say, "Do you want to call up your amendments in subcommittee?" He'll say, "Yes." I'll say, "Do you want to vote on your amendments?" He'll say, "Yes." So we go through that in subcommittee. And as soon as we get a quorum, we vote our bill right through.

A Republican described full committee activity:

> We met from 11:00 till 12:00. We reported out three bills in that time and one of them was the repeal of 14B – the

most controversial piece of legislation our Committee has
this session. We took 30 minutes on that. Sometimes, they
seem to be in a hurry and when they're in a hurry they just
go ahead and report it out. You have five minutes of debate,
someone moves the previous question, and it's all over.
They've got the votes, and when they want to do it they can.

The 89th Congress represents the extreme case. But in 1961, for example, Chairman Powell evicted the minority staff from their rooms
in the Committee office, precipitating a rancorous running feud between himself and ranking Republican Carroll Kearns for the remainder of the 87th Congress. And in the 88th Congress, for
example, Committee Democrats marked up the poverty bill in party
caucus while Committee Republicans picketed (with a sign saying,
"Open the door, Adam") outside the locked door protesting their
exclusion. ("The Republicans screamed," said a Democrat, "but it's
good for them, it's therapeutic.") No one would mistake these vi-
gnettes for pictures of life on the Ways and Means Committee. But
the point is, of course, that Education and Labor members have
policy goals they want to achieve and gladly wage a no-holds-barred
struggle to achieve them. They will battle for their goals via massed
partisan phalanx or extrapartisan guerrilla skirmishing, as conditions
of external partisanship and individual philosophy may dictate.

Our other four committees display a good deal less internal partisanship than these two. On the evidence of Table 4.2, by far the
least partisan of the six is the Appropriations Committee. The measures used in Table 4.2 probably exaggerate its lack of partisanship
somewhat, because the Appropriations Committee happens to have
a particularly strong internal norm proscribing the writing of minority reports — even when internal disagreement exists. On the other
hand, however, the existence and apparent success of the norm is
evidence of a strenuous effort to dampen such internal partisanship
as may exist. Whether or not the distance between Appropriations
and the next three Committees is as great as Table 4.2 portrays,
there is little doubt that Appropriations is far less partisan in its
decision making than the two Committees we have discussed. Its
members have all the same incentives for nonpartisanship as Ways
and Means. In pursuing their goal of House influence, they lean
hard on executive budgets. But unless they can win House support
for their decisions, neither the committee collectively nor the members individually will be influential. So Appropriations members be-

come as concerned as Ways and Means members for their reputation
and their success in the House. One requisite, they believe, is the
curbing of internal partisanship, to the end that the Committee will
come to the floor united (or, at least, apparently united) in support
of its recommendations. Under such circumstances they will maximize the likelihood of winning on the floor. Unlike Ways and Means,
however, Appropriations members face few external demands for
partisanship; so they try to minimize partisanship at the point of
decision as well as at the deliberative stage. Their guiding rule is
the norm of "minimal partisanship," a stronger and more pervasive
injunction than that of "restrained partisanship."

Two freshman members, recently transferred from Education and
Labor, described Appropriations Committee decision making according to this norm — the first at the subcommittee level and the second
in full committee:

> If there's a difference of opinion, we may pass on and then
> come back to it later. Usually we come to an agreement and
> compromise things out. Most subcommittee reports are
> unanimous reports. I never saw a unanimous report on any-
> thing on Education and Labor. I guess you could say there's
> a lot less partisanship on Appropriations.

> On Education and Labor there was a healthy partisan divi-
> sion. But on this Committee there are no Democrats or
> Republicans. There's harmony. There's no two-party system
> on Appropriations. In full Committee, the chairman of the
> subcommittee gets up and then the ranking minority mem-
> ber of the subcommittee. And they say what a good job the
> other has done. They scratch each other's backs. There's
> never any dissent. Only once in two years has there been
> any difference.

Partisanship does, of course, occur, just as nonpartisanship occurs on
Education and Labor. But the ratios of partisanship to nonpartisanship in the internal operations of the two Committees are the exact
reverse of one another, as any congressman moving from one to the
other can — plainly and vividly — see. And these contrasting ratios
can be explained, again, by different member goals and different environmental contexts.

The ideological convergence of Appropriations Committee members eases their internal effort to minimize partisanship. The same
phenomenon plays an even more important part in accounting for

the low levels of partisanship on the *Foreign Affairs Committee.* Committee Democrats and (especially) Committee Republicans have markedly more liberal leanings than their respective party colleagues in the House. And liberals (in the period 1955–1966), we assume, were more likely to define the foreign aid program — the Committee's central issue — as good public policy. Partisanship has been relatively unimportant in decision making for the basic reason that, throughout the period, all but two or three Democrats and a majority of Republicans have supported the foreign aid program. In twelve years, as Table 4.2 shows, the Committee recorded only three party disagreements. One (1961) involved foreign aid policy; but it recorded Republican objections to President Kennedy's proposed method for financing the Development Loan Fund, not opposition to the program itself. Insofar as foreign aid dominates the work of the Committee (and it does), a bipartisan majority has felt little inducement to prosecute partisanship as a means of implementing its key decision rule.

Prior to full committee markup (i.e. decision-making session) on the foreign aid bill, the Democrats caucus to see if they can reach a consensus on the amount of the authorization they will support and to discuss amendments any of them intends to propose. Pro-aid Republicans are not invited; to this extent partisanship does affect Committee decision making. But sympathetic Republicans have plenty of opportunity to offer amendments at the markup and usually can get them accepted. The "hopelessly split" Republicans do not caucus as a group, but the anti–foreign aid "minority of the minority" does, to decide which amendment to offer, how to vote, how to focus their attack. If they need staff help, they must get it from the Committee's totally nonpartisan staff. But they normally do not find partisanship a useful vehicle for the promotion of their policy goals. In the words of a State Department official, "They oppose on conservative grounds, not on partisan grounds." And a veteran leader of the anti-aid group summed up: "Foreign Affairs is partisan sometimes, but it's not the same as Education and Labor or Banking and Currency or Ways and Means. Less partisan than these . . . most of the time it comes down to a question of individual opinion rather than a party question."

Partisanship on Education and Labor and Ways and Means, we have seen, is primarily a response to environmental partisanship. Foreign Affairs works in response to executive-led coalitions that make strenuous efforts in exactly the opposite direction — seeking bipartisan, consensus support for their foreign policy initiatives. Executive branch prescriptions of nonpartisanship are closely bound to the more general argument that the Committee should support the President, regardless of his party. And these sentiments evoke a sympathetic response inside the Committee. The day he took over chairmanship of the Committee, under a Republican president, Dr. Thomas Morgan said:

> I intend to try to further bipartisanship on the Committee; and the aid bill will be presented on that basis in the House. I have always believed in the old Vandenberg theory of bipartisanship.[3]

And seven years later, a Committee member described the practice thus:

> There's a feeling on the Committee that you don't want to exacerbate partisan feelings if you don't have to. That's the feeling. And after all . . . (the majority of Republicans) we get them, so you don't want to drive them away. . . . Doc will say many times, "It makes no difference; under Eisenhower, Kennedy, or Johnson we did this." He'll often make this appeal. I've heard it several times when some partisan questions will be raised. I won't say he does it every time there is a conflict, but he sets the atmosphere of the Committee. There's a feeling that the executive has to have a free hand here, as much as possible.

"Sometimes, of course, the members get partisan," said a State Department leader, "but they'll never admit it. Partisanship is a dirty word on the Committee and nobody wants to be called a partisan." He was, of course, happy about the condition, concluding, "Nonpartisanship is usually observed on the Committee and that's the important thing." Surely the Committee members' foreign aid policy goals and their environmental pressures are both conducive to a low level of partisanship. And this will continue until such time as a Committee majority can decide what strategy it will substitute for the executive "free hand."

In Table 4.2, the *Post Office Committee* displays the same low

---

[3] *New York Times*, February 9, 1958, p. 62.

degree of partisanship at the stage of decision as Foreign Affairs. Its three partisan reports were written during the Eisenhower years, when the Committee's clientele-oriented Republicans followed their President, providing a majority for pay increases (1955) and rate increases (1956, 1957) deemed too low and too high, respectively, by the affected postal groups. Eight Democrats joined their clientele allies in opposing each Committee action. In the election year of 1960, all but one Republican and Chairman Murray stood with the clientele groups and against the President on the postal pay raise bill; and a bipartisan Committee majority spearheaded the successful override of Eisenhower's veto of that bill. Since then, Committee Democrats and Republicans have operated in an atmosphere of low partisan intensity — broken only by a small but unorganized minority of the minority. For a group whose strategic premises involve the close adherence to clientele desires, partisanship is not relevant. "No, no, it's not partisan," said one Republican, "because with the exception of two or three mavericks, the members realize the power of the postal workers." The 1965, anti-Murray rule changes were voted in by sixteen of seventeen Democrats and five of eight Republicans — including the ranking minority member.

In terms of their individual goals, no two sets of committee members could be farther apart than those serving on Post Office and Foreign Affairs. One group wants committee service to help them get re-elected; the other group wants to help make policy on an international scale. We found their environments, however, to be strikingly similar. Relative to the other four committees, these two inhabit simple, monolithic environments — the one strongly dominated by a small set of clientele groups, the other strongly dominated by the executive branch. For both committees, the dominant environmental element has worked hard to depress partisanship, thereby helping to account for the low levels of partisanship in both cases. It seems reasonable for any environmental element (other than the political party) to want to keep down conflict inside the Committee if the element has a strong, monopolistic position in the environment. For the exacerbation of partisanship means that two opposing positions will be argued, in which case the monopoly-like external element stands to lose some of its support and some of its pre-eminence. Besides, parties become useful as leaders of policy coalitions only when some organization is needed to aggregate plural environmental interests. All other things being equal, we might speculate, the more monolithic the committee environment, the less the partisanship inside the Committee.

Interior Committee members uniformly describe their Committee as low in partisanship. And the reason is clear. Neither of its decision rules could be implemented under conditions of partisanship. Its members could not meet their re-election goals, and the clientele groups with which they are in greatest sympathy would not be served. To the contrary, cross-party cooperation is absolutely essential if members are to get projects for their districts and extend sympathetic treatment to Western-oriented interests. The direct relationship between individual member goals and bipartisan internal decision making was stated by two members.

> There's a kind of cohesiveness in the Committee that overrides partisan considerations. The key here is that there aren't any ideological issues. You don't hear the Republicans saying we can't afford this or that. And the reason is that everyone has a project in his district that he wants or will want.

> Interior is not partisan like some other committees here. You don't have the bitter partisan fights you do on some committees. . . . Look at the membership. Most of the members are from the seventeen western states. The issues are thrashed out in the Committee. If you can't get a whole loaf take half a loaf, if you can't get a half take a slice, and if you can't get a slice take a crumb. . . . There's no friction, you see, and that's how you get cooperation. The man you squash today, so to speak, you may need his help tomorrow.

Its members have been attracted to Interior precisely because they sought loaves, half-loaves, slices, and crumbs; and they have devised an appropriately low-partisan decision-making process through which to obtain them.[4] As far as the protection of Western interests are

---

[4] It is interesting in the light of James Murphy's recent work emphasizing partisanship on the House Public Works Committee that two Interior members who also sit on Public Works should spontaneously comment about Interior, "It's not a partisan committee. It's just the opposite from Public Works." Public Works would appear to be populated by constituency-oriented members and to operate amid highly partisan environmental constraints. Its strategic premises are, therefore, a kind of cross between Interior's project-oriented guidelines and Education and Labor's party-oriented guidelines — in Murphy's

concerned, there, too, partisanship would be counterproductive, because the conflicts, as we have seen, simply do not cut that way. A Committee member explained: "What you get is not Republicans fighting Democrats, but conservationists against the commercial users. These things cross party lines. You get Easterners versus Westerners."

It is a further indication of success in depressing partisanship that Wayne Aspinall, Chairman of the Committee through 1972 * and an ardent Westerner, worked so amicably and cooperatively with ranking Republican John Saylor, an ardent Easterner. Said a Republican:

> Saylor and Aspinall work so completely together it wouldn't make any difference who was chairman. They don't let politics in. When someone brings up something political, they put the lid on right away. It couldn't be less partisan.

The two men had some strong policy disagreements — over conservation and public power; and in that sense, the preceding comment overstates its case. What Aspinall and Saylor shared was a desire to maintain the Committee's reputation for careful, expert, and independent handling of its legislation and, consequently, the confidence of the House. To this end, they worked in conspicuous harmony on all internal procedural matters and compromise on substantive matters wherever possible. Aspinall yielded to Saylor because Saylor's support on the House floor helped legitimize the Committee product in the eyes of non-Westerners. Saylor yielded to Aspinall because he could not beat Aspinall head-on in the Committee; and by acting as "constructive critic" internally he could help to shape bills substantively, while at the same time preserving sufficient external unity to retain the Committee's floor reputation. Saylor, it should be noted, comes from a coal mining area in Pennsylvania and has his own constituency-re-election goals to achieve on the Committee.

This strong House orientation of the Interior Committee derives not, as with Ways and Means and Appropriations, from any special House interest in the Committee's work. It emerges rather, as we

---

terms "routinization" and "partisanship." See "The Empty Pork Barrel: Partisanship and Routinization in House Public Works Committee Decision Making," a paper presented at the American Political Science Association Meeting, Washington, D.C., 1968.

* Chairman Aspinall was defeated in a primary election in September, 1972. As of January, 1973, James Haley of Florida became Chairman.

94 CHAPTER FOUR

noted earlier, out of the Committee's strategy for insuring passage of its many small bills and allaying non-Western fears regarding its few controversial ones. We might generalize from the three committees that, however derived, a strong committee concern for its success (i.e., winning, plus respect and confidence) on the House floor acts as one of the most important regulators of internal committee partisanship. All things being equal, the greater their concern for floor success, the more a committee's members will act to depress internal partisanship.

PARTICIPATION-SPECIALIZATION

Because of the overwhelming magnitude of its task and its large size, the *Committee on Appropriations* divides its labor among a dozen or so subcommittees, ranging in size between five and eleven members. Each subcommittee has jurisdiction over a cluster of executive agencies, and each produces a separate appropriation bill. The work of the Committee — holding hearings, examining budgets, marking up bills — is done in and by the subcommittees. Furthermore, subcommittee members lead the discussion in full committee, dominate debate on the floor, and go to conference with the Senate on their particular bill. Each Committee member serves on two or three subcommittees. And he participates in Committee decision making almost exclusively in his subcommittees and through his subcommittees. Table 4.3 compares the number of subcommittee and full committee meetings for each committee in 1963 and 1964, thereby providing a crude indication of the locus of internal participation. It shows that the Appropriations Committee had the greatest number of subcommittee meetings, the fewest number of full committee meetings, and the highest ratio of subcommittee to all committee meetings of any of the six committees.

Though one cannot infer this from Table 4.3, Appropriations members have made a virtue out of a necessity by achieving the House influence they seek in the context of subcommittee participation. They have made the subcommittee structure work to promote their individual goals by giving to each member nearly certain influence within the restricted scope of his subcommittee activity. In order to preserve the subcommittee structure and member influence within it, the Committee has elaborated a more complex set of informal decision-making norms than have the other five committees.

First, there is the norm of subcommittee autonomy which restricts

Table 4.3
Subcommittee and Full Committee Meetings,
88th Congress[5]

	Number of Subcommittee Meetings	Number of Full Committee Meetings	Total Number Meetings	Subcommittee Meetings as a % of total
App.	590	24	614	96
E.&L.	363	40	403	90
Int.	374	82	456	82
P.O.	119	44	163	73
F.A.	186	135	321	58
W.&M.	0	180	180	0

participation to one's own subcommittee. Said a veteran member of the Treasury-Post Office subcommittee.

> Why you'd be branded an imposter if you went into one of those other subcommittee meetings. The only time I go is by appointment, by arrangement with the chairman at a special time. I'm as much a stranger in another subcommittee as I would be in the legislative committee on Post Office and Civil Service. Each one does its work apart from all others.

Second, there is the norm of reciprocity, whereby all nonsubcommittee members accept the recommendations of the subcommittee in the full committee. "It's a matter of 'if you respect my work, I'll respect yours.' " "It's frowned upon if you offer an amendment in the full committee when you aren't a member of the subcommittee."

Third, there is the norm of specialization, which grows out of subcommittee autonomy and operates as a rationale for reciprocity. Each subcommittee specializes; and nonsubcommittee members defer to expertise. "It's considered presumptuous to pose as an expert if you aren't on the subcommittee." "You don't go barging into another man's field unless something is patently wrong."

Fourth, there is the norm of apprenticeship, which holds that newcomers should spend a little time learning committee norms and subcommittee subject matter before he starts participating fully in its work. As two subcommittee veterans advised freshmen:

> Work hard, keep quiet, and attend committee sessions. We don't want to listen to some new person coming in here. But

[5] Figures for Table 4.3 are from Joint Committee on the Organization of Congress, *Final Report on Organization of Congress*, 89th Congress, 2nd Session (Washington: U.S. Government Printing Office, 1966), p. 65.

> after a while, when you know what you are doing, we'll listen
> to you.
>
> Follow the (subcommittee) chairman until you get your
> bearings. For the first two years, follow the chairman. He
> knows. He's been around a long time. Then take more of a
> part yourself.

When these four decision-making norms are combined with the
norm of minimal partisanship, then the internal structural conditions for subcommittee unity, full committee unity, full committee
influence, and, ultimately, individual member influence are present.

For the two dozen or so subcommittee chairmen and ranking
minority subcommittee members, observance of these participation-
specialization norms brings almost certain influence in the House —
as much as most full committee chairmen or ranking minority committee members. Appropriations newcomers are not always happy
about the restricted scope of their participation. "It's frustrating as
hell. You feel shut out — and you are!" But if they are content (as
most are) to endure a brief apprenticeship, the rewards of influence
soon become evident. A second-year man described the sequence:

> The first year you let things go by. You can't participate.
> But you learn by watching the others operate. The next year
> you know what you're interested in and when to step in. For
> instance, I've become an expert in the school lunch program.
> The (subcommittee) chairman said to me, "This is some-
> thing you ought to get interested in." I did, and now I'm the
> expert on the subcommittee. Whatever I say on that, the
> other members listen to me and do what I want.

So long as his subcommittee regards him as the specialist, and so
long as full Committee members defer to the subcommittee, this
one Committee member may be the most influential man in Congress on the school lunch program. He may even find this small area
of influence useful in dealing with other members of the House.
And these are, after all, the goals that led him to the Committee in
the first place.

The Committee members' strategic premises do not require any
one particular internal structure to secure their implementation. But
the arrangements we have just described, along with minimized partisanship, appear well enough suited for such implementation to
underwrite their continued observance. For example, members per-

ceive of their subject matter as manageable by a series of independent decisions, all of which can be made by compromising along a dollars-and-cents continuum. These perceptions and the decision making by autonomous and unified subcommittees provide strong mutual reinforcement. For another example, a restricted scope of decision making helps members obtain the kind of intimate, detailed knowledge of an agency that facilitates budget cutting. Members believe that in order to uncover unnecessary expenditures, one must "dig, dig, dig behind closed doors day after day" in "the salt mines of Congress." And they use their knowledge of "the facts" and their style of "hard work" to help sell the House on the necessity for budget reductions.

There is, of course, the chance that the opposite result may develop out of intensive subcommittee specialization — what we have called elsewhere "the interest-sympathy-leniency syndrome" [6] — and bring program support without budget reduction. Subcommittee assignments are patterned so as to hedge against this syndrome by assigning some members to subcommittees in which they have no personal experience and in which their constituency has no interest. And the apprenticeship period is used by elders to socialize the newcomers in the perceptual and logical underpinnings of budget cutting. On the evidence, they have a good deal of success; but if they fail, the very compartmentalization of the Committee keeps any spending virus isolated — this took place, during the period studied, in two subcommittees, Health, Education, and Welfare and Agriculture.[7] In the end, of course, the Committee's decision rules call for a balance between budget reducing and program support decisions, and the subcommittee structure gives some support to each.

In many ways, participation and specialization practices on the *Interior Committee* are a pale imitation of those on Appropriations. For instance, Interior has a similarly durable subcommittee structure, which is the main locus of every member's participation. When the Committee was formed by the Legislative Reorganization Act of 1946, it was a confederation of six previously existing standing committees. Two of the six were combined, a new one was added, and the pre-1947 standing-committee structure became the subcommittee

[6] Richard Fenno, *The Power of the Purse* (Boston: Little, Brown, 1966), p. 141.
[7] *Ibid.*, pp. 212–214, 364.

structure of the new committee. A tradition of moderate subcommittee autonomy and influence sprang from these roots and has continued since. Subcommittees are not as compartmentalized as they are on Appropriations, mainly because there are only six, and every member sits on three of them. Ranging in size from sixteen to twenty-one members, they are more nearly a replica of the full committee than any Appropriations subcommittee could be. Hence, the elaborate system of norms to insure subcommittee autonomy and influence are absent from Interior. Nonetheless, like Appropriations, decisions tend to be made in subcommittee and accepted by the full committee. Two subcommittee chairmen explained:

> I'd say that in my twelve years on the Committee, eighty per cent of the bills, once they go through the subcommittee and are reported out, go through the full Committee with no problems. The membership overlaps so much on our subcommittees, you don't run into trouble with the full Committee. Most of the bills are reported to the full Committee unanimously.

> About 95 per cent of the time the subcommittee recommendation on what policy ought to be reported out (to the floor) is accepted; but if you are talking about the actual substance and wording of the bill, then I'd reduce the figure to about eighty per cent.

Sometimes major controversial bills, e.g., the Wilderness Bill, are considered immediately in full Committee. Even considering occasional deviations, the percentage of subcommittee meetings is high, as revealed in Table 4.3.

For the individual member, concerned particularly about constituency benefits, the subcommittee system provides an avenue for extensive participation. Each member states his preferences for subcommittee assignment, on the basis of his constituency's interests. The chairman grants as many as he possibly can; and members are quite satisfied with their assignments. Once on a subcommittee, a member often has opportunities to hold *ad hoc* subcommittee hearings on district projects in the district itself, with all the attendant benefits of local publicity. Specialization in one's subcommittee work and reciprocity across specializations are present, just as they are on Appropriations. But on Interior, specialization is primarily the result of each member's constituency-based interest in his subcommittee area. And deference to specialization plus reciprocity within and across subcommittees will often take the form of a member-to-member negotiation for exchanges of support for their constituency projects. For instance:

> *Mr. Burton* (*R. Utah*): I think the Dixie Project has worked its natural course and it is before us today and we hope that we can have your support.

> *Mr. Udall* (*D. Arizona*): I think when the roll is called up yonder, that I will be found in support of the legislation or something very much like it. . . .

> *Mr. Burton:* I want my colleague to know that I am sure when the roll is called up yonder, he will find me in support of his aspirations as far as water is concerned. . . .

> *Mr. Udall:* I am hopeful that we can work this thing out so that both Dixie and projects we need lower down on the Colorado can help each other.[8]

Advice from Committee veterans to Committee newcomers is liberally sprinkled with hints like these on how to secure one's projects: "He'd better make sure he's up on what affects his district or he won't have to worry about anything else. He'd better specialize in constituency matters." "I'd put that (constituency specialization) at the top of the list. That's number one. And be tolerant with other people who have different interests back home to worry about." The advice takes and works. "I can't think of a committee where there's more cooperation or camaraderie than ours," exulted one Westerner. "More legislation is passed by the Interior Committee than by any other one." Decision-making characteristics of this sort are as useful to the individual member with senatorial ambitions as they are to the member seeking re-election to the House.

The Interior Committee member, unlike his Appropriations Committee counterpart, is quite free to determine for himself the scope of his participation. Nor is his participation seriously restricted by his juniority. Committee elders advise the newcomer to "do your homework," "read the previous hearings and reports," "study, study, study" — and in this way they mean to emphasize that subject mat-

---

[8] Committee on Interior and Insular Affairs, *Hearings on the Dixie Project, Utah,* before the Subcommittee on Irrigation and Reclamation, 88th Congress, 2nd Session (Washington: U.S. Government Printing Office, 1964), p. 76.

ter competence, not social philosophy, is the relevant basis for achieving one's goals on the Committee. They do not mean to impose an apprenticeship; the necessity for achieving one's individual goals before the next election will not permit it. Accordingly, a central tenet of internal decision making is, "Everyone has an equal right to be heard. No one's throttling anyone on Interior." And freshmen consider themselves equal participants. "I feel no constraints," said a first-term Republican about subcommittee hearings. "You have to wait your turn to ask questions, and they start with the senior members. I understand it's not like that on all committees — some chairmen run all over you if you're a freshman." Newcomers consider Interior "the best training ground for active participation and debate in the House."

If members are to achieve their individual, project-oriented goals and at the same time process their distinctively large number of bills, participation must not only be equal but orderly and efficient as well. The Committee was one of the first (if not the first) in the post–1947 period to write its own set of supplementary (to those of the House) rules providing for majority control of Committee activity, while protecting individual member rights. These rules are — in the formal sense at least — a model for participatory democracy; and they were copied by Education and Labor and Post Office during their later democratizing efforts. Once the rules were written, the Committee proceeded to adhere religiously to them. And this adherence gives to the Committee its distinctive self-image as orderly, efficient, and fair. "Everything is formal. You have to raise your hand, get recognition, yield the floor, and all that." "The chairman bangs the gavel and we go through every step. We can skip a step only by unanimous consent, and this is not taken unless the ranking minority member is there. It's very strict and fair." "We just go through every bill line by line. Every member has a chance to offer amendments, just as they do on the floor, under the five-minute rule — Republicans and Democrats right down the line." [9] Observance of these careful parliamentary procedures help, obviously, to dampen partisanship. It would be hard to devise an alternate internal struc-

[9] Excellent examples can be found in: Committee on Interior and Insular Affairs, *Hearings on Marketing Area of the Bonneville Power Administration* before the Subcommittee on Irrigation and Reclamation, 88th Congress, 1st Session (Washington: U.S. Government Printing Office, 1963), pp. 12, 107–109, 253.

ture better suited to the implementation of members' goals and environmental demands. "You ask around Capital Hill," said one, "and you'll find that Interior probably does the best job of them all. As for efficient handling of the work load and that sort of thing, we are very fast."

Education and Labor is the third committee which appears to operate with an active subcommittee structure. And while it is true, as Table 4.3 indicates, that most of its members' time is spent in subcommittee activity, the participation-specialization characteristics of Education and Labor are very different from those of Appropriations or Interior. Prior to 1959, the Committee operated with *ad hoc* subcommittees set up to deal with specific bills. In 1959 it established five permanent standing subcommittees. In 1961, these were changed to six — three for labor policy and three for education policy — of about ten members each. To this core has been added, from time to time, less permanent ones, for a total of nine in 1961 and eight in 1965. Only the poverty bill (in 1965–66) was taken directly to the full committee. The 1959 and 1961 rules changes were designed, in part, to insure the widest possible participation of all members. And such is the case. Every member serves on two or three subcommittees; members say that "you can get practically any subcommittee you want so everybody is happy with his assignments." Unlike Appropriations, and more, even, than Interior, "everybody gets his shots in" on Education and Labor. A new member of the Committee declared:

> I never dreamed the older members would have allowed us freshmen to contribute so much and participate and get into the legislative process as much as we have. I thought we would have to break the seniority system. But on my subcommittees I participate, get amendments passed, and open doors I never thought I could. I was amazed at how little restraint and restriction is placed on us. I think Education and Labor is unique in the use that is made of freshmen.

Life on the Committee, members say, is "just the opposite of what the myth and fiction of seniority would have you believe," "Freshmen even get to go to conference on this Committee." There would seem to be ample opportunity for each member to pursue his policy goals. Indeed, there is far more opportunity than the formal subcommittee structure reveals.

In the first place, subcommittees are not autonomous, as in the case of Appropriations, but highly permeable. A member commented:

> I have friends on all the other subcommittees. I talk with
> them constantly about what is going on and we plot strategy.
> I'm very seldom surprised by anything that comes out of any
> of them. . . . I'm chairman of a labor subcommittee, but
> I'll fight like hell for things I want in education. I'm having
> an argument now with the subcommittee on higher educa-
> tion. I think I've won, but if I haven't I'll go to the full com-
> mittee and raise hell there.

In the second place, unlike both Appropriations and Interior, subcommittee decisions carry very little weight in the full committee.
"On some two-bit, piddling little bill, the full committee will say,
'that's what the subcommittee recommends, we'll vote it through.'
But on major bills, the subcommittee has no standing with the full
committee." A veteran describes the full committee meeting:

> The members of the subcommittee always have the first
> crack at the legislation they report. They explain it and they
> are allowed to talk first. Then everyone pitches in. We ques-
> tion the subcommittee, we crossexamine the subcommittee,
> and they'd damn well better be able to answer the questions.
> That's true of the freshmen, too — they participate as much
> as anyone else. . . . Everybody gets in the swim in full
> committee. Very few pieces of legislation get through the
> full committee the way they come out of subcommittee.
> Maybe a few noncontroversial bills, but not the major ones.
> They are all amended in full committee. Sometimes I
> wonder why we have subcommittees at all.

The fact that a member participates extensively in his subcommittee
does not mean, on Education and Labor, that he cannot also participate intensively in the work of other subcommittees — at subcommittee or full committee level.

On Appropriations, participation is restricted; on Interior, it is less
restricted; on Education and Labor, it is unrestricted. Appropriations
and Interior members restrict their participation, in the interest of
their individual goals — in one case to enhance House influence, in
the other case to attend to one's constituency. Education and Labor
places no restrictions on participation so that its members can be
free to pursue their interest in good public policy. Their lowest-
common-denominator decision rule, calling for policy individualism,

requires this kind of internal structure. Thus we are brought back again to the Committee members' view of their subject matter as essentially ideological and hence quite manageable in terms of their prior experience and social philosophy. If every member's policy opinion is as valid as the next fellow's, why should anyone be denied the opportunity to pursue his policy goals at any point in decision making? Given the extent of members' participation, it is impossible to develop a high level of specialization or expertise. There would be little reward for these in terms of members' goals, for they would not bring deference on policy. Again their perception of subject matter is important.

> Expertise? Hell, everyone thinks he's an expert on the questions before our Committee. On education, the problem is that everyone went to school. They all think that makes them experts on that. And labor matters are so polarized that everyone is committed. You take sides first and then you acquire expertise. So no one accepts anyone as impartial.

When Committee members say that they "specialize" in education or labor matters, they mean that they have a special interest in one field or the other. They do not mean that others defer to them in decision making. Nor, of course, do members defer to the committee's staff. One reported: "The staff isn't very influential. I doubt if anyone relies on them on policy. They may furnish technical information, that's all. Policy positions are pretty well taken beforehand." It is a self-fulfilling evaluation, therefore, when members criticize, as they do, the quality of the staff. Staff turnover is, under such working circumstances, predictably high.[10] Of course, members will sometimes defer to the political judgment or the political blandishments of party leaders. But that is a different matter.

On those occasions when partisanship is not totally controlling, the Committee's high-participation, low-specialization characteristics will dominate internal decision making. A participating Health, Edu-

---

[10] Of the six men who acted as professional staff for each of the standing subcommittees when they were established in the 87th Congress, only one remained at the beginning of the 88th Congress — and he had changed from an education to a labor subcommittee. Of the six who manned the standing subcommittees in the 88th Congress, three stayed to begin the 90th Congress. And of those, only one remained at the outset of the 91st Congress. During the four Congresses from 1961 to 1968, every standing subcommittee had *at least* three different staff men in charge of its operations.

cation, and Welfare executive supplied the following perspective on the process:

> Our greatest trouble with the committee is that they are a bunch of smart asses — they think they know everything there is to know and the trouble is they don't. They don't do their homework, they don't know what is in the bill when they pass it or after they pass it even. When they get in executive session, they all think they are experts and no one will listen to anyone else. It's wild. They will nitpick on some little item for two hours and then pass the whole rest of a two billion dollar bill out in forty-five minutes. They have a very cavalier attitude toward staff. The staff is weak generally and wouldn't dare talk up to these strong personalities. The staff doesn't count for anything — compared to the staff on the Senate side. House committee members don't even know what they are talking about. In some ways it may be good. If a member is with us, he goes all the way. But if he gets the bit in his teeth and wants some very bad amendment, he won't listen to reason. He may shout and bang his fist on the table and very often no one in the committee will want to take him on. No one knows what he's talking about anyway, so he gets by. There is nothing we can do about it. The work habits of the members are terrible and it makes for bad legislation. These habits become the norm. . . . The younger members of the committee have a unique opportunity. They can get amendments in the bill, amendments galore. They can speak up and participate all over the place. Nothing about being seen and not heard on this committee. They can make speeches knowing that no one will contradict them, because nobody knows enough. No one knows the bills. For the freshmen, this is very exhilarating, but from our viewpoint it is demoralizing. It is hardly a good legislative process. These young people learn that they don't have to do any work. They can just come in and sound off. Legislation is not passed on the basis of reasoned arguments. It is a matter of who can shout the loudest or bang his fist the hardest.

To a considerable extent Committee members are doing what they came on the Committee to do. The process is not, as with Interior, orderly and efficient. As a Democrat serving on both committees put it:

> We do give careful consideration to (Interior) legislation. Every "t" is crossed; every "i" is dotted; every comma is in

> the right place . . . On Education and Labor, we don't con-
> sider all bills thoroughly. The "t's" aren't crossed; the "i's"
> aren't dotted; and the commas aren't there.

But Education and Labor decision making is, say the members, "stimulating," "exciting," "explosive," "pyrotechnical." And most of them like it. "It's never a dull committee," said one, "it isn't like Appropriations, which would be awfully boring—to me anyway." An alumnus of the Committee, now unhappily ensconced on Appropriations, agreed: "Education and Labor was creative and exciting work. It's considered an honor and a promotion to go on Appropriations. But I feel like a glorified accountant."

Ways and Means is one of the very few House committees (three in the 88th Congress) that function without subcommittees. Its relatively small size makes feasible full committee decision making. And the rationale offered by Committee members emphasizes their perception of their policy subjects as of immense national importance. Therefore, so the members reason, every member must legislate on the basis of first-hand knowledge of every subject.

> The things we deal with are so important and have such
> major consequences that we don't use subcommittees. I
> wouldn't want to have to rely on subcommittees for bills
> with such consequences. . . . We want to know what's
> going on.

> The historic tradition of the Committee is that each member
> is an integral part of the Committee. It's a small committee
> and each member has to keep informed on everything.

So long as there are no subcommittees, specialization will remain at a low level on Ways and Means. As the work of Education and Labor makes clear, there is no inexorable logic linking subcommittees and specialization. But Ways and Means members often make the link in explaining the absence of specialization "The Ways and Means Committee does not specialize because we don't have any subcommittees." "I am so damn glad we don't have subcommittees, because if you broke things down into three or four parts you wouldn't know what's going on. . . . All the members want to know what's going on in everything." It is probably true that if the incentive to specialize exists, subcommittees are a necessary condition of that specialization. At present the incentive does not exist on Ways and Means. Neither influence in the House, nor writing a bill that will pass, nor prosecuting partisanship requires specialization.

The first two can be achieved by the kind of responsible, carefully architected judgment expected by the House, and the second can be achieved by observing party allegiance in voting. So long as the full Committee performs accordingly, incentives for subcommittees and/or specialization will continue to be absent.

Members participate in lengthy full-committee executive sessions. So also, for most of the deliberative phase, do executive officials (and sometimes clientele groups). This is the stage at which bipartisan consensus building is emphasized, and everyone participates freely. For the newcomer, however, an apprenticeship norm — less restrictive than that of Appropriations — exists. The idea is that it takes time to acquire a good working grasp of the Committee's complicated subject matter and to develop good judgment in handling it. While learning, say the Committee's elders, freshmen should participate modestly and knowledgeably.

> I'd advise a new member to work as hard as he could and get familiar with everything. . . . I wouldn't advise anyone to specialize in minutiae . . . you just can't do it. . . . If he wants to be effective, he will have to master the subject. He can participate, but if he's wise he'll comment only if he knows what he's talking about. He'd better not show his ignorance. I tell him to listen to the more senior members and follow their advice, pretty much. After all, we've been around for years and over everything time after time.

> He'd be a fool to jump right in except for asking questions for information. I'd tell him to participate right away, however. No reason why he shouldn't be active right away. The members with the seniority know the subject pretty well and they lead things. I wouldn't tell him to specialize in anything; just be familiar with everything we do.

These prescriptions call for knowledge and participation but not specialization.

New members share the perception of subject matter that regulates their participation. They are impressed, if not overwhelmed by its difficulty. "The Committee won't hear much from me for a while." "I study hard." If they are frustrated, it is not because (as with Appropriations newcomers) their participation is restricted to a few subjects but because they have such a wide range of subjects to master. "I used to leave the meetings with a headache, truly a headache." On the other hand, they feel that as soon as they know what they are doing they can participate. "If I have any questions, I can ask them. I get a chance to participate . . . no problems." And participation is bipartisan. "In Committee deliberations," wrote a Republican freshman to his constituents, "I have as much chance to influence legislation as anyone else. This has given me many personal satisfactions I would not have had on a more partisan committee." The Committee's apprenticeship norm is nothing more than a reminder of the more basic self-restraining "responsibility" norm. All members accept this as necessary to the achievement of their individual goal of influence in the House.

On the *Foreign Affairs Committee*, as the figures in Table 4.3 suggest, the important arena for participation is the full committee. Second only to Ways and Means, Foreign Affairs has the most active full committee and the highest percentage of full committee meetings of the six committees. Desirous of making public policy and able to agree on the extent of their activity only on the foreign aid bill, all members naturally want to participate fully in this one important decision of the year.

> If you had subcommittees, the full committee would take it apart all over again. It's the one bill of the year. It's not like Education and Labor, where you have all those big bills. You can't reverse this process and have subcommittees. We have only the one big bill every year.

In 1957, the foreign aid bill was broken up into segments and parceled out to regional subcommittees. But when the bill reached the House floor, the subcommittee chairmen defended their respective segments with such varying degrees of skill, enthusiasm, and knowledge that the whole thing "fell of its own weight" for lack of coherence and coordination. Only a very few members still think subcommittees would help on this important bill. Indeed, so ingrained is the tradition of handling important matters in the full Committee that the Peace Corps, the Arms Control and Disarmament Agency, and resolutions such as Tonkin are also treated in full committee.

The Committee has a fairly elaborate array of standing subcommittees (nine in the 88th Congress) supplemented on occasion by special *ad hoc* subcommittees (one in the 88th Congress). Some of them are regional in their jurisdiction (e.g., Europe, Inter-American Affairs) and some pertain to the problem areas (e.g., International

Organization, State Department). Members serve on from two to four of these and experience little difficulty getting placed on the subcommittees that most interest them. The crucial fact about these subcommittees is simply that very little happens there. With the exception of the subcommittee handling State Department regulations, they report out almost no legislation. Their function is one of information gathering, to which end they hold hearings and consume information. Members speak of them as "more for research and study than legislation" or "more conversational than legislative." They also describe them as "really minor things dealing with picayune matters." "Africa never meets except to welcome an ambassador."

> I've been on the Europe subcommittee for five months and I haven't even heard NATO mentioned, haven't even heard the word. I read my hometown newspaper to find out what's happening to NATO. . . . The subcommittees have displayed absolute irrelevancy in foreign affairs, amazing irrelevancy.

Lacking a legislative charter and inclined to spend time on less than central matters, subcommittees tend to become "inactive," "dormant," or "slow." In the 89th Congress, three subcommittees did not meet at all, and a fourth was nearly defunct. One had not met for five years. Subcommittee chairmen lack incentive — "if you are a beaver, you can call a lot of meetings. I don't" Ordinary members succumb to more pressing priorities. "Once we are finished with the foreign aid bill, you can't get the members to come. They think it's all over and they have too many other things to do." In such a context members have plenty of opportunity to participate and to specialize. But in such a context neither activity will help them meet their individual policy goals. Nor, for those members pursuing outside career ambitions, does attentiveness to detailed subcommittee work seem productive in running for the Senate.

The only participation that counts occurs on the foreign aid hearings and markup. And here, specialization counts for little. Everyone participates equally, and no apprenticeship of any sort obtains. As on Education and Labor, the other policy-oriented Committee, expertise and deference are nonoperative. "You can go on there and become an expert overnight." "Every man is his own foreign policy expert." In the hearings, the Committee operates under the five-minute rule for questioning witnesses, with Democrats and Republicans taking turns, "from left to right, very fair." Some members chafe under the five-minute restriction, applied more out of consideration for key executive branch witnesses than for meaningful Committee member participation. "The five-minute rule means you can't ever develop a line of questioning. The witness will filibuster on one question; he won't really answer it, and then he's out of time." But the restriction hits all members equally. Full Committee markup sessions are more leisurely and less restrictive. Any member can offer as many amendments as he wants and no one is cut off from speaking on the amendment. A member who sits on Foreign Affairs and Interior described the two markups as "completely different":

> Interior (is run) strictly according to the rules. We meet at 9:45 and that doesn't mean 10 o'clock. Nobody speaks out of turn — no one. You have to have the proper recognition to speak, to offer amendments. On the other hand, Foreign Affairs — we sit around and have general discussion. How they ever keep a record of that I'll never know. It's the most disjointed, disconnected committee.

Foreign Affairs is a policy-oriented committee, lacking a complete set of decision rules; Interior is a constituency-oriented committee, with an operational set of decision rules.

Given all that we have said about member support for foreign aid, the main proceedings in full committee are an anticlimax. On the main lines of disagreement, positions have been established in their respective caucuses by the majority and by the "minority of the minority." Executive officials sit in the anteroom if information be needed. All that cannot be predicted are the "country amendments," often the result of constituency interest, which committee members want to append and executive officials wish to avoid. A Democratic administration stalwart described this aspect of the markup:

> Someone's got some silly amendment he's offering because he already has a press release out on it and he wants to say he tried to get the Committee to do this or that but they rejected it — or maybe they didn't. He's running against Tito this week or Sukarno or Castro. Maybe he's just been to Togoland and seen a "Yankee go home" sign; or he's mad because they tore down our library and he wants to get back at "never-never land.". . . I lean back to take a look at who's not there, who's asleep and not paying attention,

> who's ready to spring an amendment from his vest, who's
> breathing heavy, and whose nostrils are dilated. . . . You
> have to watch out.

Shades of decision making inside Education and Labor! But these
are minor flurries over details, not the main contest. That has already
been settled. In the end, Foreign Affairs seems much less participatory than Education and Labor and provides much less involvement,
as we have already said. Two members who transferred from Education and Labor to Foreign Affairs summed up: "Education and
Labor was a much more active Committee. The legislation flows
through there like water." "On Education and Labor, I was *too*
busy. On Foreign Affairs, all we do is handle the foreign aid bill
and go on trips."

For the *Post Office Committee*, as for Foreign Affairs, internal
norms are less important for understanding participation and specialization than is the sheer amount of Committee activity. As
Table 4.3 indicates, Post Office has been, in terms of the number of
meetings, the least active of the six committees. Table 4.2 reveals,
relatedly, that Post Office reported out the fewest pieces of "major
legislation" of the six committees, with Foreign Affairs reporting
the next fewest. Post Office members attributed much of this inactivity to the internal stalemate over strategy between Chairman
Murray and the clientele-oriented members. At least, this was a
cause of inactivity susceptible to internal remedy. And it was to raise
the level of Committee activity and thereby increase overall member
participation and member specialization that a large majority of
members voted to adopt the Committee Rules of 1965.

The major change was the creation, for the first time, of eight
standing legislative subcommittees. Prior to 1965, the Committee
had had only four subcommittees, all of the "investigative" rather
than legislative. On legislative matters, *ad hoc* subcommittees would
be created and subsequently disbanded. The net result was to restrict member participation, member specialization, and legislative
volume. Two of the rebellious leaders vented member complaints.

> Murray would appoint some fluffy subcommittee, a tem-
> porary sort of thing, with mostly newcomers. They'd issue
> some half-assed report which no one would read. . . . We'd
> read the hearings and then come in and vote. Of course
> there wasn't that much legislation to handle. . . . With

the old subcommittees, they were temporary and you couldn't learn about any one thing. But with permanent subcommittees, you can absorb information from the witnesses and you can become an expert.

We have two functions: one, legislate, two oversight. And we weren't performing either. During the last two years our Committee passed eighteen bills. Now, I don't rank effectiveness by numbers but many of these were minor little things. We're a third-rate committee and I think we should be a first-rate one. Look at what we handle. The most important thing we wanted, and there were lots of things, was subcommittees so we could specialize and do our job.

Under the new rules, every member sat on three subcommittees, and as an inducement to support the rule changes, the 1965 freshmen were given their first and second choice of subcommittees. The number of subcommittees was dictated not by natural subject matter divisions but by the desire to secure the allegiance of the eight most senior Democrats. The remainder of the rules, copied closely from those of the Interior Committee, were designed to bring order, dispatch, and fairness into full-committee procedures, which had become meandering and dilatory under the purposeful neglect of Chairman Murray.

If it be asked why Post Office members did not seek to increase their overall level of activity before 1965, a major reason is simply that most members of the Committee, as we have said, are not terribly interested in the Committee. They do not come to it with purpose, they give it less of their time than their other committee, they use it for constituency advantage while they serve on it, and they leave it as soon as they can. This scenario is not valid for all members, but for enough so that any serious commitment to internal change was hard to come by. Table 4.4 presents some corroborating evidence. Post Office has the highest average turnover of the six committees, and the highest percentage of freshman appointees. Turnover among majority party Democrats (who were most likely to favor change) was especially high, averaging 49 per cent for the five sessions, as against 27 per cent for the Republicans. These conditions militate against a large number of interested members — against the solidification of a revolutionary leadership and of followers with strong incentives to participate in a revolt. Common in-

Table 4.4
Committee Turnover[11]

	Percentage New Members Per Congress – 85th–89th						Percentage Freshmen Among Total No. of Appointees 1955-1966	
	85	86	87	88	89	Avg.		
P.O.	40%	44%	44%	40%	36%	41%	74%	58/78
Int.	16	39	39	46	42	36	73	64/88
E.&L.	23	30	29	32	23	27	69	52/75
F.A.	19	28	27	24	17	23	30	21/69
W.&M.	4	36	16	20	28	21	4	2/52
App.	12	24	8	24	32	20	14	14/100

[11] This computation does not take into account anyone who remained on a committee less than six months. If it took them into account, turnover figures for Post Office would be even higher.

ertia and respect for tradition doubtless often played a part. So, too, did the occasional success of the Committee's majority in working around their recalcitrant chairman.

When the change came, the overall aim seemed to be to increase the Committee's gross level of activity and, particularly, to render greater assistance to clientele groups. The vehicle was the new subcommittee system. And the method was the assertion of leverage over the executive branch. In the 89th Congress, the Committee's activity level rose palpably. A top Post Office Department official reported the reverberations.

> Once a congressman gets a subcommittee, he has to come up with some plan for the betterment of mankind. Or else he will go back to campaign and his opponent will say, "He's chairman of a subcommittee and what legislation has he brought out — nothing. . . ." That's what has happened on Post Office and Civil Service now and it's keeping us in the Post Office hopping.

Committee members felt rejuvenated and began to zero in on their traditional adversary, the Post Office Department. Prior to 1965, they felt, "Post Office paid no attention to the Committee; it was a withering arm of the House." But in the 89th Congress, "We are driving them crazy now; they are really worried. We are criticizing now, you see. We have the power and are they ever worried?" Here is how a veteran committee leader discussed the transition:

> You aren't a member of Congress and you would have had just as much influence as I had. The Department would just promulgate rules. They were happy — what the hell. (Postmaster General) Gronouski is coming here tomorrow and you know what I'm going to tell him? "It's a new day. Things have changed. They aren't going to work the way they used to." [12]

More than accomplishing anything specific, Committee members seemed pleased to be in motion and making progress. "We were a third-rate committee; we are a second-rate one now."

That the Committee can ever become a first-rate one or that

---

[12] An early example of this "new day" will be found in Committee on Post Office and Civil Service, *Hearings on Zip Code System in the United States Postal Service*, 89th Congress, 1st Session (Washington: U.S. Government Printing Office, 1965) pp. 9–18; 445–448.

internal specialization will ever give it much independent leverage over the executive branch seems doubtful. So dominated by clientele groups is their environment and so easy is it to meet their individual goals by yielding to such domination, it does not appear that they have any durable incentives for developing an independent competence. "The Post Office Committee is the creature of outside groups" summed up a veteran member. "They found out years ago that if they could control our membership, they could control our product. They have to; we're their lifeblood. . . . And they've been very successful at it." The monolithic environment, in short, dampens internal participation and specialization, regardless of stirrings among the members.

Again, the similarity with Foreign Affairs is compelling. As a companion piece to the foregoing comment, a Foreign Affairs member summarized: "One generalization you can make is that the Committee is more reflective of the executive than any Committee I know of. We do just about what the State Department tells us, and we don't do anything they don't want us to." And a member who serves on both committees sees environmental dominance as rendering them "two of the most insignificant committees in the House." He said: "Foreign Affairs is a disgrace because all Doc Morgan does, just like a rubber stamp, is give the Administration everything it wants. . . . Post Office is a disgrace in a different way. Individual members are owned by the postal unions. Post Office is subservient to the unions." The judgment is harsh, but the comparison is apt. Their many decision-making similarities result from the strong conditioning force of similarly monolithic environments.

LEADERSHIP

By all accounts, internal and external, Chairman Wilbur Mills dominates decision making in the Ways and Means Committee. The following comment by an AFL-CIO official strikes the common note:

> Wilbur Mills runs that Committee. . . . It simplifies our problem because all you have to do is deal with Mills. . . . Once Wilbur gives his word, my worries are over. Oh, I keep up contacts with the other members. But Mills is the Committee.

Viewing influence as a reciprocal phenomenon, John Manley has persuasively argued that the necessary condition of Mills's leadership is the support of his fellow Committee members. He has written, "Contrary to the impression one sometimes receives from newspaper stories about the 'all-powerful' Chairman Mills, he is perhaps as responsive to the Committee as the Committee is to him." [13] More baldly stated, Mills is influential in the Committee because he gives its members what they want. Taking a similar tack, we have contended that the most critical fact about *any* chairman is his relationship to the strategic premises espoused by the bulk of his committee's members. The critical fact about Mills is that he agrees with and helps implement his Committee's decision rules. By helping the Committee to write a bill that will pass the House and to prosecute partisanship, he helps give them what they most want — influence in the House. And, so long as he does so, they are content with his decision-making leadership.

Though he sits atop a formal structure that is highly centralized, he does not impose his policy will on the other members. With the desire for floor success uppermost in mind, he does everything he can to facilitate and achieve a consensus on every bill. He has said, "I think if I can get a vast majority of the membership of the Ways and Means Committee to agree on something, that I've got a vast majority of the House to agree on the same thing." [14] Close observers testify to his passion for "vast majorities." "He is happiest when all twenty-five members agree and the House is unanimous." "He wants at least twenty votes." If his aim is consensus, his technique is compromise. "He is a consensus seeker. He never pushes things to votes, we reach a compromise." "He leads by compromising." He listens patiently and at great length to all members. And he is a practitioner of responsible partisanship. "If he started by saying, 'I'm for the Administration position,' then the Republicans would gang up; but he doesn't do this." "If Wilbur said, 'what the hell, there are fifteen votes, why not vote it through, why waste all this time' then of course it'd be different." As part of his consensus-building efforts, Chairman Mills consults and cooperates closely with ranking minority member John Byrnes throughout the deliberative stage.

[13] Manley, "Wilbur D. Mills," *op. cit.*, p. 464. With a couple of additions, this section is a paraphrase of Manley's rich, path-breaking article on Mills.
[14] As quoted, *Ibid.*, pp. 448–449.

The proximate sources of Mills's influence are his subject matter expertise and his feel for the distribution of opinion in the House. As Committee members see it: "He knows the tax code inside and out, and he knows what Ways and Means has done for the last twenty years." "He counts the heads in Committee; and he counts the heads in the House; he's always counting." Technical competence and political viability are the ingredients of what House members call "a good bill," one they can support. And Committee members usually trust Mills's judgment in both respects. Mills's unique contribution to the Committee's decision is an architectural one — fixing the final form of the bill, deciding when a consensus has been built. A high-ranking executive official described the final Committee markup on Medicare in 1965.

> The key thing was Mills's taking the Byrnes proposal and incorporating it into the bill. His problem was to get enough votes on the floor to defeat the recommittal motion. He was looking for consensus. . . . All the time he had me up there testifying, dragging me back and forth over all the alternatives, he was searching for a formula that would take some of what the Administration wanted yet would be neither what the Administration wanted nor what the opposition wanted. It would be a Mills's bill. . . . At the time it happened, I thought he was playing cat and mouse. Wilbur usually takes three steps forward and two steps backward, one step sideward to the right and two steps sideward to the left before he does anything. But when he turned to me suddenly and asked if I could weave the two proposals together, the electric lights lit up and began to flash in my mind. Then I knew what he had been doing. I said "Yes, sir. . . ." And everybody in the room knew then that it was all over. The rest would be details. In thirty seconds, a two-billion-dollar bill was launched and the greatest departure in the social security laws in thirty years was accomplished. But that's typical of the Committee — the search for a formula that will neutralize the opposition and pass the House.

And, with the eventual support of eighteen Committee members, it did.

To continue with the subject of Medicare, however, it must be noted that from 1961 to 1964, Chairman Mills opposed his party's leaders on that very subject. And so we are led to ask whether Mills adheres to the second strategic premise of the group — the prosecution of partisanship. While shaping a consensus, does he, nonetheless, act in a partisan fashion at the point of decision? The answer to both questions seems to be a qualified "yes." In the mix of restrained or responsible partisanship, his enthusiasm is clearly for restraint and responsibility. His idea of consensus building envisions not only Republican participation but, if possible, Republican votes at the decision stage. As a realist, he knows this is not always possible; and so, reluctantly, he also practices policy partisanship. As one executive official said, "Sometimes he'll give up and settle things by a party vote, but he prefers not to." When the chips are down in Committee, Mills votes like a Democrat with the Democrats. On the fifty-nine minority reports listed in Table 4.3, Mills "voted" with the majority of Committee Democrats in every case but one. On the whole, he has been responsive to the policy wishes of Democratic leaders in the House and White House — on the trade bill of 1962, the recurring debt limit proposals, social security extensions, tax reduction in 1964, the extension of corporate and excise taxes, unemployment compensation. There have been some massive exceptions — on Medicare and, later, the tax surcharge of 1968. In both cases, Mills and his party leaders bargained to a compromise. But the bargains were slow in coming, and Democratic party leaders sometimes criticize his consensus-building procedures for resulting in tardy, conservatively-inclined decisions. Chairman Mills, like every member of the Committee, balances two strategic premises. As to winning on the floor, he performs optimally; as to policy partisanship, he performs less than optimally.

In subtle matters of balance among potentially conflicting decision rules, personal factors are probably critical. Wilbur Mills is an Arkansas Democrat, in the moderate-to-conservative wing of his party. And if he does not respond with alacrity to the party-led policy coalitions of his environment, his personal policy conservatism is one reason. More speculatively, a temperamental cautiousness may account for his preference for "vast majorities," as well as his reluctance to risk floor defeat by a partisan sharpening of the issues. A more liberal, less cautious chairman might increase policy partisanship and rely on smaller, partisan majorities — even at the risk of occasional floor defeat. Different individuals will strike different balances while still adhering to the two decision rules. And at this point, of course, the play of the seniority rule is crucial.

As to the particular balance struck by Mills, it must be concluded that it gives top priority to the decision rule Committee members themselves value most — success on the House floor. It is probably true that for reasons of his personal House influence, Mills hates to lose on the floor; but it is even more true that for reasons of Committee influence in the House, Mills wants to win on the House floor. So do his fellow Committee members. And they, like Mills, want to win in a style that will enhance the long-run reputation of the group — exuding a maximum of substantive competence and a minimum of partisan bickering. When Mills resisted his Democratic Presidents on Medicare and the tax surcharge, he did so partly because he judged that victory on the floor could not be assured. While other Committee members disagreed with that judgment or believed that a partisan commitment by Mills himself could have altered the situation, they shared the desire for ultimate victory. Short-run differences between Chairman and member are outweighed by Mills's ability to deliver in the long run. In the words of a veteran member, "You hear some criticism of Wilbur, but he has a high regard for the Committee. He takes care of it, respects it, and acts to insure its effectiveness on the floor." For *any* Chairman of the House Ways and Means Committee, that qualifies as the ultimate achievement and the ultimate praise.

Two committee chairmen, of those studied, have dominated the internal life of their committee and have done so with the approval of the majority of the membership. One is Wilbur Mills. The other is Wayne Aspinall.* The *Interior Committee* has a vastly different decision-making process from that of Ways and Means — more decentralized in organization, more formal in procedure. But, like Mills, Aspinall agrees with his Committee's decision rules and has used his chairmanship to help implement them. Thus he works to pass a large number of bills through the Committee and the House and to protect Western user interests in the more controversial cases. The members, in turn, grant him his pre-eminence. If there is a consensus opinion of their Chairman, it is that expressed by one member who said, "Aspinall is probably as good a chairman as you'll find. He dominates the Committee in a fair way."

The most commonly used adjective in describing Aspinall is

* Again it should be noted that Aspinall was defeated in his 1972 primary election.

"fair." Primarily, the word has been used in reference to his careful observance of Committee rules, which he helped institute and which guarantee full and equal participation by all individuals. With most members desirous of reaping particular benefits from the process of decision making, it is of enormous importance that they view it as fair. They do; and they attribute it not just to the rules but to the Chairman's exemplary devotion to them.

> We are the best-run committee, from a parliamentary stand-
> point, in the House. Everything is done according to the
> book. *Aspinall is fairness personified.* He bends over back-
> ward to be fair.

As Table 4.4 indicates, Interior is a high-turnover Committee with a perennially large freshman contingent. Aspinall, "the old school-teacher from Colorado," more than any of the other chairmen, works to guide, help, and socialize the newcomers. And they think of him as extremely "fair" in this sense too. The freshmen say: "He has a reputation of being a very fair man and I've found him to be. He's kind of like a schoolteacher who likes to explain a lot of background stuff for the members. And it helps." "Aspinall is fair, thorough, a helluva guy. It's great training. He spends as much time with the freshmen Republicans as with the freshmen Democrats."

At the beginning of each Congress, he holds what he variously calls an "orientation," "indoctrination," or "get-acquainted" session with the Secretary of the Interior and his top-level aides, primarily for the education of new members. During the session, all members have the opportunity to "ask questions which may be pertinent to general matters or which may be pertinent to matters within their own districts." [15] Aspinall primes the executive officials to tell the newcomers how accessible they are and how they can be reached. And he prods them to emphasize their special willingness "to give the facts whenever any problems arise within a member's district." [16] From the outset, therefore, Aspinall indicates that he understands their constituency oriented re-election goals. They, in turn, under-

---

[15] Committee on Interior and Insular Affairs, *Hearings on Programs and Activities of the Department of Interior*, 86th Congress, 1st Session (Washington: U.S. Government Printing Office, 1959), p. 1.

[16] Committee on Interior and Insular Affairs, *Hearings on Policies, Programs and Activities of the Department of the Interior*, 89th Congress, 1st Session (Washington: U.S. Government Printing Office, 1965), p. 16.

stand that he as chairman will have something to say about the achievement of those goals. One member noted:

> I need a couple of little Indian bills and a land bill I've got to get out of this Committee. All of us have — they're our bread and butter. Wayne doesn't say anything explicitly, but you know that if you cooperate, you'll get your bills out of Committee. And if you don't, you may not.

So long as he does not use this power frequently or arbitrarily, it is surely an aid to his internal domination.

The Chairman also socializes the newcomers as to Committee pride and Committee independence.

> Wayne Aspinall is an old schoolmarm. He gives us civics lectures up there in the Committee about the three coordinate branches. He tells us we don't have to accept the administration bill or the Senate bill — that we are going to take our time and do it in our own way. We are schooled in that philosophy of independence.

It is within this context of Committee independence that Chairman Aspinall makes a distinctive contribution to decision making, by acting as the funnel through which all legislation must pass. With the great bulk of Interior legislation, as we have said, the question is not "whether" but "when." And it is Aspinall who decides "when." He fixes priorities, fixes subcommittee agendas, and decides when a bill shall move from the hearings phase into the decision phase. In a situation where traffic control is an absolute necessity, he acts as chief controller, coordinating the work of his subcommittees and regulating the flow of legislation. A top Interior Department leader observed:

> The Committee is an amalgam of interests (and). . . . The pressures in the Committee are centrifugal — everyone is off someplace different from everyone else. That's why Aspinall's leadership is so important. In a half-dozen conversations between Aspinall and Secretary Udall, we learn what Congress is ready to take up and which projects are likely to come along in a year or two.

Conservation-minded executive officials do not always appreciate the Aspinall slowdown — especially when subsequent Committee decisions tilt toward user interests. But they recognize the effective leadership he displays. One remarked:

> If we can get by Aspinall, we are in good shape. . . . He is
> very sensitive to the interests of the people who live in his
> district — to the cattlemen, for instance, and mining. We've
> had some classic battles with him over grazing policy. He
> prides himself on running a model committee, and he does.
> He's a fine chairman — one of the best. All our problems
> boil down to getting along with the chairman.

For preservationist clientele groups, Aspinall is the *bête noir* for
holding up such matters as the Wilderness Bill and the Scenic and
Wild Rivers Bill. They are correct in attacking him as the effective
leader of the slowdown. But they are wrong if they think his Committee disapproved of the results.[17] As a high-ranking Interior Department executive said: "Without him, there would have been no
Wilderness Bill. He grafted a whole new concept on our bill. He
knows how to reconcile interests. He knows what his Committee
will do."

Quality control is another necessity when the volume of legislation is so great. And here again, orderly procedure helps. Chairman
Aspinall makes an additional contribution by participating actively
in the work of his subcommittees. He is a member *ex officio* of each
one, and he attends most subcommittee meetings — often dominating the questioning even though he does not preside. In markup
sessions, he forces careful examination of every line of the least important bill. Members criticize him as an "old maid," a "stickler,"
and "a perfectionist" in the markup of Interior bills. And the impa-
tient ones complain that "we sit there and nit-pick for hours on
something when most of us don't give a God damn about the outcome." But they admit that he knows more about the Committee's
work than anyone else, and that he controls subcommittee decision
making because of it.

> He has total control of the Committee and I mean total
> control. You can't get the subcommittee chairmen to do any-
> thing, they won't budge without his say-so. He runs a water-
> tight ship. He knows so much no one can keep up with him.

---

[17] For a good example of this overpersonalized and, hence, misdirected kind
of criticism, see Richard A. Cooley and Geoffrey Wandesforde-Smith, *Congress
and the Environment* (Seattle: University of Washington Press, 1970), p. 232.
For Aspinall's own rebuttal of such criticism, see Committee on Interior and
Insular Affairs, *Hearings on the Wilderness Preservation System*, 88th Congress,
2nd Session (Washington: U.S. Government Printing Office, 1964), pp. 1291–
1292.

For those who might protest, another contributed:

> He has the power to embarrass you by knowing more than
> you do about your bill. And that's strong medicine around
> here where no one has the time to become an expert on
> everything. But Aspinall is — on everything within his juris-
> diction: I'm in my forty's and he's in his seventy's; but he's
> in here before I am and leaves after I do.

Aspinall hires the Committee's relatively small but highly professional staff (ten in 1964) and keeps it attached to the full committee (i.e., to him) rather than to the separate subcommittees. The
Chairman's total immersion in decision making leaves the subcommittees less autonomous than they would be under a less domineer-
ing and less knowledgeable chairman.

A final perspective from which to view much of Chairman Aspinall's behavior inside the Committee is his orientation toward the
House floor. Believing as he does that "no man passes a bill in the
House unless he has the confidence and trust of his colleagues,"
Aspinall works to build a reputation for himself and for his Committee that will win respect and pass bills on the floor. From the moment
hearings on a bill begin, Aspinall is anticipating the floor context — how many reclamation projects the House will buy this year,
what the non-Western members will object to, whether the timing
is propitious. Consider, for example, these Aspinall comments from
two reclamation hearings in 1960:

> We are nearing the end of the session and we have a limited
> amount of time. These kinds of projects can be lost by just a
> little failure of proper timing. It would be far more impor-
> tant to you folks in Nebraska if you came up with the proper
> timing, something like San Luis (Project) did yesterday, and
> received approval next year than to have your bill defeated
> this year. . . . These are difficult situations when we get to
> the floor of the House.[18]

> In this committee we are favored by having some critics of
> the reclamation program. You would be surprised that some
> of these people who ask questions which seem to be rather

embarrassing — you would be surprised to know that what they are asking is not necessarily to show any opposition to the project, but it is to get the project in position so that we may carry it on the floor of the House.[19]

Doubtless, as it is with Mills, winning is a matter of pride for Aspinall. But also, as with Mills, Aspinall's performance is immensely valuable to his Committee members. Not an end in itself, as with Ways and Means, floor success is of critical instrumental value to Interior members anxious to deliver tangible benefits to their districts. Committee members are, therefore, pleased with their floor reputation. And they credit Aspinall: "The guys on the floor have confidence in Aspinall. When he says green is green, by God it's green." "I don't think Aspinall has ever gone down on the floor, at least I can't remember a time." "When you come to the floor with the Interior Committee, you feel like a member of the varsity team. You're right up there with the best. It's not like Foreign Affairs or Education and Labor." By now, of course, we realize that the decision rules of Interior prescribe a different kind of floor performance than those of Foreign Affairs or Education and Labor. But the point is that Chairman Aspinall runs his Committee in a way best calculated to accomplish its floor tasks. And therein lies one cornerstone of his internal influence.

Ways and Means and Interior have had committee chairmen who functioned by consensus. So, too, has the *Appropriations Committee*, in the person of Clarence Cannon, for most of the period and, later, George Mahon. Each has worked to aid the Committee in its budget-reduction strategy and, subsequently, in holding its reduction on the floor, thereby insuring House influence for the Committee and for its members. With one notable exception, both have felt that the program-support aspect of their decision strategy would take care of itself and that their influence as chairmen should be exerted to keep coalitions of the executive branch plus House members from raiding the Treasury. But neither man, in contrast to Mills and Aspinall, could be said to dominate decision making inside his Committee. The tradition of subcommittee autonomy and influence is, itself, so deeply rooted — as a source of House influence

---

[19] Committee on Interior and Insular Affairs, *Hearings on the Norman Project, Oklahoma* before the Subcommittee on Irrigation and Reclamation, 86th Congress, 2nd Session (Washington: U.S. Government Printing Office, 1960), p. 61.

for Committee members — that Appropriations chairmen can affect subcommittee decision making only marginally. One of the Committee's important norms provides for minimal interference by the Chairman in subcommittee affairs, thereby proscribing anything like Wayne Aspinall's immersion in subcommittee decision making — let alone the consensus building of Wilbur Mills. So the Appropriations Chairman plays his most influential part *within* the subcommittee structure, as chairman of one of the many subcommittees — Cannon on the public works subcommittee and Mahon on the defense subcommittee. He does sit *ex officio* on all subcommittees and does (along with the ranking minority member) participate as a voting member at all subcommittee markup sessions. But here, too, he is expected to intervene actively only on rare occasions. He hires the Committee staff members and assigns them to subcommittees; but he is expected to change staff assignments only at the request of, or with the consent of, the subcommittee chairman. Executive branch officials understand the essential limitations of the chairmanship. To them, "our committee" means their subcommittee, and "the chairman" means the subcommittee chairman. Only the cluster of agencies that confronts the Chairman *as* subcommittee chairman knows him, worries about him, or is affected by him.

The Appropriations Committee functions with a complex set of informal rules (or norms) but few formal ones. When the Committee meets at the beginning of each Congress, it perfunctorily passes a resolution empowering the Chairman to appoint all subcommittee members and fix the jurisdictions of all subcommittees. These are his important formal sources of influence. But they, too, are circumscribed — in appointments by seniority norms, which hold that once appointed to a subcommittee, a member stays there, moving up the seniority ladder until he becomes subcommittee chairman. Of course, promotions from a less important subcommittee (District of Columbia, say) to a more important one (Defense) are possible. And it is in his original appointments, in his "promotions," in his extra appointments to subcommittees, and in his abolition of subcommittees that the Chairman exercises some influence internally. Similarly, by creating new subcommittees and enlarging old ones, the Chairman can generate rewards for those members who support him when he so requests. Between 1947 and 1961, Chairman Cannon manipulated subcommittees and their size so as to create an impressive sixty-four additional subcommittee appointments and used them as bargaining counters with his membership. "When Cannon wants someone to go along, he says, 'maybe there's a chairmanship of a committee coming up for you.'" He was known among the members as a man who "deals by rewards and punishments" or "deals on a promise-reward basis." He could be particularly stingy in rewarding freshman members until they had served a satisfactory apprenticeship. Chairman Mahon has been far less stringent about this, trying to give each freshman a good subcommittee assignment. But it should be noted that of the five subcommittee systems we have studied, Appropriations is the only one whose members do not routinely state their preferences and receive them at the hands of the Chairman. Perhaps policy goals and constituency goals are so obviously linked to specific subcommittees that member preferences cannot be avoided by any Chairman who would retain internal influence, whereas the goal of influence in the House can, after all, be achieved on a subcommittee handling any subject matter.

Given the Committee's extraordinarily decentralized, compartmentalized structure, the Chairman derives some influence from the sheer scope of his activity. For he is the only member with a general idea of what is going on in all subcommittees, and he is the person who schedules the flow of subcommittee business from one decision-making stage to the next. To this informational superiority is added general legislative experience — and together they command a certain increment of deference from the members. "Of course the Committee wouldn't follow him if it didn't want to," said a member about Cannon. "He has a great deal of respect. He's an able man, a hardworking man." Cannon was the author of the House manual of parliamentary procedure and totally the master in any procedural tangle. "You can't argue with Cannon," Committee members would say. "He wrote the book." The question arises, then, what does the Chairman want from the members? To what ends does he put such influence as he has? He has acted, first, to bolster the strategy of budget reduction and, second, to strengthen observance of those internal norms that maximize unity on the floor, hence protecting their budget cuts. In sum, both chairmen used their formal sources of influence, their example, and their persuasion to insure Committee behavior that would give the members what they wanted. It might be, as we said earlier, that some other pattern of activity could also bring them influence in the House. But the one we have described certainly does. And that fact underlies its longevity.

In appointing subcommittee members, both chairmen have sought to insure budget reduction by not assigning people whom they suspected of having predetermined reasons for supporting especially large appropriations — a principle very different from the interest-oriented principles governing subcommittee appointments on other committees. Cannon said: "No member of the Committee should be obligated by his supporters to a certain appropriation. He should be able to take a judicial view of appropriations, a neutral view." And Mahon agreed: "Putting men on subcommittees where they have a vested interest in the subject matter should be avoided wherever possible. . . . The factor of objectivity is one of the considerations in making selections." The Committee's ranking minority members have followed the same principle on the Republican side. The only noteworthy exception was Chairman Mahon's deliberate stacking of the budget-cutting foreign aid subcommittee on behalf of a program-support strategy in 1964 — at the urgent behest of his fellow Texan, President Johnson. (The policy results of the move are shown in Table 6.11.) In rearranging subcommittee jurisdictions, Cannon often worked to guard against the interest-sympathy-leniency syndrome — abolishing separate service panels on the defense subcommittee, for example, when he felt subcommittee members were becoming too "buddy-buddy" with particular services. When they have intervened at markup time, both chairmen have done so on behalf of budget reduction. Said one subcommittee chairman: "Of course, Mr. Cannon and Mr. John Taber (ranking minority member) are always in favor of the low figure — always looking for a cut. In all the markup sessions I've attended, I've never seen any friction between (them)." Another recalled pressure from Chairman Mahon: "George said to me, 'You're putting too much in your bill. You've got to take some out. . . .' So I went home and thought it over and worked like fury to take some money out of the bill and I found five items I could cut."

Some of the ardor that Cannon and Mahon have bestowed on the Committee's budget-reduction strategy is a consequence of their own conservatism. And it is here that "the personality of the chairman" and, hence, the consequences of the seniority rule come into play. But the idea that the Committee's job is to cut expenditures by reducing budgets is held by Committee liberals as well as conservatives. As one of the most liberal of the members put it:

> I suppose I came here a flaming liberal; but as the years go
> by I get more conservative. You just hate like hell to spend

all this money. It's an awful lot of money. I used to look more at the program, but now I look at it in terms of money . . . you come to the point where you just say, "by God, this is enough jobs."

Such a view would be espoused — to a substantial degree — by *any* Appropriations Chairman. So would any Chairman uphold the intricate system of supporting norms. Chairman Cannon, especially, worked constantly to socialize Committee newcomers. When one announced he was going to write a minority report, thereby violating the norm of minimal partisanship, he learned something. He reported later: "The Chairman was pretty upset about it. It's just a tradition, I guess, not to write minority reports. I didn't know it was a tradition. . . . The Chairman said it just wasn't the thing to do." Committee unity on the floor is the ultimate and critical product of the norm system. And Cannon regularly preached observance of it and of its supporting tenets, in the full Committee meetings. In his words:

> I tell them we should have a united front. If there are any objections, or changes, we ought to hear it now and not wash our dirty linen out on the floor. If we don't have a bill that we can all agree on and support, we ought not to report it out. To do that is like throwing a piece of meat to a bunch of hungry animals.

Clarence Cannon, like Wayne Aspinall, was a former schoolteacher. And, like Aspinall, he taught his Committee members the forms of behavior that were most likely to give them what they wanted — in this case, influence in the House. Every really effective House committee chairman not only shares his committee's strategic premises but also articulates, extols, explains, rationalizes, exemplifies, and, by any other means available, teaches those premises to the committee's members.

Education and Labor had two entirely different chairmen — in personal qualities, leadership styles, and impact on Committee decision making. They had only one thing in common. Both lived by the Committee's harsh rules of policy combat and were eventually deposed by majorities invoking those rules against them. As one would expect on a policy-oriented committee, the root difference between them concerned policy. And, as one would expect on such a highly permeable committee, each man functioned simultaneously as a Committee leader and as a policy coalition leader.

Aside from his support of a few well-established programs attractive to rural areas (i.e., vocational education and library services), maintenance of the status quo was Graham Barden's chief policy goal. On major bills like minimum wage and federal aid to education, his aim was to prevent their enactment or, failing this, to delay and water them down. From 1955 to 1958, the internal lineup was thirteen Republicans and two Southern Democrats opposed to fifteen liberal Democrats — a policy stalemate tailored to Chairman Barden's objectives. As best he could, therefore, Barden ran the Committee as an outpost of the Southern Democratic-Republican "conservative coalition." As one Committee Democrat said in 1961:

> You never had any leadership under Barden, not majority leadership. Under Barden you had a club. He was a Republican; there's no doubt about that. He was a Democrat in name only. Under him, you had a coalition. And it was very skillful. The coalition ran things until 1959 when Ways and Means decided to enlarge the Committee.

Other Democrats spoke of the "Barden-Eisenhower leadership" of the Committee. The central fact about Adam Clayton Powell was his membership in the liberal-Democratic policy coalition. For most of the period, he cooperated with fellow Democrats on and off the Committee to win approval for liberal legislation — federal aid to education, the poverty program, minimum wage, to name a few. Said a Democratic member in 1965:

> We have been a more productive committee in the last year and a half than the New Deal. You talk about Roosevelt's one hundred days — what the hell, look at what we've done. It has been under Powell's chairmanship and you've got to give him credit for that.

The other members of his policy coalition were lavish in praise of Powell's work — Speaker McCormack credited his "brilliant and courageous leadership" and President Johnson spoke of his "brilliant record of accomplishment." [20]

From their policy differences flowed differences in the leadership behavior of the two chairmen. A veteran staff man explained:

> You can't get away from the fact that the Chairman has power. Barden used it to block legislation; Powell uses it to

[20] *Congressional Record*, Daily Edition, October 10, 1966.

push legislation through. And one is as arbitrary as the other. During executive session, after a few minutes of debate, Powell will listen to anyone who moves the previous question. He'll put it to a vote and if it carries, debate is shut off. Barden would never even recognize anyone who moved the previous question. You could make the motion, but he'd let everyone keep on talking.

Barden exercised a far more centralized brand of leadership, however, than Powell. For most of the time, he worked only with *ad hoc* subcommittees, choosing them and occasionally, even, chairing them himself. And he kept a close procedural watch on Committee business. From 1955 to 1960, Committee expenditures averaged $76,000 per year.[21] He kept the Committee staff small (eleven in his last year of control), kept them attached to the full Committee, and hired them all himself.[22] Powell favored a more decentralized system of autonomous subcommittees — whose meetings he never attended and whose work he never supervised. Two Committee members recalled:

> He set up subcommittees and let everyone go his own way. He treated us like adults. He allowed us to use our own initiative. And we pumped out that great society program like it was going out of style — this bill, that bill, one after the other. It was a decentralized committee and we got results.

> He lets each of his subcommittees run free and do what they want. It's a hell of a way to run a railroad. It's like turning the railroad over to the engineers. There are a lot of engineers — each one with his own train and his own cargo. He loads it up, gets at the wheel and off he goes. And when each comes to the end of the line, we take up the bill. It's quite a system. Timing is all slapdash, no priorities. But it works.

Powell expanded the staff (to forty-two in the first year of his control), and the Committee spent an average of $316,000 per year

[21] *Congressional Record*, Daily Edition, March 6, 1963, p. 3345.
[22] For more on Barden's leadership technique, see Richard F. Fenno, "The House of Representatives and Federal Aid to Education," in Robert Peabody and Nelson Polsby (eds.) *New Perspectives on the House of Representatives* (Chicago: Rand McNally, 1969), Chapter 12. A good case study of Barden in action is: Gus Tyler, *A Legislative Campaign for a Federal Minimum Wage — 1955* (New York: Henry Holt, 1959).

during the first Congress (89th) of his chairmanship.[23] He allowed each subcommittee to hire its own permanent staff and to spend its own budget. Clientele and executive branch members of the coalition had all their working contact, not with Powell but with the subcommittee chairmen. The contrast to Graham Barden was great. The contrast to a chairman like Wayne Aspinall was nearly total.

Powell's contribution to decision making consisted mainly in moving subcommittee recommendations through the Committee's Democratic caucus and/or the full Committee and to the House floor as quickly as the ratio of policy partisanship to policy individualism would allow. He wanted his chairmanship to be judged by the large number of bills passed. And he wanted the kind of credit that coalition members — from House to White House — showered upon him. For he traded heavily on that credit to furbish his image as a powerful leader of a nationwide black constituency.[24] An implicit bargain — autonomy for the subcommittees, credit for the chairman, and good public policy for the liberal-Democratic policy coalition — was the basis for normal decision making during the Powell chairmanship. But as soon as the Democratic majority on the Committee and their coalition allies off the Committee came to believe that Powell was positively damaging their policy cause, they moved to create an institutionally powerless chairmanship.

The coalition's complaints were twofold. The first was personal. It involved Powell's temperament — his inattentiveness to Committee business and the occasional unfathomability of his behavior. A Committee Democrat commented "He's erratic. He'll call a meeting, cancel it; call a caucus, cancel it. . . . You talk to the White House guys — he's made their lives miserable. The problem is they can't rely on him." And a Labor Department executive said:

> The quixotic unpredictability of Powell is our greatest problem. He creates so many uncertainties for us. . . . With Powell you never can tell what he's going to do or why he will do it. . . . Sometimes when you think Wilbur Mills is going right, he surprises you and goes left. But when he does this, his behavior has something to do with getting support

[23] *Congressional Record*, Daily Edition, March 6, 1963, p. 3345.
[24] For one example of the payoff to Powell in the black community, see Mervyn M. Dymally, "The Legislative Record of Adam Clayton Powell," *The Black Politician*, January, 1971, pp. 16 ff. And see Powell's own insertions of coalition leader praise into the *Congressional Record*, October 10, 1966, pp. A 5211–5212 — one of which is reprinted in the prior article.

somewhere. It grows out of the logic of the political process, and eventually you understand it. But when Powell turns left instead of right, it grows out of the personality of the chairman and you may never understand it.

A subcommittee chairman complained: "You can't reach him. The Committee members can't reach him. The Speaker can't reach him." And a staffer noted: "He just doesn't want to take the time with legislation. His attention span is short. As they say, when he gives a thing weighty and thorough consideration, he'll attend to it for three minutes." Powell's highly publicized extracurricular escapades — an adverse judgment in the courts, pleasure trips at government expense, payments to his wife for Committee services never rendered — supplied additional evidence of an erratic personal style. And these things accelerated the desire of his coalition partners to insulate themselves from the indeterminacies of his behavior.

The second complaint involved (as did the first indirectly) policy. Chairman Powell employed his prerogatives to delay the transmittal to the Rules Committee of three bills dear to the hearts of the liberal-Democratic coalition — the repeal of 14B in 1965, the situs picketing bill of 1966, and the antipoverty bill of 1966. In each case, Powell's action stemmed from his desire to bargain for greater policy benefits for black people — for a Fair Employment Practices Commission bill, for more hiring of blacks in the construction trades, and for more poverty money for Harlem respectively. Whether his bargaining technique was designed for personal image building or whether it was designed for immediate policy results is a moot point. In terms of his policy preferences and his perception of his constituency, he was acting as a policy individualist *par excellence*. But in each instance he was thwarting the immediate policy goals of the coalition. "He has refused to bring up the situs picketing bill," said an AFL-CIO executive. "That has our people all inflamed. It has gone through every normal process and he won't bring it up." The initiator of the internal revolt, Sam Gibbons, charged that Powell's delay of the poverty bill had "thwarted the will of the majority of the Committee" and "put the poverty bill in serious jeopardy." [25] A Committee Democrat said:

> We got fed up the way things were running downhill. We were trying to get the poverty bill through the Rules Com-

25 *New York Times,* September 16, 1966, p. 1; *Washington Daily News,* September 13, 1966, p. 12.

mittee and onto the floor, but Adam just wasn't around.
. . . We decided to write some rules that would make it
possible for the Committee to function without a chairman.

That, by vote of twenty-seven to one, is what the Committee did in
September of 1966.

In view of the national publicity given to some of Chairman
Powell's extra-Committee exploits and his eventual loss of his chairmanship altogether, it is hard to assess the causes of this action. But
primarily, we would argue, Committee members revolted against
Powell for the same reasons they had revolted against Barden seven
years earlier — disagreement over policy and policy tempo, and under the same facilitating conditions — lopsided Democratic majorities. The comparison may seem odd in view of the wide area of
agreement between Powell and his colleagues and in view of his
usual willingness to let the legislation flow through the Committee.
The problem was that the strong partisan Democratic majority,
which had been waiting for this opportunity since the mid-1930's,
would not tolerate *any* policy individualism on the part of the chairman. Doubtless Powell's personal behavior hurt the image of the
Committee. But Education and Labor members do not worry much
about their image. They do not even have a sense of their Committee as an institution — just a battleground. Their concern is for
policy, and they view their chairman's job in policy terms.

When Gibbons explained the revolt, he gave first priority to
policy reasons:

I think Mr. Powell's actions have become so damaging to
the programs we have in our Committee and so reflect on
the integrity of Congress that this type of action stripping
Powell of chairmanship powers is necessary.[26]

Committee members' intolerance was partly a personal intolerance
— of Powell's erratic, unpredictable, frustrating personal style. But
it was more a policy intolerance — of Powell's unwillingness to act
when, as, and if the Democratic majority wished. And Education
and Labor has no protective norms, no tradition of deference to its
chairman to shield him from intolerance of his policy. Policy individualism, we have said, is a way of life on Education and Labor.
Members pursuing policy individualism expect to be outvoted when

[26] *Washington Post*, September 16, 1966, p. 8.

they cannot win a majority to their view. When the wayward member is the chairman, the only way to "outvote" him is to strip him of his special institutional resources and make him as subject to majority rule as every other member. Powell's downfall (inside the Committee) came primarily because he would not process *all* legislation as quickly as he processed most legislation. Had he been willing to act as the mouthpiece for any Democratic majority, he would not have been deposed. In the highly partisan environment of the 89th Congress, the Democrats stood ready to outvote anyone who at anytime and in any way stood athwart the total achievement of their policy goals. Neither their action nor our explanation of it should startle anyone familar with the intensely political and highly volatile nature of Education and Labor's decision rules and its decision-making processes.

The behavior of any committee chairman must be analyzed within the context of his committee's strategic premises and, particularly, in the light of individual members' goals. Whatever his personal characteristics, temperamental or ideological, this context puts limits on the kinds of behavior he can engage in and still retain his leadership, and it sets forth positive guidelines for his success and effectiveness inside the Committee. The chairman of the *Foreign Affairs Committee* is severely hampered in giving his members what they want because they do not really know what they want — not sufficiently to standardize and operationalize their desires in a satisfying set of decision rules. They know only that they favor the foreign aid bill; and insofar as their policy goals are attainable by supporting foreign aid, their chairman can help. Beyond that, there is considerable membership frustration, about which any chairman can do very little, given the vagueness of members' goals coupled with the environmental dominance of the executive. Chairman Thomas Morgan has operated effectively within this constraining context. Where the members have a strategic posture — on foreign aid — he has worked to implement it. Where the members remain indecisive, Morgan has yielded to executive branch initiatives. And he has expended the rest of his energy soothing members' frustration — thereby preventing their unhappiness from developing into some kind of aimless internal convulsion.

Not one of the chairmen thus far discussed was described by his committee members as distinctively "kind" or "nice" or "gentle." But that is the affective language used to describe Chairman Mor-

gan. His aim as chairman is to maintain the committee's effectiveness within its present scope by keeping the group free of animosity.
As he puts the prescription:

> You have to be close to the members of your Committee.
> You have to be cooperative. You have to help them with
> their problems. I try to talk to all of them and to help them
> in every way I can. I do that — whether they are on the ma-
> jority or on the minority side. The members think I am
> friendly, understanding, and fair to them. We don't have
> animosity on the Committee. In *Time Magazine,* they said,
> "Morgan kills his enemies with kindness." There's a lot to
> that.

The overwhelming impression conveyed by the interviews is simply
that Committee members *like* their chairman. An experienced Democrat, in stating that he preferred Morgan as chairman to any of the
half-dozen or so next senior Democrats, said: "I like Doc. He's a
nice guy. He's no Fulbright, no great scholar. But he's for the (foreign aid) program and so am I. He cracks jokes; no one gets upset."
Others noted: "He likes to run the Committee, and he does, in such
a way that no personal feelings are hurt and no one gets upset. He
does not like to ruffle anyone's feathers."

His major technique is simply to "bend over backward to let
every one have his say" in the committee, and to keep a fairly loose
rein on the members, who say: "He is tolerant. . . . He lets everybody talk himself out." "He sits there and absorbs, absorbs, absorbs
— like a sponge." "Doc Morgan is so kindhearted. Suppose you were
testifying and you had ten minutes left, he'd say, 'What the hell, go
ahead, the hell with the rules.'" The Committee has no special set
of rules and no member said he wanted any. They don't need them
to insure democracy (like Interior) or majority rule (like Education
and Labor) or chairman responsiveness (like Post Office). Besides
which, they like their chairman so much personally that they would
not do anything to hurt or offend him. One declared:

> I would say Doc is not as forceful as he might be. . . . He's
> an effective chairman. He does not dominate the Committee
> in an autocratic way, but 99.9 per cent of the time he gets
> what he wants in the Committee. He gets what he wants in
> a gentle way. I suppose if he were stronger, as I wish he were,
> I wouldn't like him as much as I do.

What the unhappy members really want is an expanded scope of activity for the Committee. One explained: "He's a perfectly delightful man, so I have nothing against him personally. . . . But he's the State Department's man. As a result, this precludes any aggressive or imaginative activity on the part of the Committee."

As always, the positive prescriptions are vague. Sometimes there are intimations that if only Chairman Morgan were like Senator Fulbright, things would be different: "Hell, Fulbright is an initiator of ideas. Doc likes peace and quiet." Doc isn't that kind of guy (like Fulbright). He's a politician, a Pennsylvania politician." Yet even some of those who want the Committee to do more defend Morgan against these vague stylistic prescriptions. Said one:

> The proof is in the pudding. Look at the way he got the (aid) bill through. He anticipates objections and amendments . . . and trouble on the floor. He has a good sense of the House and he works quietly. Look at the trouble Fulbright has with his Committee and the bill the Senate's bringing to conference! That's no way to do it. Doc is very skillful. Really, there's an air of the unsung hero about all of it.

The House Committee is, of course, not the Senate Committee — does not have its constitutional prerogatives, its institutional importance within the parent chamber, or its traditions of foreign policy debate. It is only another mark of member frustration that some should blame the chairman for their own uncertainties in goals and strategic premises. It is highly doubtful that *any* chairman can lift the members of Foreign Affairs by their own bootstraps out of their malaise; if he cannot, then the benign chairman they now have seems well suited to helping them live with it.

Post Office Committee chairman Tom Murray was the only one studied who operated over any length of time in a manner contrary to the strategy and goals of a sizable majority of his Committee. He worked, *not* to help his members get what they wanted but to promote executive branch wishes. His chief weapons were the presidential veto and a sufficiently large Republican-Southern Democratic, conservative coalition vote to sustain it. Ideologically, and temperamentally, he was not an activist. And he slowed down Committee work, not by dint of his parliamentary prowess *a la* Graham Barden but by sheer inertia. He would delay organizing the Committee until March or April, and he would simply disappear from the Committee rooms for stretches of time. In his last year or two, advancing age robbed him of whatever vigor he had once had. His members thought of him, by turns, as "a dictator" because he would not appoint subcommittees, and as "ineffective" for his inability or unwillingness to run such Committee meetings as were held, in an orderly fashion. The rules changes of 1965 were designed to remedy both defects — to decentralize decision making in subcommittees and to institute binding rules of procedure. They provided for regular meeting days and empowered a vice-chairman to do anything the chairman could do, should the chairman absent himself.

A Committee member who served on Interior and Post Office compared, lengthily and vividly, decision making under an effective and under an ineffective chairman:

> Aspinall's a marvelous chairman. He knows more about that jurisdiction than any other person in the country, bar none. He's in at 8:00 A.M., works all day, no social life. He dominates those subcommittee chairmen; they have no autonomy at all. He's with them every step of the way. And everything's by the numbers, according to good parliamentary procedure. When we wanted rules for Post Office, we followed Aspinall's rules. He lets everybody talk, he's fair. He'll say if a freshman has anything to say, let's hear it. Aspinall's the best chairman anyone could have. It's time consuming, time consuming as hell; but it's run perfectly. On the other hand I'd go over to Post Office and it was a miserable mess. Everyone yelling and shouting, 'Who's got the floor?' 'I don't know.' 'Is there a quorum?' 'Who cares.' It was utter chaos. . . . Screaming, fighting, a miserable mess . . . and all old Murray would do was stare off into space. . . . When we did want to do something, we'd meet in Morrison's office, then leave by twos so no one would get suspicious. Then we'd come in, vote cloture, and get a bill out. But even after we ran a steamroller over Murray in committee, we'd have to prod him to go before the Rules Committee for a God damn rule.

The comparison speaks for itself. If it is even half true, Chairman Murray qualifies as Exhibit A in any case against the seniority rule. When the Committee voted its set of rules, Chairman Murray "just sat there" and, in the end, voted in favor of them.

The rules changes "took everything away from Murray but his gavel." In the 89th Congress, the effective Committee chairman was

Vice-chairman James Morrison, the next most senior Democrat, a man who stood foursquare with the strategic premises of the group. Morrison had long been a key member-spokesman for clientele groups. A staff man spoke of the decision making under Morrison.

> It's like hauling coals to Newcastle. He was the ramrod behind the reorganization anyway. He has the power to act in the absence of the chairman, and the chairman is absent a good bit of the time. He can approve travel funds, call meetings, change the time of the meetings.

"It's working very satisfactorily," said Murray. But he had "lost interest" in participating. "Tom has thrown in the towel," said one member. "Sometimes he comes to meetings and sometimes he doesn't. He's resigned to it. He doesn't struggle any more." The other members divvied up the subcommittee assignments without paying any heed to the nominal chairman. And the remodeled Post Office Committee turned to the business of meeting the goals of its members.

We have tried to demonstrate, in this chapter, that each committee's internal decision-making processes are shaped by its members' goals, by the constraints placed upon the members by interested outside groups, and by the strategic premises that members adopt in order to accommodate their personal goals to environmental constraints. One overall comparative dimension suggested by the independent variables of the analysis involves the relative impact of the members themselves and of external groups on decision-making processes. We might think of the dimension as *decision-making autonomy*. The greater the relative influence of the members, the more autonomous the committee; the greater the relative influence of outside groups, the less autonomous the committee. Making only the grossest kinds of distinctions, it appears that Ways and Means, Appropriations, and Interior are more autonomous decision makers than Foreign Affairs, Education and Labor, and Post Office. That is, members of the first three committees have a more independent influence on their own decision-making processes than do the members of the second three. For Ways and Means we might mention the restraints on partisanship and the leadership of Wilbur Mills;

for Appropriations, there are the specialization and internal influence of its subcommittees; for Interior, there are its participatory democracy and the leadership of Wayne Aspinall. The sources of committee autonomy are not always the same, but the result — a marked degree of internal, member control of decision making — is the same. With the other three committees, it is the environmental impact on decision making that seems most noteworthy. For Foreign Affairs, it is executive domination; for Education and Labor, it is the permeation of partisan policy coalitions; for Post Office, it is clientele domination. The three more autonomous committees emphasize expertise in decision making more than the three less autonomous ones, suggesting that perception of subject matter is related to decision-making processes.

The clustering of committees with regard to decision-making autonomy parallels the clustering noted in the last chapter, based on some similarities and differences in the committees' decision rules. Appropriations, Ways and Means, and Interior have, in common, a consensus on decision rules, a House-oriented set of decision rules, and decision-making autonomy. The three characteristics are probably closely interrelated. But the main thrust of our argument would be that the first two contribute to the third. When a committee's members agree on what they should do, they are more likely to be able to control their own decision making than when they cannot agree on what to do. When a committee's decision rules are oriented toward success (i.e., winning plus respect and confidence) on the House floor, the committee will have a greater desire to establish its operating independence than when its strategies are not especially concerned with floor success. House members, we recall, *want* their committees to be relatively autonomous, relatively expert decision makers. They are more likely, therefore, to follow and to respect committees that can demonstrate some political and intellectual independence of outside, non-House groups. Whether or not distinguishing the two clusters of committees will, in turn, help us to differentiate and explain committee decisions is a question we will keep in mind as we turn to a discussion of that subject.

Before moving to the final subject of House Committee decisions, however, we think it would strengthen our analysis to stop and compare — as to the four variables thus far discussed — our six House Committees with their six counterpart committees in the Senate.

CHAPTER FIVE

Senate Comparisons

In what respects, if any, do our House committees differ from their Senate counterparts? And in what respects, if any, are the patterns among our House committees duplicated among their opposite numbers in the Senate? Answers to these questions will enrich our discussion of the six House committees, by delineating more clearly the impact of institutional factors on committee behavior. Cross-chamber comparisons also add dimension to the discussion of committee decisions in the next chapter. Our comprehension of the six Senate committees is less detailed and less extensive than for the six House committees. But it is sufficient, we think, to strengthen the analysis of our House committees and to confirm the usefulness of the line of argument developed for that analysis.

MEMBER'S GOALS

Senators hold the same range of personal goals as Representatives — *re-election, good public policy, influence in the chamber,* and *career ambitions beyond the chamber.* Like House members, they perceive committees to be differentially useful in the pursuit of these goals. Our interviews with Senators (though fewer in number and, thus, more tentative) reveal patterns linking member goals and committees, patterns similar in most respects to those found in the House.

Senators are attracted, for example, to their Committees on *Interior* and *Post Office* for the same reasons of constituency service and re-election as are Representatives. Echoing their fellow Westerners in the House, Senators of both parties described the Interior Committee's obvious attraction for them.

> I wanted Interior because I come from a Western state and
> the Committee deals with matters like dams, parks, recrea-

tion, mines, public lands — all especially important to the
so-called public lands states. Everything I can get from the
Committee — big dams, mining, outdoor recreation, parks —
helps me back home.

Senators who seek Post Office membership see it, too, as helpful in
achieving their re-election goals. "It's a committee you go on to get
reelected. That's why I went on. It's good for mobilizing the workers, civil servants, and so forth." As in the House, no member of
either the Senate Interior Committee or Post Office Committee
sought these assignments primarily to further his goals of policy or
influence. It should be noted, however, that the same re-election goal
makes Senators and Representatives attentive to quite different constituencies. Generally, Senators face larger and more varied constituencies than House members. And this fact can produce cross-chamber
differences in committee behavior even while member goals remain
the same.

Senators on the *Labor and Public Welfare* and *Foreign Relations*
Committees also sound very much like their opposite numbers in the
House in stressing their policy-oriented goals. On each committee,
members describe a personal interest in the subject matter as the
prime source of the committee's attraction. A Labor Committee
Democrat said, "My entire background made me interested," where-
upon he detailed a lifelong concern for education and manpower
problems. Another, who had previously served for ten years on Education and Labor, cited a lifelong interest in "promoting good labor
laws and uplifting working conditions." Urban-state Democrats seem
to give the same secondary emphasis to constituency service and re-
election goals as do their House counterparts. Beyond the obvious
tie between labor unions and the Committee, a factor strengthening
the emphasis on constituency is the Senate Committee's added jurisdiction over health and some veterans' benefits. One Democrat
noted:

> The Committee's no good (politically) on the House side;
> it is good on the Senate side. Over there, they get all the hot
> potatoes and none of the plums. Here, we have some plums.
> Health — you can't get a purer plum than that.

And another, referring to veterans' education, exclaimed, "There's
political gold in them thar hills." Still, Committee selectors have not

always found it easy to fill Democratic vacancies.[1] And some Democrats have come to the Committee knowing that it is a political liability. "I have sometimes thought," said one, "that some of my enemies who wanted to see me defeated engineered my appointment to Labor. But I went on because of my interest in education." Republican Committee members emphasize the electoral risks of membership even more. They describe membership as "a chore" and claim to have great difficulty finding candidates. Thus, two freshmen had to be drafted to fill vacancies in 1965. In sum, for those members positively attracted to the Senate Labor and Public Welfare Committee, the dominant motivation is the promotion of their policy interests. Some also find it electorally advantageous. But the countervailing impact of those who view membership as a political liability keeps the goals of constituency service and re-election in a strictly subordinate position.

Senate Foreign Relations Committee members emphasize the same longstanding interest in foreign policy that motivates Foreign Affairs members. "I've always been interested in foreign affairs. That's about it." "In college — even before that — I was interested in foreign affairs. I've read *Foreign Affairs* for forty years. I'm just interested." "It has always been in my mind — since I was a little boy." None of the eight Senators interviewed mentioned re-election benefits. And one argued, in agreement with most members of the House committee, that "from a political standpoint, the Foreign Relations Committee is not a good committee to be on," specifying:

> It's a political liability. . . . You have no constituency. In my re-election campaign last fall, the main thing they used against me was that because of my interest in foreign relations, I was more interested in what happened to the people of Abyssinia and Afghanistan than in what happened to the good people of my state.

Several Senators mentioned the "prestige" of the Committee. None, however, claimed that this prestige could be translated into an extra measure of personal influence in the Senate, and none asserted that the desire for inside influence led him to the Committee. The Committee's prestige would seem to be of external rather than internal

---

[1] Joseph S. Clark, *The Senate Establishment* (New York: Hill and Wang, 1963), p. 82.

value — which may explain why the Committee does seem to attract Senators with career goals focused, beyond the Senate, on the White House. Such men are not likely to speak openly of these ambitions. But it is not accidental that Senators Estes Kefauver, John Kennedy, Hubert Humphrey, Eugene McCarthy, Edmund Muskie, and George McGovern sought (and the middle four gained) membership on Foreign Relations prior to their presidential candidacies. Membership on the Committee provides national visibility plus a chance to demonstrate close association with, if not substantive competence in, the presidentially critical area of foreign affairs. As a career launching pad for a minority of its members, Foreign Relations, again, resembles Foreign Affairs. Only the objects of their "progressive ambition" are different. But the dominant goal of most members remains participation in the making of good foreign policy.

The two Senate Committees whose members' goals differ most from their House counterparts are *Appropriations* and *Finance*. With Appropriations, there is a similar pattern with an important difference in emphasis; with Finance there is a different pattern altogether from that of Ways and Means.

Senators come to the Appropriations Committee, they say, because of its power.[2] "It's the most important and powerful committee in the Senate." "Appropriations appropriates, and that's power." As members of the purse-string committee, they have special status inside the Senate. "It's a magical title, a badge of distinction to be on Appropriations. Even though you are at the bottom of the Committee, you are respected." The rhetoric is familiar. And, in general terms, the dominant goal of Appropriations members is the same in both chambers — inside power. The difference lies in the almost simultaneous and universal connection that Senators make between having a special degree of influence and using it to further their goal of re-election through constituency service. The freshman Senator, who spoke of the Committee's "magical title," added:

> On Appropriations you can, just by the flick of the hand or
> by a personal endorsement, get things for your state that
> you couldn't get otherwise. . . . My main interest is Foreign

[2] Much of the material concerning the Senate Appropriations Committee in this chapter is taken from Richard Fenno, *The Power of the Purse: Appropriations Politics in Congress* (Boston: Little, Brown, 1966), Chapters 10, 11. Individual citations will not be made, however.

Relations, but I was told that Committee wouldn't do me any good back home.

"It's a power committee," said a veteran Southerner. "There's a lot of development going on in my state. I know I can get more for my state on this committee than on any other committee." In his study of the Committee, Stephen Horn concludes: "Control over the country's purse strings, with its concomitant power over programs and agencies, is attractive to only a few members primarily because of national policy interests. Most desire Appropriations first of all because of what membership can do for their state." [3]

The focus on the goal of re-election sharpens when Senators compare their reasons for seeking their multiple assignments. One sought and remains "on Foreign Relations because I like it and on Appropriations because I can, realistically, get more benefits for my state." Another sits on Labor "even though it is a (political) risk, because it has exciting issues"; he subsequently picked up Appropriations to offset this electoral liability. He pointed out, "I had all these people trying to defeat me, and as a defensive mechanism I went on Appropriations." The Committee's opportunities for serving re-election aims by benefiting constituencies are more widely appealing to Senators than to Representatives because most Senatorial constituencies generate a heavier and more diverse set of demands for federal money. The legislative assistant of a large state Appropriations member explained:

> When you've got a fast-growing state with millions of people, you've got a lot of eggs in the appropriations basket — military installations, flood control, urban renewal, rivers and harbors, reclamation, agricultural research, and so forth. People I never heard of before come in here with their tin cups looking for dollars. Public officials — county supervisors, city councilmen, game wardens, and so forth — write to us all the time. That's why the Senator wanted to get on the Committee — so perhaps they'll all remember us and do us a favor at election time. That's the selfish motivation that guides most men on Appropriations.

No Senator with a broad constituency could fail to see the re-election benefits of Appropriations membership — the more so if he can add it to one or two other committee assignments. When he articu-

[3] Stephen Horn, *Unused Power* (Washington: Brookings, 1970), p. 11.

lates the goal of inside power, he gives it a more definite and specific slant toward his constituency than does his counterpart in the House.

Senators on the Finance Committee — in sharp contrast to House Ways and Means members — make no mention of the goal of inside influence. To be sure, Finance Committee Democrats lack the special incentive of a committee on committees function; but even so they are not concerned about their status inside the Senate. Instead, they emphasize about equally the pursuit of policy and re-election goals. In language more reminiscent of Education and Labor or Foreign Affairs than of Ways and Means, they describe their Committee as "important" because of its subject matter. And the opportunity to participate in making important public policy attracts them. A liberal Democrat and a conservative Republican commented:

> I'm not sure I wouldn't put Finance as the most important committee in the Senate. Not as much prestige as Foreign Relations but more important. The Committee's jurisdiction includes so many issues vital to the nation. . . . I thought then and I think now that a crying need in this country is for an equitable system of taxation. That's the reason (I went on Finance).

> I was in business, and so after I was elected I simply went through the list of committee titles to see which ones were most closely connected with business. I was business-oriented. If you asked me, I'd say Finance and Foreign Relations are the two top ones. Appropriations is a dog's life. You don't have any influence over policy.

For most Committee members, their policy goals shade imperceptibly into their constituency-reelection goals. "I was attracted to the Finance Committee because it is the committee that is closest to the business interests of my state." No state is without an array of businesses for which tax and trade decisions are of monumental import — oil, liquor, sugar, tobacco, textiles, minerals, chemicals, and insurance were among those mentioned by the eight Senators interviewed. And while none described the quid pro quo between the decisions that were helpful to these interests and forthcoming campaign contributions, enough has been written about it to make the inference seem reasonable.[4] One antimedicare member observed that in his

---

[4] See, for example, Frank V. Fowlkes and Harry Lenhart Jr., "Congressional Report: Two Money Committees Wield Power Differently," *National Journal,* April 10, 1971, p. 795.

re-election campaign, "I organized the healing arts like the healing arts have never been organized. I got the doctors, nurses, druggists, interns, pharmaceutical people out working for me." David Price, in his study of the Finance Committee, emphasizes the constituency basis of the members' policy concerns in this way:

> Senators with widely differing ideological viewpoints and vary- ing constituency and group ties had a strong incentive to seek membership and a voice in Committee affairs. For many members, this included perusing legislation and offer- ing amendments with an eye to the welfare of a group or region. For relatively few, however, did it mean an attempt to formulate and develop original or far-reaching policy pro- posals.[5]

Both the emphasis on policy and the strong tie between policy and constituency-re-election goals contrast sharply with the personal goals of the members of Ways and Means.

A summary comparison of the six pairs of committees reveals one noteworthy difference. The member goal of influence inside the chamber is not as prominent for any Senate committee as it is for the two House committees, Appropriations and Ways and Means. In the case of Senate Appropriations, the expressed desire for inter- nal influence is linked closely to and thus diluted by constituency service-re-election goals. In the case of Senate Finance, it is simply nonexistent. If we could adduce a generalization, it is that Senators are less concerned about using their committees to enhance their inside influence than are House members. If there is an explanation for this generalization, we are most likely to find it in the immediate environment of Senate committees — that is, in the parent chamber itself.

ENVIRONMENTAL CONSTRAINTS

INSTITUTIONAL ENVIRONMENT. Senate and House committees op- erate in quite different institutional environments. Each chamber presents the members of its committees with its own constellation of opportunities and constraints. And committee members' goals are affected accordingly. The root institutional differences between

[5] David Price, "Who Makes the Laws: The Legislative Roles of Three Senate Committees," unpublished manuscript, Yale University, 1969, pp. 301– 302.

Senate and House are those of size, procedure, constituency, and tenure. They, in turn, combine to produce very different decision-making structures in the two chambers. The smaller size of the Senate makes it possible for each individual Senator to have more of an impact on chamber decision making than the individual House member — both as a matter of proportional weight and as a matter of procedural opportunity. Small size is conducive to a flexibility and informality of procedure that makes any collective Senate action uniquely dependent on the consent of each individual Senator. Coming as he does from a more heterogeneous constituency, the average Senator will want to exert his influence on a greater range of chamber decisions than the average Representative; and he will promote and preserve a facilitating internal structure. A Senator's public status (the result of size, constituency, and tenure differences) makes it easier for him to command the publicity resources with which to develop a national constituency; he can popularize a national problem or press a national candidacy. Senators who wish to avail themselves of this opportunity, as increasing numbers now do, will support an internal Senate structure that allows them to highlight their individual identities.

Senators, in sum, want to, can, and do sustain a decision-making process that is more individualistic and gives greater influence to the individual legislator than is the case in the House. We shall be offering support for this generalization throughout the chapter.[6] But one particularly interesting bit of support derives from House members' reactions to Senate decision-making styles in their conference committee confrontations. When brought face to face with Senators, House members are most impressed by the frequency with which Senate conferees defend items in their bill on the grounds that these items represent the identifiable desires of an individual Senator. As House conferees see it, an individualistic style of decision making has produced the Senate bill and continues to dominate the bargaining in conference. The following accounts are by an Appropriations and a Ways and Means veteran:

> Someone on the other side will say, "Senator so-and-so wants this project," or, "Senator so-and-so is interested in this

---

[6] Support for this proposition can be found in Lewis Froman, *The Congressional Process* (Boston: Little, Brown, 1967), and in Randall B. Ripley, *Power in the Senate* (New York: St. Martin's, 1969). Froman makes House-Senate comparisons; Ripley stresses the growing internal "individualism" of the Senate, 1955–1969.

item." That Senator isn't even on the Committee and hasn't attended the hearings, but he wants something and the rest look out for him. He isn't even in the conference room, but he's in there just the same. It's a club and they are trying to help him out. Maybe he just spoke to the Chairman or the clerk and said, "I want this in," and they'll fight for him in conference.

All the Senators are interested in is getting their amendments into these tax bills, when we come to conference. They make no bones about it; they're very open. They'll sit down for God's sake and say, "Now let's see, whose amendment was this? Oh yes, it's ————, and I told him I would support it. We are going to stand firm on that."

As we might expect, members of House-oriented committees are the quickest to sense an institutional difference in decision-making styles — and to be most critical of any recognizably Senatorial style.

The important corollary of this institutional difference is that *decision making inside the Senate is much less of a committee-dominated process than it is in the House.* For where it becomes necessary, as in the House, to circumscribe the activity of individual members and rely on fairly inflexible procedures and where the countervailing pressures toward individualism are of only modest intensity, the tendency to rely on formal collectivities for decision making is strong. And this tendency, of course, magnifies the importance of committees. In the House, the individual member's influence on chamber decisions is exerted, almost wholly, within and through his committees. Senators operate within no such constraints. A Senator with long experience in both chambers pointed up the contrast:

The House is a body of 435 struggling individuals whose only chance to have an impact is through their committees. The office of Senator is such, the prestige of office is such that a Senator can dabble in two or three areas that aren't necessarily in his committees. A House member can't do this.

Senate committees are important as arenas in which decisions are made. But they are not especially important as sources of individual member influence — not when compared with House committees. That is, a Senator's committee membership adds far less to his total potential for influence inside his chamber than a Representative's committee membership adds to his potential for influence in his chamber. And members of the two chambers formulate their com-

mittee-oriented personal goals accordingly. Thus, our earlier finding
— that Senators are less likely than House members to pursue the
goal of inside influence via their committee memberships — can be
explained by the differing realities of decision making inside the two
institutions.

On the Senate side, the most marked characteristic of committees
is, as we might expect, their permeability. They are not kept exclusive in their membership or autonomous in their operating procedures. Unlike the House, no Committee is given a special status as
an "exclusive" committee. Every Senator serves on at least two and
often three committees. In the 89th Congress (see Table 5.1) more
than half the members of our six House committees had only one
standing committee assignment, and the rest had but two. All members of our six Senate committees had at least two assignments, and
more than half of them had three or more. Senate committee memberships overlap and intertwine, thus linking each committee to
almost every other committee. In the 89th Congress, eight members
of our six committees chaired one Senate standing committee while
serving as members of two others. These multiple assignments keep
committees interlocked and help to dilute the importance a Senator
will attach to any one committee membership. Committee prominence is further diminished by the absence, in the Senate, of such
protective barriers as closed hearings and closed rules which, in the
House, are guarantors of committee autonomy and committee influence. Should a Senator have trouble dealing with a Committee (be
he a member of it or not), he can easily take his case to the Senate
floor where he has all the time he wants to argue his position — in a
context where the presumption in favor of the committee position
is much weaker than it is in the House.

Table 5.1
Number of Committee Assignments

Members of Six Committees, Senate and House, 89th Congress

Number of Assignments	Number of Senators	%	Number of Representatives	%
One	0	–	119	57%
Two	33	43%	91	43%
Three	37	49%	0	–
Four	5	7%	0	–
Five	1	1%	0	–
	91		210	

It is convincing evidence of the comparatively modest status of Senate committees that the Senate Appropriations Committee, whose members alone emphasize their inside power, should make perhaps the outstanding exhibit of committee permeability. In the 89th Congress, its members averaged between two and three standing committee assignments, and seven of its members were chairmen of other standing committees. In addition, Senate rules provide that three members from each of eight other Senate committees shall join the Appropriations Committee as full participants in decisions affecting those committees. If we add these twenty-four outside Senators to the regular twenty-seven, we find that about *half* the Senate participates directly in the work of this especially powerful committee. Furthermore, the Committee holds all its hearings in open, public session. Its nonexclusive membership and its accessibility to other Senators make it prototypically a Senate Committee and practically the antithesis of its House counterpart. For all the talk of their inside power, the members of the Senate Committee wield nowhere near the amount of independent influence over their colleagues that House Appropriations Committee members wield over theirs. A member of the Committee with earlier service in the House noted:

> The Appropriations Committee isn't nearly as important over here as it is in the House. Over there, it's life or death for a member. He has to get his project approved by the Appropriations Committee and they're very tough. Over here it's much looser. It's much easier for the individual Senator to get his projects in the bill.

Appropriations membership does not, accordingly, confer a "badge of distinction" in the Senate chamber nearly as prestigious as it does in the House. Aspirants to this Senate Committee understand the difference, and that is why they emphasize a narrow, constituency-oriented influence, in contrast to the broader, chamber-wide influence emphasized by House Appropriations members.

Assertions about the widespread distribution of influence and committee permeability in the Senate should not be taken to mean that Senators find all committees equally desirable. They do not. Some committees are more coveted and harder to get on than others. Even if a Senator has ample opportunity to amend a committee bill on the floor, his chances are better if he works inside the committee.

And even if the Appropriations Committee is easily permeated by nonmembers, it is easier still for a Senator to get what he wants if he is a member. Because of the multiple assignments, Senators rarely have their preferences put to a hard, meaningful test. When a Senator can gain Foreign Relations without giving up Appropriations, or gain Finance without giving up Foreign Relations, or gain Appropriations while keeping Labor and Post Office, a detailed transfer matrix paralleling that of Table 2.2 is not very useful. Two other indicators provide, however, an adequate picture of the relative attractiveness of the six. They are: first, the number of Senators transferring off each committee as a percentage of the total number of transfers to and from the committee; second, the number of freshmen appointees as a percentage of the total number of appointees to each of the six committees. The rankings, along with House committee comparisons, are displayed in Table 5.2.

Table 5.2
Preference Rankings — Six Senate Committees

	Transfers *From* Committee As Percentage of All Transfers To and From Committee[7] 1949–1969			Freshman Appointments As Percentage of All Appointments To Committee 1955–1966		
Foreign Relations	6%	2/32	(18%)*	0%	0/17	(30%)*
Finance	11	3/28	(10%)	18	3/17	(4%)
Appropriations	14	6/42	(15%)	15	3/20	(14%)
Interior	53	9/17	(61%)	76	25/33	(73%)
Labor & Public Welfare	63	15/24	(57%)	62	18/29	(69%)
Post Office	78	29/37	(65%)	60	15/25	(74%)

*Corresponding House Committee Figures in Parentheses.

The three most desired Senate committees are the same as those in the House. And, as in the House, a large gap separates the three most desired from the three least desired. Too fine a point probably should not be put upon gradations within the two categories. But it must be noted that, by every measure used here (and elsewhere), the most attractive Senate Committee is Foreign Relations.[8] And by every cross-chamber comparison made, Senate Foreign Relations occupies a consistently higher ranking than House Foreign Affairs.

[7] Transfer column adapted from: George Goodwin, *Little Legislatures* (Amherst: University of Massachusetts Press, 1970), pp. 114–115.
[8] See, for example, Donald Matthews, *U.S. Senators and Their World* (Chapel Hill: University of North Carolina Press, 1960), p. 149.

Senators give primacy to Foreign Relations, we think, because the subject matter area is the one in which the Constitution has given the Senate, as distinguished from the House, special prerogatives, namely, the authority to ratify treaties and approve the appointments of diplomats. Foreign policy is to the Senate what money policy is to the House, a special institutional preserve and critical to the power of the institution within the American political system. Within each chamber and across the two chambers, the institutionally important committees are the most attractive ones. In the House, where committees are so central to decision making, the members of the institutionally important money committees are accorded distinctive inside influence and distinctive working autonomy. In the Senate, where committees are less central to decision making, no such added importance is bestowed upon the members of the institutionally important foreign policy committee. Foreign Relations may be especially attractive, but it is not especially influential, at least not by dint of parent chamber wishes. If, therefore, the members of the Committee should try to parlay the special status of their subject matter into special influence for the Committee, they would have to work against, not with, the grain of the Senate's internal decision-making processes.

When House members grant a special degree of influence to a committee, House leaders work to insure the future responsiveness of that committee by closely superintending the committee assignment process. In addition to the conventional criteria of appointment, they often apply an institutional criterion, e.g., "a responsible legislative style." Given the lower estate of Senate committees, we would expect to find less superintendence and less concern for institutional criteria. Such does seem to be the case. Among the Republicans in the Senate, the most senior applicant for a vacancy routinely gets what he wants — modified only by the understanding that no man should sit on more than two of the more desirable committees. The Democratic Steering Committee does exercise discretion, but lessened it by adopting the Johnson Rule in 1953, which assures every freshman of a "major" assignment before other vacancies are filled. For most committees there are no contests. For Foreign Relations, Appropriations, and Finance, there usually are. And it is in these situations that such factors as seniority, leadership preference, steering committee composition, geography, philosophy, and institutional criteria come into play. On the evidence, institutional criteria are employed only against the most dedicated institutional "out-siders," and even then with flagging zeal. Senators Wayne Morse, Paul Douglas, Joseph Clark and William Proxmire, four of the more publicized "outsiders" of the period, were denied and passed over for membership on the Foreign Relations, Finance, Foreign Relations, and Appropriations Committees respectively. Sometimes seniority criteria were preserved by drafting a more senior man to "run" against them (the Senate's version of cooptation), sometimes not. But, in every case, the institutional criteria were relaxed, and each of the four eventually received the assignment he was earlier denied. For some of these men, it is probable that philosophical cri-teria were at least as important as institutional ones. If "outsiders" eventually get the committees they want, it seems likely that for the Democrats, as for the Republicans, seniority is the most common criterion; and most committees are self-selected. The committee as-signment record, such as we know it, modifies only slightly, if at all, our generalization that Senators evince less of an institutional inter-est in their committees than House members do in theirs. No Senate committee operates within an institutional environment like that which constrains the House Committees on Ways and Means and Appropriations.

POLICY ENVIRONMENT. There are not many differences among the policy environments of Senate and House committees. With few exceptions, each pair of committees considers the same subject matter and confronts the identical policy coalitions. Such differences as there are, center on those pairs of committees in whose institutional environments we have already found some differences. The presence or absence of parent chamber interest, it seems, affects all other in-terested outsiders. As chamber interest declines, other environmental influences become more salient. When chamber interest is constant, similar policy subjects attract similar policy coalitions. Three Senate Committees — Finance and Appropriations (where chamber interest is less) and Foreign Relations (where chamber interest is greater) — inhabit somewhat different policy environments from those of their opposite numbers in the House. Three others — Labor, Interior and Post Office — live in environments very similar to those already de-scribed for their House counterparts. We shall give these latter three no special consideration here.

For all the same reasons that the administration is prominent in the policy environment of the Ways and Means Committee, so, too, is it active in that of the *Finance Committee*. Wherever tax, trade, and welfare policies are involved, executive and party interest run strong. Of at least equal importance in the Finance Committee's policy environment, however, are clientele groups. "No Committee in the Senate . . . ," writes Price, "was the target of more wealthy, powerful, or politically active interest groups than Finance." [9] And it is clientele prominence on the Senate side that marks the difference in the policy coalitions facing the two taxing committees. A *National Journal* comparison of the two committees describes Ways and Means as "a quiet pond" and Finance as "a cauldron" in respect to clientele clashes. It says, "The pressures, by all accounts, are most intense along the legislative path that leads through the Senate." And it adds, with regard to the Finance Committee:

> Most of the outside pressure comes not from the White House or even from broad-gauged interest groups like the AFL-CIO or the National Association of Manufacturers, but from special interest groups like the oil lobby, the coal lobby, and the cement lobby.[10]

Finance members describe these same "special interests" as being involved in their very appointments to the Committee. Two Democrats claim to have been blocked for a long time by "the oil interests primarily" and by "the oil interests, the insurance interests. . . . , all the big interests." Two Republicans, whose paths to membership were smooth, said that "some business groups may have been involved" and "all economic groups watch these assignments carefully." From start to finish, therefore, the Finance Committee's relations with clientele groups are characterized by an intensity not matched by Ways and Means.

Clientele groups, of course, express an interest in Ways and Means activity. But they are held in check by those attitudes and practices of the Committee that stem from its constitutional prerogatives and its special place within its parent institution. Since all revenue bills start in the House and since Ways and Means always acts first, every disappointed clientele group descends on the Senate Committee seeking last resort redress. Thus the intractable legislative sequence concentrates a heavier and more intense volume of clientele activity on Finance. This concentration is further insured by the Ways and Means practice of drafting its own bill from a rather general admin-

[9] Price, *op. cit.*, pp. 301–302.
[10] Fowlkes and Lenhart, *op. cit.*, pp. 795, 804. For the same emphasis, see Manley, *The Politics of Finance, op. cit.*, Chapter 6.

istration message, which means that clientele groups cannot know in advance the specific provisions on which the Committee will act. While Ways and Means is making its decisions, however, the clientele groups are in close touch. Once the Committee has acted, of course, the closed rule protects the Committee's decision from amendment on the floor. Because of their institutional interest in Ways and Means behavior, House members have guaranteed the Committee a high degree of autonomy, in return for which the Committee's members are expected to manifest a sense of responsibility and a special degree of responsiveness. Ways and Means is supported by its parent chamber, then, in espousing a set of attitudes and procedures that give it some counterweights in coping with clientele pressure. Senate Finance operates with no such counterweights; and clientele groups are much more dominant in their environment. Correlatively, Finance members do not feel constrained to manifest any special degree of responsibility or responsiveness to their parent chamber.

The policy environment of the Senate *Appropriations Committee* is dominated by the executive branch. Like its House counterpart, it acts upon a budget prepared by the executive agencies. More than the House Appropriations Committee, however, the Senate group confronts policy coalitions in which their chamber colleagues and supporting clientele groups play an independent part. Whereas the aggregating of interests for presentation to the House Committee is virtually monopolized by the executive branch, supporting legislators and outside groups come independently to the Senate Committee. Here again, because of their institutional concerns, House members have allowed their Appropriations Committee to operate autonomously within the House and to constrict all incoming access routes. In contrast to this, the Senate Appropriations Committee appears extremely permeable. The legislative sequence, too, is the same as it is for tax bills, with the Senate acting last and receiving the brunt of special appeals for addition or restoration of funds. Because the House Committee acts in secret, clientele groups will not usually know what has happened until there is too little time to take action in the House. The effect in the Senate Committee is described by a member:

> The Senate always gets the bill after the House has dealt with it. Every group or interest or community that feels aggrieved comes over here and asks us to put the money back

> in. We get all these appeals because we're the court of last resort. A lot of Congressmen will come over here, too, and ask us to help them out.

And, as another Senator exclaimed:

> All the appeals are for increases. No one ever testifies against an appropriation. It's ten to one, one hundred to one in favor of raising them. . . . I've never had a single person ask me to reduce an appropriation — unless it's a Senator opposed to something. You may get that. But no interest group has ever called me and asked for a lower appropriation.

As with Ways and Means and Finance, a set of institutional conditions that are present for House Appropriations and absent from Senate Appropriations make for differences in the policy environments of the two groups.

With the two foreign policy committees, the opposite tendency occurs. Without question, the policy environment of both these committees is dominated — overwhelmingly so — by the executive branch. But in the field of foreign affairs, the Senate has been given special constitutional prerogatives. And because of these prerogatives, the members of the Senate take a special institutional interest in the subject matter. That is, Senators generally think of the Senate as having a distinctive contribution to make in foreign policy, and they may act to protect their right to make it. The *Foreign Relations Committee's* topmost place in the prestige hierarchy reflects the extra special appeal of this particular policy area to members of this particular institution. Here, then, the Senate's foreign policy interest makes the policy environment of the Foreign Relations Committee somewhat less monolithic than that of Foreign Affairs. For Senate opinion *may* contend with executive opinion, confronting the Committee with strongly held differences of viewpoint and giving the Committee some leverage in dealing with the executive branch. We emphasize the word "may," because the potential inherent in the Senate's institutional concern may or may not be capitalized. One reason why it may not be capitalized is that Senators have done nothing to give their Foreign Relations Committee any special operating autonomy or corporate influence. As noted earlier, Foreign Relations is kept as permeable and as collectively unimportant as all other Senate committees. Senators make no exceptions — not even in the one area of paramount institutional in-

terest to them. We should not be surprised to find this ambivalence
having its effects on the behavior of the Foreign Relations Committee.

STRATEGIC PREMISES

Strategic premises (or decision rules) are overall guides to committee decision making, which most of a committee's members believe
will enable them to accomplish their personal goals within the
existing set of environmental constraints. Where either goals or
environment are different for a Senate committee from those of a corresponding House committee — as they are for Finance, Appropriations, and Foreign Relations — we would expect to find the greatest
differences in the resulting strategic premises. The decision rules we
have adduced for Senate committees are even more tentative than
those we have described for the House. We conducted fewer interviews; Senate committees are smaller in size; and our impressions can
be more easily skewed by one or two members. Moreover, the pervasive individualism of the Senate militates against a consensus on any
strategic premises. We offer both our verbal and our numerical pictures of the six Senate Committees with considerable hesitancy.

Finance Committee members must pursue their policy and their
constituency-re-election goals in a markedly pluralistic environment.
Their policy subjects draw the serious interest of the executive
branch, party leaders, and clientele groups alike. It is the concentrated concern of clientele groups, however, that is distinctive.
And it is the reciprocal attentiveness of Finance members to their
clientele's expectations that produces the Committee's most durable
strategic premise. Except for their broadly ideological policy goals,
Committee members find that they can achieve a high proportion of
their personal goals by extending sympathetic treatment to clientele
groups. Price commented, in this regard, that only three out of the
seventeen members had "serious misgivings about using their committee position to promote home state or other interests." [11] Wherever their policy goals have a strong constituency flavor or wherever
constituency-based clientele groups press them directly, Finance
members can help themselves by helping clientele groups. They are
encouraged in this stance by the conditioning force of the legislative

----

[11] As quoted in Fowlkes and Lenhart, *op. cit.*, p. 795.

sequence in which they always act after the House has passed its bill and in which they always are besieged by groups appealing House decisions. Committee members have standardized their decision context by assuming that the House has given general form to the bill and that their task is to deal, by amendment, with the remaining "hot spots" in that bill.[12] Their decision strategy, then, is *to give remedial assistance to clientele groups who appeal to them for redress from House decisions.* "Most of our work," observed one member, "has to do with the special effects of general legislation, what you might call special interest amendments. . . . We have to spend a lot of time taking care of the people who might be hurt." [13] "We give everyone a second chance," said another, "the administration, too." Chairman Harry F. Byrd, for his own conservative reasons, endorsed the "appeals board" strategy. As one member said,

> The old man won't begin a bill unless it's sent over by Ways and Means. He's a stickler on this. Of course, one of the reasons is that he's opposed to doing anything anyway.

But the strategy is neither inherently conservative nor liberal. Byrd's successor, Russell Long, was a great deal more liberal; but he believed, too, "that the Committee should be an arena for interest aggregation and amendment." [14] This strategic position is the converse and the complement of that of Ways and Means. Whereas the House Committee sees itself as responsibly fashioning an interrelated policy whole, its Senate counterpart sees itself as providing piecemeal remedies for people who feel ill served by that House policy. Whereas the House Committee is strongly constrained by its institutional environment, the Senate Committee is not.

What, then, of the broader goals of the Finance Committee's members? And what of the similarly broad programs of the executive branch and of the parties? What strategic premise has the Committee produced for coping with their kinds of expectations? In the same situation, Ways and Means members have developed a distinctive measure of policy partisanship. There is no abstract reason why Finance could not develop a similar premise. But they have not. Tables 5.3 and 5.4 show one reason why. Unlike Ways and Means,

[12] *Ibid.*, p. 803.
[13] Price, *op. cit.*, p. 314.
[14] *Ibid.*, p. 299.

Table 5.3
Senate Committee Conservative Predisposition
(Mean Conservative Coalition Scores, 86th–89th Congress)

	Democrats			Republicans			Total		
	Comm. Membs.	Other Senate Membs.	Diff.	Comm. Membs.	Other Senate Membs.	Diff.	Comm.	Total Other	Diff.
App.	48	29	+19	67	65	+2	54	41	+13
Fin.	37	33	+4	77	63	+14	51	43	+8
P.O.	34	34	0	65	66	-1	44	46	-2
F.R.	28	35	-7	71	65	+6	42	45	-3
Int.	19	37	-18	71	65	+6	35	47	-12
L.&P.W.	16	37	-21	57	68	-11	30	47	-17

Table 5.4
Senate Committee Partisan Predisposition
(Mean Party Unity Scores, 84th–89th Congress)

	Democrats			Republicans			Total		
	Comm. Membs.	Other Senate Membs.	Diff.	Comm. Membs.	Other Senate Membs.	Diff.	Comm.	Total Other	Diff.
Int.	71	65	+6	72	66	+6	72	65	+7
L.&P.W.	75	64	+11	64	68	-4	71	66	+5
P.O.	73	65	+8	65	68	-3	70	66	+4
F.R.	67	65	+2	66	68	-2	66	67	-1
Fin.	60	67	-7	71	66	+5	65	67	-2
App.	62	67	-5	67	68	-1	64	67	-3

the Finance Committee's members (in the period under study) display no ideological divergence along party lines. Finance Republicans are a faithful replica of those on Ways and Means — more conservative and more partisan than their Senate colleagues. But Finance Democrats are the reverse of their Ways and Means counterparts, being more conservative and less partisan than their fellow Senators. "It's a conservative committee, more conservative than the Senate," said one Democratic member. And Manley concludes that "the bipartisan, conservative coalition has dominated the Finance Committee for many years." [15] The Committee has had a conservative policy majority, but not a partisan policy majority. And for ten of the twelve years under study, the possibilities of policy partisanship were further blunted by a very conservative chairman, Harry F. Byrd. The Committee's conservatives, however, have not been cohesive enough or programmatic enough to develop an operating premise of their own. The Committee's conservative Democrats, on whom the durability of such a premise would depend, have been too unpredictable. While they are not often very responsive to Democratic administration wishes, sometimes they are. Perhaps the most general reason for a lack of policy partisanship is simply that Finance members are policy individualists. Surely their constituency-related goals draw them in this direction. And even their broadest policy goals may be more idiosyncratic than programmatic. Price takes this view when he writes:

> Few Finance Committee members had inclinations toward independent or extensive policy involvement (by the Committee) in the first place. Others, like (Russell) Long, (Albert) Gore, (Paul) Douglas, (Abraham) Ribicoff, (Vance) Hartke, and (Harrison) Williams seemed less likely than most Senators to be encouraged or deterred by the prospects their committee offered them for success. Their involvement was often motivated by a desire for publicity, by determination to take a "principled" stand, or by a quest for an activist image — motivations upon which the consensus-building capacities of the Committee were likely to have little impact.[16]

The Finance Committee's second strategic premise is, then, one of *policy individualism — each member to pursue his own view of good*

[15] Manley, *op. cit.*, p. 297.
[16] *Ibid.*, pp. 307–308.

public policy in concert with whatever allies he can find. When members come to a committee in pursuit of policy goals and there are no disciplining forces — such as parent chamber constraints or partisanship — emanating from the environment, policy individualism is the only available strategic premise.

Senate Appropriations Committee members face a relatively simple strategic situation. Individually, each wants appropriations for his state; collectively, they confront executive agencies, clientele groups, and fellow legislators who want more money than they have been granted by the House. They are mindful of the abstract desirability of economy, but neither their own goals nor dominant environmental expectations can be met by budget cutting. Conversely, their special incentives and pressures direct them toward program and project support. In pursuit of their individual goals, their strategic premise is *to approve the constituency-based appropriations requests of each Committee member.* And in response to environmental demands, their strategic premise is *to act as an appeals court, giving appropriations relief to those who have suffered excessive reductions at the hands of the House.* Implicit in both decision rules are moderating considerations of reasonableness (size of request), fairness (fair shares for claimants), and legitimacy (executive agency support). Otherwise, the first rule is quite straightforward in reflecting the members' desire for influence. The second rule reflects the Committee's standardization of its decision context. As Committee members see it, the House has already acted, has made budget reductions, and has probably made many excessive reductions (often deliberately in expectation of Senate restorations). Since Senators have neither the time nor the inclination to take up agency requests *de novo,* and since agencies and their supporters will petition only in case of a House reduction, it simplifies the Committee's task to consider its normal function as that of an appellate court.[17] And while, like any such court, it will deny some appeals, its working assumption is that the overall thrust of its money decisions will be more liberal than will those of the House Committee. "They call us the

---

[17] Stephen Horn questions the continued accuracy of the "appeals-court" description of the Senate Committee. His thesis is that most of its subcommittees now begin their hearings before the House makes its appropriations decisions. But it remains true that Senate Committee decisions are always made after House Committee and House decisions. This aspect of the sequence, we would argue, is what underpins the "appeals court" strategy of the Senate group. See Horn, *op. cit.,* pp. 72–82.

'upper body' because we 'up' appropriations, and it's true," commented a Senate Committee member. "We cut some, but usually we raise appropriations."

In view of its tendency toward liberal decision premises, one may be surprised to note that our indicators show the Senate Appropriations Committee to be the most conservative committee of the six. On second thought, however, one realizes that the members have adopted their decision rules for reasons quite independent of their social philosophies. And, in any case, we have described their posture as liberal only *in comparison with that of the House Committee.* We have characterized direction rather than magnitude. And doubtless a more liberal committee would produce more liberal decisions than the committee we are studying. The Committee's lopsidedly conservative membership reflects mainly the impact of seniority on the committee assignment process, in a period when Southern Democrats and conservative Republicans were overrepresented among senior Senators. But these men were not attracted to the Committee as a forum in which to practice their conservatism. Far from it. A veteran Republican conservative offered the most widely held explanation of why the Senate "ups appropriations":

> House members only have one district to please. They may have one interest they have to cater to. They can get elected by looking after one thing; and they just say the hell with everything else. You've got some pretty mean and ornery fellows over there. You ask the agencies and they'll tell you we're a lot more lenient over here. A Senator has a whole state to look after.

A common corollary holds that the six-year term frees Senators from the countervailing impact of those short-term national economy moods to which House members, campaigning at two-year intervals, must often respond. The logic of both these arguments is institutional, not philosophical. A set of strategic premises emphasizing budget cutting — as on the House side — probably requires a conservatively inclined committee. But the strategic premises adopted by the Senate committee require no particular set of ideological — or, for that matter partisan — predispositions.

Members of the *Senate Foreign Relations* Committee want to participate in making foreign policy in an environment dominated by the President and the executive branch. Their strategic problem is similar, therefore, to that of Foreign Affairs; and Foreign Relations members, too, have been troubled by uncertainty and frustration in devising a solution. Because of the Senate's institutional prerogatives in the foreign policy area, the Senate Committee's efforts have taken a different tack than those of the House Committee. And because of those institutional prerogatives, the unhappiness of Senate Committee members has been that much greater. The top aide of one member exclaimed:

> My boss is interested in foreign affairs. He broke his back
> to get on the Committee. It's fine to be interested in some-
> thing. But unless the Committee does something, you'll just
> sit there and get ulcers. What good is membership on a com-
> mittee when it doesn't influence the course of events? The
> Committee is supposed to have prestige. But I don't under-
> stand the prestige bit either. How can you get prestige when
> you don't do anything? I don't understand why anyone
> would want to be on that Committee.

Venting his dissatisfaction, Democrat George Smathers resigned from the Committee in 1965, after two years of service. "Foreign Relations is the biggest fraud in the Senate," he said. "It handles only one big bill a year — foreign aid. And everything I heard in closed-door briefings was no different than I'd read in the papers." [18] No self-respecting Senator will content himself, as so many Foreign Affairs members do, with a job definition calling for passage of the foreign aid bill and support for the President on everything else. Whereas the foreign aid bill gives the House Committee its vital entree into the foreign policy field, Senators view it as a modest part of their broad-ranging "advise-and-consent" responsibilities. Committee Chairman J. William Fulbright described the foreign aid bill as a "plague" on his group. "That cursed thing took up three-quarters of our time. No member really liked it. They were bored with it. It about destroyed the spirit of the Committee." [19] Foreign Relations members have struggled to find a strategic posture that would give them the extra scope and the extra independence in making foreign policy that the Constitution prescribes. During the period under study, they tried three different strategies, none of which

[18] As quoted, *Washington Post*, March 26, 1966, pp. A1 ff.
[19] Brock Brower, "The Roots of the Arkansas Questioner," *Life*, May 13, 1966.

proved wholly satisfactory. All, however, provide a contrast with the strategic efforts of the House Committee.

Their first strategy of the period was one whereby Committee members would *presume in favor of executive branch requests, provided only that the executive would maintain, in exchange, a close consultative relationship with the Committee.* Reaching for the very same metaphor that House Chairman Morgan did, Senator Fulbright said, on assuming the chairmanship in 1959, "No football team can expect to win with every man his own quarterback. . . . The Foreign Relations Committee is available to advise the President, but his is the primary responsibility." [20] The Senate Committee, unlike its House counterpart, felt justified in asking for a special degree of consultation. This strategy was established under Arthur Vandenberg, when the Committee participated in and gave solid bipartisan support to America's postwar revolution in foreign policy. A Democratic President needed the support of a Republican Senate; President Truman and Secretary of State Acheson worked closely with Chairman Vandenberg; Vandenberg worked to keep his Committee united behind the policy, to which he and they made minor contributions; executive attention added to Committee prestige; the unanimity of the Committee made it influential inside the Senate; its prestige and its influence re-enforced the President's need to consult with it. Such were the circumstances during "the golden age" of the Committee. This strategy of conditional support for the executive has had considerable durability. It remained as the dominant Committee strategy — despite Committee members' complaints about the inadequacy of executive consultation ("We're in on the crash landings, but not the takeoffs") — during the early part of the period studied. And it endured as a strategy for crisis situations through the Gulf of Tonkin Resolution in 1964.

A second strategy, which waxed as the first one waned, was *policy individualism.* "Every man his own policy" is a fallback strategy for every policy-oriented committee — especially for any Senate committee. But the sense of institutional responsibility held by members of this Committee (as it is not by the House Committee) encourages them twice over to speak out on foreign policy. Policy individualism is always at least a minor strategy on Foreign Relations. But in the mid-1960's, it became the dominant one. Committee

[20] *Washington Post,* September 22, 1965, p. E4.

members' disagreement with President Johnson's Vietnam policy, plus their feeling that they were not, in any case, being consulted, destroyed the earlier decision rule. Committee members repaired to their individual views. "There are," said one, "nineteen men on it and they represent twenty-one and a half different viewpoints." [21] Using the Committee as their platform, members participated in the national policy debate. But they were unhappy that the Committee, as a committee, was not capitalizing its potential for influence. In January 1966, a Democratic opponent of the Administration summed it up:

> The Committee is in disarray. It cannot shape any consensus. And if the truth be known, the President and the Secretary of State probably like it that way. . . . So long as we are split, we cannot be influential. We cannot offer a challenge to them. . . . No one speaks for the Committee. Every member speaks for his own position. Right now, dissent comes from various individual Committee members. The only solid, unified position comes from the Administration. . . . The Committee used to be the most venerable, the most prestigious committee in the Senate. Now it is in a bad state of disrepair.

Members of the Finance Committee are reasonably content to follow the decision rule of policy individualism. For them, it is a hunting license to recruit their own policy coalitions in the kind of pluralistic policy environment that offers good prospects for success. For Foreign Relations members, however, policy individualism is a less attractive way of achieving their policy goals. For they seek policy participation in a monolithic environment where the executive branch is the exclusive leader in coalition building. And long experience tells them that they are more likely to be successful in coping with the executive branch if they can agree on a less individualistic approach to their tasks.

As the period ended, the Committee had begun to develop a third strategic premise. It was *to make the Committee the spearhead in strengthening the institutional independence of the Senate in foreign policy making.* It was an effort to pull the Committee up, as it were, by the institutional bootstraps of the Senate. As such, it involved a line of justification that is not so readily available to the

---

[21] As quoted, Marvin Kalb, "Doves, Hawks and Flutterers in the Foreign Relations Committee," *New York Times Magazine*, November 19, 1967, p. 56.

House Foreign Affairs Committee. Senate Committee members can standardize their decision context as one in which the Senate's special prerogatives have been eroded during a long period of executive dominance. They can claim that both the Senate and the Committee have far too long been ignored, with the result that a constitutional imbalance exists in the making of foreign policy decisions. They can point out that the Foreign Relations Committee should take the lead in reasserting Senate prerogatives and should act independently of the executive to redress the balance. The appeal of this strategy lies in its institutional content. It can unify a Committee whose members still hold differing policy views by sublimating, rather than substituting for, policy individualism. And by unifying the Committee, it provides the basis for a revival of Committee influence within the Senate. A strategy calling for assertions of institutional independence is not very specific. Its earliest manifestation came in the public hearings on Vietnam in early 1966, with the Committee acting as a forum for the discussion of alternative policies beyond those of the administration. These and later hearings were an effort to influence the executive indirectly and publicly rather than directly and privately as in the older, Vandenberg strategy. In defending the hearings, Chairman Fulbright argued that "it is the function of the Senate and of the Committee to create a dialogue and to have a discussion about foreign policy." "The hearings," he believed "suggest the possibility of a reinvigorated Senate participating actively and responsibly in the shaping of American foreign policy." [22] The strategy could well take other forms. It remained in the process of evolution as the period ended.

Senate Interior Committee members seek goals of constituency service and re-election in a clientele-dominated environment. In the abstract, their strategic situation is the same as that faced by House Interior Committee members. Like their House counterparts, Senators on the Interior Committee are entrepreneurs on behalf of the interests of their constituents. Describing the Committee as their "obvious," "natural," "clear," and "number-one" choice, they come to it eager to help their states. They are as much the leaders as the led in their relations with the policy coalitions of their environment. Indeed, like House Committee members, Senate Interior members claim to feel no clientele pressure at all — though they often speak

[22] Statement of Senator J. W. Fulbright before the Subcommittee on Separation of Powers of the Judiciary Committee, July 19, 1967, Press Release, p. 11. This is the best statement of the third strategic premise.

of working jointly with state and local groups on behalf of legislation affecting their constituencies. As Table 5.5 indicates, Senate Interior is an overwhelmingly Western Committee — much more so, even, than the lopsidedly Western House group. Far Westerners make up eighty-seven per cent of the Senate Committee, whereas they make up "only" fifty per cent of the House Committee. Out of their mutual understanding and their mutual self-interest, they easily adopt a decision rule identical to that of the House Committee — *to secure Senate passage of all constituency-related, Senator-sponsored bills*. The core of the rule is, of course, to secure favorable Committee action on their own bills. "There's a rule around here," said a top staffer, "that when a Committee member has something he wants for his state and it does not affect other states, they let him have it." Furthermore, he said:

> If the Committee is faced with a problem where a Democrat who is not on the Committee is opposed to a Republican who is on the Committee, they will be very reluctant to oppose the Republican. They will support the Republican — unless it's a matter of national policy.

The great bulk of the Committee's work does not consist of "national policy" questions. In implementing this decision rule, Senate Committee members display none of the House Committee's concern for their image and their performance in the parent chamber. Senate Interior members see themselves as hospitable to the requests of their colleagues; they do not believe their colleagues harbor any particular suspicion of them because of their Westernness; and they take no special precautions to insure chamber passage of their bills. They assume, in other words, the permeability of their Committee and a consequent ease of Committee-chamber relationships. Adding to this sense of ease, Westerners are in fact less of a minority and less isolated in the Senate than in the House. The seventeen reclamation states plus Alaska and Hawaii make up thirty-eight per cent of the Senate's membership but only twenty-six per cent of the House's membership. As an institution in which small states are relatively powerful, the Senate is altogether a more Western institution than the House.[23]

---

[23] Barbara Hinckley has recently noted that Westerners receive a disproportionately large number of committee chairmanships in the Senate. Barbara Hinckley, *The Seniority System in Congress* (Bloomington: Indiana University Press, 1971), pp. 46, 110.

Table 5.5
Regional Representativeness of Senate Committees
84th–89th Congresses

Percentage of Man-Years Service on
Committees by Region

Average Percentage Senate Seats by Region		Appropriations		Foreign Relations		Finance		Labor & Public Welfare		Post Office		Interior	
	%	%	Difference	%	Difference	%	Difference	%	Difference	%	Difference	%	Difference
East	20%	18	-2	23	+3	16	-4	40	+20	12	-8	11	-19
South	22%	31	+9	23	+1	32	+10	15	-1	21	-1	3	-19
Border	10%	6	-4	4	-6	11	+1	8	-2	24	+14	0	-10
Midwest	22%	18	-4	33	+11	27	+5	14	-8	27	+5	10	-12
Far West	25%	27	+2	19	-6	15	-10	22	-3	16	-9	+87	+62
Total	99%	100		102		101		99		100		101	
Representativeness Score		21		27		30		34		37		122	

What strategic posture do Senate Committee members take when confronted with the standard conservation versus commercial user conflict? In the House Committee, the conservationist position is likely to be taken by some of the non-Westerners, with a majority of the membership leaning toward the user position. But in a committee made up almost exclusively of Westerners, how are such controversies structured and solved? Applying the logic of intraCommittee conflict in the House, one might guess that the Senate Committee, lacking any non-Western conservationist contingent, would be even more user-oriented than the House Committee. But such is not the case. The Senate Committee's stance is the reverse of the House Committee. It is: *to provide, in the context of legislation balancing the interests involved, for the adequate preservation of land and water resources*. One explanation for this difference can be seen in Table 5.4, which displays the lopsidedly liberal predisposition of the Committee. The liberalism of its Democrats is nearly as great as that of Labor Committee Democrats and makes Interior nearly as liberal, overall, as the Labor group. Although we cannot equate liberals with conservationists (or vice versa), it does seem likely that the more liberally inclined a political group, the less sympathetic it will be to the economic interests of commercial users. A related explanation for the difference between Senate and House Interior Committee strategies lies in the nature of their constituencies. Senators have larger, more diverse constituencies, less easily dominated by a few economic interests. A Senator must do more balancing of interests, and conservationists will loom larger in these calculations. Constituency differences may explain both liberal and conservationist predispositions in the Senate. A Senate Committee member explained:

> Senators represent entire states. Since the popular election of Senators, they have been responsive to all the people of the state. House members represent more the rural areas; but Senators are concerned about city people as well. These people are the ones who feel the need for outdoor recreation. And the sportsmen — they are becoming increasingly numerous and they tend to gather in the cities. That's why the Senate Committee is more in favor of conservation than the House Committee.

An Interior Department official made the point when he said, "(Senator) Tom Kuchel (Calif.) isn't a Western Senator; he's an urban Senator. He wants a redwoods policy that conforms with the wishes of Los Angeles, and not the wishes of Del Norte County." The one group is as constituency-oriented as the other. But the constituencies they see are different.[24]

Labor and Public Welfare members seek the same policy goals in the same pluralistic, highly partisan environment as the members of Education and Labor. And they develop the same two strategic premises. One prescribes *policy partisanship*. The other prescribes *policy individualism*. Labor Committee Democrats are the most liberal and the most partisan of all of the six sets of Democrats. And the partisan premises of the Committee grow primarily out of their attachment to the core programs of the Democratic party. One Committee Democrat commented:

> We're so damn liberal. The establishment said let's put all those screwy bastards on Labor; what the hell, no one cares about it. Pretty soon we found we had the bit in our teeth. We were passing most of the New Frontier, and now the Great Society.

Conservative Republican members see the Democratic side as "stacked," and some think that "we should have stacked the Committee a long time ago just like the Democrats." But the Committee has had as much appeal for Republican liberals and moderates as for the party's conservatives. And the result is that the Committee's Republicans have been, collectively, the most liberal and the least partisan of the six Republican contingents. (See Tables 5.3 and 5.4) Thus, a dosage of extra partisan-policy individualism has come from the Republican side of the aisle — from men like Jacob Javits, Clifford Case, John Sherman Cooper, and Winston Prouty. The Committee's Democrats — liberal and activist — are even more supportive of policy individualism and in no sense view themselves as merely responding to initiatives taken in the policy environment. In his

---

[24] According to the Urban, Suburban, Rural classification in *Congressional Quarterly almanac,* 1963, pp. 1170–1184, the averages for the Senate and House Committees were very similar. House Committee member constituencies averaged 21 percent urban, 8 percent suburban, and 71 percent rural. Senate Committee member constituencies averaged 23 percent urban, 10 percent suburban, and 67 percent rural. But, whereas only four of seventeen Senators (24 percent) had *no* urban constituents, fifteen of thirty-three (45 percent) of the House Committee's members had *no* urban constituents.

study, Price emphasizes the degree to which the Committee's business results from the "political entrepreneurship" of its members:

> The Calendar of the Labor and Public Welfare Committee was . . . crowded . . . with proposals formulated or independently championed by its members. These bills reflected a wide variety of policy interests and a general desire for new or accelerated federal activity in every area of LPW jurisdiction.[25]

It would be difficult to compare the ratios of policy individualism to policy partisanship on the House and Senate Committees. But the policy individualism of the Senate group surely is the more solidly reinforced by conditions in its parent chamber. As a strategic premise, policy individualism is more likely to be adopted by Senate than by House committees. And where it is adopted by a Senate committee, it will be that much easier to implement.

The strategic premises of the *Senate Post Office Committee* do not differ from those of the House Committee. At least not so far as we could discern, in interviewing men whose interest in and commitment to the Committee were tenuous. The starting point for understanding the Committee is this typical comment by one member:

> I didn't ask for Post Office. It was the only vacancy when I came and that was it. I said, "Don't I get any choice?" They said, "That's all there is left."

Every member serves on two other committees. To a man, they view it as "a minor committee" that "doesn't take much time." One Chairman of the Committee spent a little more time than the others, he said, because "I have to talk to the employee groups more often. . . . And when they have banquets, I'm expected to go. So it takes more time." The Committee's members live in the same clientele-dominated environment as the House Committee members. And, in pursuit of their constituency-re-election goals, they have developed the same decision rules as the House Committee calling for favorable action for those groups. They are: first, *to increase employee pay and keep postal rates down* and second, *to accede to executive branch wishes when the alternative is no pay raise for federal employees.* Unlike the House Committee, there was no disagreement

---

[25] Price, *op. cit.*, p. 440.

on these premises between the members and their chairmen — Olin Johnston (1955–1964) and Mike Monroney (1965–1966).

Senators are, however, slightly less sympathetic to employee groups than are Representatives. A postal employee group leader stated flatly that "we are closer to the House." And he elaborated:

> We take our draft over to the House Committee and compare it with theirs and work out the legislation. We work informally with the Senate staff, too. But it's not like the House where you get right in there and feel like a partner in writing the bills.

Clientele groups have a greater influence on the House Committee than the Senate Committee, we think, because such groups have a greater marginal utility for the re-election of some House members than for any Senator. The reasons are mainly institutional ones. Senate constituencies are larger (thus diluting the impact of any one interest), and Senators run for office less often (thus diluting the frequency of contact). A postal employee leader said, "The House Committee is more liberal. That's because they have a two-year term and have to face the public every two years." The argument is a curious reversal of that applied to appropriations matters. But "the public," for Post Office Committee members, doubtless consists only of employee groups. Senators usually react to postal clientele groups the same way as House members do. But their ties to these groups are weaker. Hence, their willingness to move from their first decision rule to their second one is correspondingly greater.

DECISION-MAKING PROCESSES

The decision-making processes of a committee, we have argued, follow directly from the strategic premises of the committee members and indirectly from member goals and environmental constraints. To the degree that these three variables are similar for a corresponding pair of House and Senate committees, we would expect the internal processes of the two committees to be similar. Since all Senate committees exist in a different institutional environment from their counterpart House committees, however, some across-the-board, chamber-wide differences in decision making should be evident. Before we examine the Senate committees separately, we should call attention to two such institutional conditions that make the decision

processes of all six committees different from their House counterparts.

First, *Senators do not specialize as intensively or as exclusively in
their committee work as House members do.* Since decision-making
is less committee-centered, there is less reward in committee-based
specialization. Since committees are more permeable, it is easier for
the committee nonmember to involve himself in any committee's
subject matter. And, since he serves on so many committees and
subcommittees, the average Senator must, perforce, spread his efforts
over a greater span of subjects than the average Representative. Senators commonly draw these comparisons: "A member over there is
only on one committee. They aren't all over the lot like we are.
They can work on one thing." "They do a much better job clarifying
the bill. . . . It's not because they have better qualifications or better staff but because House members don't have to serve on so
many committees." "With four committees, two major and two
minor, you can't devote your time to one (committee) like you can
in the House." "On any bill in the House, you are going to have
more experts than you have in the Senate." For Senators seeking to
develop national constituencies, specialization becomes important
for its effects outside the committee and the chamber. Since it is less
directed at one's committee colleagues, it is a less significant ingredient of internal decision making. As Nelson Polsby has put it, "For
the Senate, specialization seems to mean finding a subject matter and
a nationwide constituency interested in the subject that has not already been pre-empted by some senior Senator." [26] Whether for inside
or outside consumption, Senatorial specialization becomes, much
more heavily than in the House, staff specialization. And, given the
individualism of Senate decision making, personal staff influence as
well as committee staff influence gets magnified in the process.

A second across-the-board difference is that *Senate committee
chairmen have less potential for influence inside their committees
than House chairmen.* This condition results, too, from the greater
individualism of Senate decision making. A veteran Senator generalized: "Senate chairmen don't have the dictatorial power that House
chairmen have. If Senators have differences of opinion, there's only

[26] Nelson Polsby, "Strengthening Congress in National Policymaking," in
Nelson Polsby (ed.) *Congressional Behavior* (New York: Random House,
1971), p. 7.

so much the chairman can do to get agreement." And a staffer put the same point more colorfully:

> No committee chairman in the Senate, no matter how strong he is, can keep the kind of tight rein on his members that a strong House chairman can. Over there, the members are herd-bound. Over here, we have one hundred prima donnas. House members aren't treated as individuals. That's why nine out of ten of them want to come over to the Senate. They want to be treated as individuals, not herded around in committees. They look over here and see every Senator wheeling and dealing and doing what he wants to do and it's like the rich man looking across the river into heaven.

To the committee member, anxious to preserve his individual identity, the chairman is one among equals. From the chairman's point of view, he is not likely to be able to attend to committee business as single-mindedly as a House chairman. It is frequently said of an influential House committee chairman — of Mills, of Aspinall, of Cannon among the ones we have studied — that "the committee is his whole life." It is a description which one *never* hears about *any* Senate committee chairman. They, like all Senators, admit to being spread too thin and having too little time to devote to any one aspect of their job. There were no revolts or hints of revolts against the chairman on any of the six committees — mostly, we think, because there was so little to gain thereby. The hand of a Senate chairman simply does not lie so heavily on his committee as that of a Barden or a Murray or a Powell — or, a Mills, an Aspinall, a Cannon.

As a consequence, then, of the Senate's individualistic mode of decision making, specialization and leadership are less important inside Senate committees than inside House committees.

An added difference that promotes an individualistic mode of decision making inside Senate committees is their relatively small size. As Table 5.6 (in comparison with Table 4.1) shows, five of the Senate committees are just about half the size of their House counterparts and the sixth (Finance) is about two-thirds as large. For all the reasons that the smaller size of the Senate encourages greater individualism in Senate decision making than is possible in the House, so, too, does the smaller size of Senate committees make for greater individual influence inside Senate Committees than is likely to happen inside the committees of the House. Senators often

Table 5.6
Committee Membership by Party:
84th–89th Congresses

	App.	*L.&P.W.*	*F.R.*	*Int.*	*P.O.*	*Fin.*
84th Cong. 1955–56	12D-11R	7D-6R	8D-7R	8D-7R	7D-6R	8D-7R
85th Cong. 1957–58	12D-11R	7D-6R	8D-7R	8D-7R	7D-6R	8D-7R
86th Cong. 1959–60	18D-9R	9D-6R	11D-6R	10D-5R	6D-3R	11D-6R
87th Cong. 1961–62	17D-10R	10D-5R	11D-6R	11D-6R	6D-3R	11D-6R
88th Cong. 1963–64	18D-9R	10D-5R	12D-5R	11D-6R	6D-3R	11D-6R
89th Cong. 1965–66	18D-9R	11D-5R	13D-6R	11D-5R	8D-4R	11D-6R

describe decision making in their committees by ticking off the name of each committee member and discussing his salient opinions and characteristics. House members may talk of blocs and leaders; but they rarely catalogue a committee's membership individually. Thus do habits of description reflect decision-making realities.

We turn now to describe those realities for the six Senate committees. We have found some pairs of committees to be quite similar in terms of goals, environments, and strategic premises, while others display marked differences with respect to these variables. Labor and Public Welfare, Interior, and Post Office are quite similar to their House counterparts. Finance, Appropriations, and Foreign Relations are quite different. We shall examine normal decision making inside the first three and then in the second three. And we shall do so in terms of the same variables used for our six House committees: partisanship, participation-specialization, and leadership.

LABOR AND PUBLIC WELFARE. Since our comparison of Senate Labor and Public Welfare with House Education and Labor found them similar in goals, environment, and strategies, we would expect to find them quite similar in internal structure. And they are. With respect to the presence and the antecedents of their *internal partisanship*, they are very much alike. Of our six Senate committees, only Labor prescribes partisanship as a decision rule, and only Labor displays a noteworthy degree of partisanship in its decision making. A Democratic member said: "We have monolithic votes on that Committee. . . . Eleven to five, eleven to five, eleven to five — no confusion. Actually it's four because Javits votes with us. . . . We on our side are united." Tables 5.3 and 5.4 show the potential for this Democratic, liberal unity. Calling the Democrats "a real murderers row," one of them described normal Committee decision making thus:

> The Republicans don't have a chance. They bring up amendments in subcommittee. We have a nice orderly hearing and vote them down. They bring them up again in the full Committee, we vote them down. They bring them up on the floor, we vote them down. No trouble, you see.

Conservative Republicans on the Committee describe the same party-dominated process. "The most exasperating part is looking at those ten faces, or rather, their proxies, because they are never there, and knowing you don't have a fair chance. Ten votes against you all the time." [27] Like the Republicans on Education and Labor, they emphasize the alliance between labor unions and the Democratic party, describing Committee Democrats as "stacked with union members" and "subservient to the unions" — and thus accentuating partisanship.

Like its House counterpart, too, the Senate Labor Committee has implemented the strategy of policy individualism by creating a large number of subcommittees, thereby giving individual members maximum opportunity to nourish and present their policy views. Price found that "the most distinctive characteristic of the LPW Committee . . . was its extreme decentralization." And he added, "For most members, decentralization meant freedom of movement and a high degree of satisfaction with the legislative possibilities of their committee posts." [28]

In the 88th Congress, for example, the Committee had seven subcommittees, averaging seven members each. Every member received assignments of his choice; twelve members participated as chairmen or ranking minority members of a subcommittee. Like Education and Labor, it structures a highly participatory decision-

[27] The exception was Chairman Lister Hill.
[28] Price, *op. cit.*, p. 446.

making process. But it is, by all accounts, nowhere near as volatile or disorderly or fractious as the House Committee. "It's the best organized committee I've ever seen," said one member. "The subcommittee chairmen are all interested in doing their work. If you were to ask me what I'd do to have a minimum of friction and a maximum of efficiency, I'd say, 'leave it alone'." We can only speculate as to the reasons. Some, at least, would seem to be institutional in nature. The smaller number of participants (eleven as against twenty-one on the majority Democratic side in the 89th Congress) makes for less diversity of viewpoint and eases the task of getting internal agreement. The variety of Senatorial interests beyond the Committee may make for less intense involvement by individual members. Greater Senate reliance on staff advice may reduce the tendency toward argumentativeness by establishing a common set of "facts." And, finally, the whole style of individualistic policy making is so commonly a Senatorial style that when it is practiced in Committee, it is easily accommodated. Since it is not a normal House style, it may be quite chaotic and disruptive on those occasions, i.e., in Education and Labor, when it does occur in House committees.

Another contributing factor might be the difference in committee leadership, which was more benign and less controversial on the Senate than on the House side. For all of the period, the Chairman of the Labor Committee was Lister Hill of Alabama. A moderately partisan Southerner, he was the least liberal and the least partisan of the Committee's Democrats. Republican members liked him because of his modest partisanship. And Democratic liberals saw him as a "good" to "superb" chairman because, unlike Graham Barden on Education and Labor, Hill did not try to impose his policy views on the majority when he differed with them.

> We had a mine safety bill; Hill didn't want to touch that. On the repeal of 14B, he was opposed to that. But he didn't keep us from acting on either one. He's that kind of person; he's very fair.

In one respect, he ran the Committee the way Adam Powell ran Education and Labor — by giving the subcommittees free rein. Unlike Powell, however, he pursued his individual policy interests within the decentralized structure, as chairman of one of the subcommittees. A Republican noted:

> There's no dissension with his chairmanship, largely because he doesn't try to exert any real power. He's chairman of the

health subcommittee, and health is the only thing he's interested in.

Hill was more in tune with the strategic premises of his committee than Barden and Powell were with the premises of theirs. And the internal rules Hill followed were the same rules that the House Committee finally prescribed for itself in 1966. A Senator observed:

> We have a rule in the Labor Committee that says a majority of the Committee's members can take action if the chairman refuses. . . . He (Hill) knows that we will invoke Committee rules if he holds up the legislation.

Both Committees, in other words, wanted similar structural features — decentralization, majority rule, a weak chairmanship. Education and Labor worked toward them throughout the period studied. Senate Labor and Public Welfare achieved them. With the achievement, Committee leadership became a stabilizing rather than a disruptive factor internally.

INTERIOR AND INSULAR AFFAIRS. The *Senate Interior Committee* organizes itself internally to implement the same basic constituency-re-election goals as does House Interior. And this accounts for the considerable similarity in their internal structures. In terms of the member predisposition displayed in Table 5.3, Interior looks to be the most partisan of the six Senate Committees. But, like the corresponding House group, neither its member goals nor its policy environment nor its strategic premises are partisan. It testifies to the pervading constituency orientation of Senate Interior that a committee with so great a partisan potential evinces so little actual partisanship. The logic by which members depress party feeling in order to implement their primary decision rule is the same as it is for the House Committee. Calling the Senate group "a nonpartisan committee," a Democratic member explained:

> We have good rapport. There's something about being from the West. There's an adhesive that runs through the members, an adherence to the West. I couldn't care less about silver, but on the silver issue, I'm with the other members from the 17 states. (Peter) Dominick (R., Colo.) and (Quentin) Burdick (D., N.D.) vote together on the Garrison Project, and on other projects. Can you think of any other issue on which Dominick and Burdick are together? A resolution on motherhood maybe. If (Frank) Moss (D., Utah) has a project, am I going to oppose it? I don't think there's any other group that has this.

As for the larger issues, public power does split the Committee along party lines. And some members see Committee Republicans as somewhat more inclined than the Democratic members to favor commercial users. More often, Republicans are "back and forth" on those issues. In any case, the spirit of nonpartisanship dominates. A Republican who sits on both Labor and Interior made this comparison:

> Interior is an enjoyable Committee. You never know if you're a majority or minority. We all work together. It's not at all partisan. Labor is the complete opposite. We are given no consideration. It's totally partisan.

No matter in what other arenas the Democrats and Republicans on the Senate Interior Committee may indulge their sharply differing partisan predispositions, they rarely do so inside the Committee itself.

Committee members specialize in the problems of their constituencies and pursue these interests through a subcommittee structure much like that of the House group. In the 89th Congress, six subcommittees had nine members each, and eleven Senators (out of a total of sixteen Committee members) were subcommittee chairmen or ranking minority members. Members almost always can match their subcommittee assignments to their constituency interests. As on the House side, the key subcommittee, Irrigation and Reclamation, contained more than half the full Committee membership. And the bulk of the work, members agree, is done in the subcommittees.

> Usually, once a bill is through the subcommittee, it goes through (full committee) without much change. By the time it's thrashed out in subcommittee, all the real controversy is gone.

The main difference is that the Senate Committee, by all accounts, acts with less deliberation and less thoroughness than the House group. A Committee staffer said:

> We can act much more quickly than the House Committee. We are much smaller than they are. . . . We can call a meeting very quickly. Usually there aren't too many of the members there. Just the ones who are most interested. The staff work is done and we can move right along. . . . We are much more flexible and informal.

Specialization is not as well developed as in the House; members admit that "we don't go over every bill line by line." A high-ranking Interior Department official summed it up:

> I'll bet I spend five hours with the House Committee for every one I spend with the Senate Committee. My Senate Committee business can be accomplished with a few phone calls and some political maneuvering. They play politics and want to make sure each gets what he wants. But my business with the House Committee has to be conducted right here at this desk doing my homework. It's the House that gets into the merits of the bill and develops the hard questions.

The difference may be partly a function of the makeup of the two committees — one wholly Western and one with Eastern and Southern members. But it is more probably the result of the institutional differences between House and Senate, discussed earlier.

The latter conclusion gains strength from a comparison of the leadership behavior of Henry Jackson (Wash.) and Wayne Aspinall. Jackson became chairman of the Senate Committee in the 88th Congress when the previous chairman, Clinton Anderson (N.M.), decided to become leader of another committee instead. As it was of Anderson, it was said of Jackson that his major interests lay elsewhere. And in this way, he is a prototypically part-time Senate Committee Chairman. A key Committee staff man noted:

> He's been tied up with the defense policy study. I think he's too busy and takes on too much. He's juggling dozens of balls in the air. And sometimes it's like a three-ring circus.

And an Interior Department leader compared Aspinall and Jackson:

> Aspinall is more limited and more concentrated. He doesn't have as agile and wide-ranging a mind as Jackson; but he knows his subject matter better. Jackson's primary interest is national security policy. Aspinall's (Interior) Committee is his life. The Congress is his life. He loves Congress — the House especially.

Unlike Aspinall, Jackson does not attend (much less dominate) the meetings of his subcommittees; he does not exercise traffic or quality control over Committee output. Neither does he intrude himself into the process unless his constituency is involved. One or two such intrusions were almost the only things to spur specific comment about the chairman. One member remarked: "He takes awfully good care of his own state and the Pacific Northwest and I am a little bit critical of him on this. But it's to be expected. We are all interested in our states." Thus, his activity seems to be squarely in line with the central decision rule of the Committee. His own policy views, moreover, are markedly conservationist. Lacking any sense of differentiation from the rest of the Senate and, hence, lacking any desire to build up a special reputation for his Committee, Jackson seems content to let the Committee process legislation to help its members and help conservationist interests — and to do both with dispatch.

POST OFFICE AND CIVIL SERVICE. Like the Interior Committee, the *Senate Post Office Committee* shows some potential — in Table 5.4 — for partisan decision making. But like Interior, the constituency-clientele orientation of Post Office members leaves no reason for partisanship. In a Committee whose decision-making processes are vaguely adumbrated by·its members, they do agree on its "unpartisan" or "totally nonpartisan" character. A Republican member said: "We have postmaster appointments and I've never seen any partisanship on that. . . . We just haven't had any partisan issues at all. I know I'm painting a rosy picture, but that's really the way it is." The logic of low partisanship follows that of the House Committee. In the words of a Committee Democrat: "Now Post Office isn't partisan because every member is interested in getting as much for the civil servant as he can get. We are all together on this, for political reasons." So long as the interests of their constituents are not partisan interests, constituency-clientele-oriented committees will make their decisions without much internal partisanship. And they will do so despite any partisan proclivities the Committee's members might have. Such at least is the case of the Interior and Post Office Committees in both chambers.

Further delineation of Senate Post Office decision making is difficult. Certainly there were none of the intracommittee disputes that characterized the House group. The Committee operated in the 89th Congress with five subcommittees, but their operation was routine and of little moment to the participants. The Committee Chairman could not remember which member chaired which subcommittee, let alone which members sat on which subcommittee. One member who became a subcommittee chairman commented, "There wasn't anything I could do, I got stuck." And another member couldn't recall whether the major pay raise bill had been considered in sub-committee or full committee. "Anyway, I went," he said. A top Post Office Department official confirmed the inattentiveness of Committee members when he complained: "They are so busy. You can't get close to them. You are almost embarrassed to call them up. They are harried and can't spend the time on our legislation." Mike Monroney, who succeeded Olin Johnston as chairman, spent "from 25 to 33 per cent of my time" on Committee work. And the major internal change he made was to try to increase and upgrade Committee staff. He said:

> We used to start the hearings and we'd have to believe everything the employee groups told us. Our problem is to get the kind of staff work done that will keep us from being so completely dependent on the employee groups and the executive branch.

He was hopeful that staff specialization would compensate for the inevitable senatorial lack of it, thus giving the Committee some leverage in dealing with its environment. Senate Post Office is a low-energy, low-profile committee with an operating consensus on strategic premises and some occasional disposition to assert its independence of the clientele groups that dominate its environment.

FINANCE. *Senate Finance* differs from House Ways and Means in goals, environment, and decision rules. We would expect, therefore, to find Finance members shaping different decision-making processes for themselves internally. And they have. There is, for one thing, less partisanship on the Senate side. Constituency-oriented member goals, increased clientele strength in the environment, and a strategic premise calling for the redress of clientele grievances cumulate to produce the difference. A veteran Finance member explained:

> Once in a while, it gets partisan, but not very often. What you get on the Finance Committee is a proposal that affects a certain business or a certain group in this way. A Senator who perhaps has representation of this business in his state will take a position; maybe some others will too. Constituency interest is what counts. It's all constituency, not party.

On those broad issues that might be expected to provoke partisanship — social welfare, for instance — policy individualism prevails. Calling Finance "the most nonpartisan committee in the Senate," one Democrat said that voting "all depends on the issue. You give me an issue, and I can tell you how each member will vote." Such internal patternings as result run more along ideological than party lines. He added, "If you want to use the term 'splits,' I suppose liberal-conservative would be it." In these terms, a conservative coalition of Republicans and some Southern Democrats often opposes the rest of the Democrats. "On a real controversial vote," said a Republican, "we can usually get some Democrats like (Harry) Byrd of Virginia, (Herman) Talmadge of Georgia, sometimes (George) Smathers of Florida and (Russell) Long of Louisiana. It all depends on the issue, but usually we are solid." Voting alignments of this nature are likely to be close, and the results will depend on several unpredictable Democrats. The strong clientele orientations of the members coupled with the policy individualism of Committee Democrats keep the Finance Committee from establishing partisan strategies and, hence, partisan patterns of decision making.

The same individualistic decision rules that dissipate partisanship also produce a decision-making process comprising high participation with low specialization. For reasons no member could explain ("never have had them, I guess," "it's been the historical tradition"), Finance, like Ways and Means, operates without subcommittees. And to a degree, the consequences are similar on both committees. Everyone participates freely and there is no division of labor based on specialization. The individual member, of course, specializes in (i.e., looks after) the interests of his constituents. The difference between the two groups is that the self-restraints that Ways and Means members observe in order to write bills that will pass the House are not observed on Finance, which operates with no such decision rule. To the contrary, both of the Finance Committee's decision rules encourage individual members to incorporate their constituency and/or their individual policy preferences into the bill without concern for the ultimate product. It is an informal working rule of the group that any member can get a vote on any proposal he makes. And the thrust of internal decision making is to tinker piecemeal with the House bill. "We send bills back to the House," said one member, "loaded down with amendments, but they are special interest or technical amendments. We don't do much, really, to shape policy." [29] Executive branch experts and Joint

29 *Ibid.*, p. 288.

Committee on Internal Revenue Taxation or Finance Committee staff people participate freely as they do in the House. But one comparative study notes that Finance deliberations are apt to be more brisk, less orderly, and less open to outside expertise than those of Ways and Means.[30] Committee members see themselves as "individualistic," "disorganized," and "loose as a goose." "Senate Finance has always had a tradition of being an undisciplined Committee." Certainly there is not the patient quest for consensus that characterizes the House committee. "(Chairman Russell) Long isn't like Wilbur Mills. Even if he just has a majority of one on the Committee, he'll take it to the floor and try to push it through." In the absence of any special concern that the committee bill pass the chamber intact, the pressure and the logic behind maximizing internal agreement are lacking.

Chairman Harry Byrd (1955–1965) presided over this "mannered free-for-all" with procedural evenhandedness. Members said of him: "Byrd is fair. He is one of the fairest people I have ever known." "He's not a gavel-pounding chairman at all." A Republican characterized him as "a gentleman, the perfect Southern gentleman. He's never discourteous, not even to those who oppose him." And a liberal Democrat agreed: "He has always been personally courteous with me, always courteous. . . . He's a Southern gentleman." But, he added, "It so happens I don't like Southern gentlemen." The dislike was ideological. Byrd was the archetypical, conservative Democrat and a strong advocate, therefore, of policy individualism. He did not dominate the committee internally to the degree that fellow Southerner Graham Barden ruled Education and Labor. But he threw his voting weight with the Republicans. And he kept the Committee staff small, as befits a status quo operation. The equally conservative long-time head of the Joint Committee on Internal Revenue Taxation staff, Colin Stam, worked especially closely and sympathetically with Byrd, thus tilting the weight of tax expertise toward the Committee's conservative coalition.[31] Russell Long's accession to the chairmanship did not change the individualistic pattern of decision making. Indeed, Long was described by his colleagues as one of the most "unpredictable," "erratic," and "flighty" members of the group. "You never know where he's going to be, with you or against

---

[30] Fowlkes and Lenhart, *op. cit.*, pp. 795 ff.
[31] See John Manley, *op. cit.*, pp. 307–319.

you. He's always off on some damn idea of his own." Ideologically,
he leaned toward the liberal faction; such influence as he exerted
internally helped to even the ideological balance. Most important,
he enlarged the Committee's own staff, the better to equip the members to take positive action. Committee liberals called the new staff
situation "five hundred per cent improved over what it used to be."
But the consequences for internal decision making were not clear
as the period ended.

APPROPRIATIONS. The *Senate Appropriations Committee* is the
second one whose normal decision-making processes would predictably differ from those of the corresponding House Committee. And
they do. But not with respect to internal partisanship. Neither committee adopts strategic premises calling for partisanship. On the
Senate side, decisions relating both to one's constituency and to
agency appeals are perceived as nonideological, nonpolicy decisions,
to be made by intraparty bargaining. "It's a pretty down-to-earth
committee. There's not much philosophizing here. It's a matter of
dollars and cents." "Of all the committees I've ever served on, Appropriations is the least partisan. That's because we're not a policy
committee." One member described the pursuit of constituency-
related influence:

> When we get into the domestic appropriations, everyone
> trades and it's a backscratching operation. You don't oppose
> his project because when yours comes up you are going to
> want his support. We bargain, trade. You have the econo-
> mizers, but when it comes to something in their states, they
> are in bed with the rest of us. . . . They'll take it out on
> foreign aid. You can cut that — no constituents.

Similarly, the Committee's "appellate-court" strategy calls for cross-
party bargaining and compromise over money amounts rather than
partisan battles over agency policy. A minority staff member explained:

> There's a lot less partisanship on the Appropriations Com-
> mittee — much less than on other committees. You're not
> legislating on policy, you're dealing with money. You can't
> cut a policy in half, but you can cut money that way. If one
> fellow wants one million and another wants two million, you
> can settle on a million and a half. But you can't do that on
> a policy — either you do it or you don't.

Appeals-board strategies, like those adopted by the Senate Finance and Appropriations Committees, are essentially strategies for turning all decisions into piecemeal, incremental ones. Such decisions will either negate partisanship altogether or facilitate various forms of "mutual partisan adjustment." [32]

The workload of Senate Appropriations compels the same elaborate subcommittee structure as that of the House Committee. And, of our six Senate committees, Appropriations is the most specialized. Compared with the House group, however, the striking characteristic of Senate Appropriations is the permeability of its subcommittees, the broad scope of member participation, and the resulting low level of specialization. Subcommittees are twice as large in the Senate as in the House, averaging fourteen members as against six members each in the 88th Congress. Whereas each House Committee member averaged but two subcommittee assignments, each Senator sat on an average of seven subcommittees.[33] Senate Committee members complain constantly about their lack of time and their inability to give in-depth attention to their multiple subcommittees. But they would not organize internal decision making any other way. They have devised a structure perfectly attuned to their pursuit of constituency-related influence. The more subcommittee memberships they have, the more access points they get for the purpose of extracting constituency benefits from the process. A man with experience on both Appropriations Committees explained: "If you're a member of a subcommittee, you can get preferential treatment. If there's a ten-million-dollar appropriation for something, I can usually work with the clerk and get some of it for my state. They trade a lot more over here (than they do in the House Committee)." Senators do not need to become specialists or even attend hearings to influence their subcommittees' decisions. A newcomer observed:

> They come to subcommittee markup after never having been to the hearings and say, "I want more money for a hospital in my state. We need it." And the chairman will say "O.K.," and the Senator leaves. If I attend the hearings and the markup, I can get almost anything I want.

[32] This concept is found in Charles Lindblom, *The Intelligence of Democracy* (New York: Free Press, 1965).

[33] The full Committee handled the foreign aid appropriations; it has been counted as a subcommittee in these totals.

Subcommittee decisions become, for the most part, the decisions of
the Committee — except that full Committee meetings are regarded
by nonmembers of subcommittees as one more opportunity to make
a constituency-based pitch for funds.

> The full Committee follows the subcommittee 98 per cent
> of the time. The only changes are to raise the appropriations
> when some Senators who are on the full Committee, but not
> on the subcommittee, ask to have projects put in. They are
> almost always granted.

The entire process is much less oligarchical than in the House. In
the House Committee, subcommittee assignments are sometimes
parceled out deliberately to members who have no personal interest
in the subject matter, as a structural prop for the budget-cutting
premise. On the Senate side, members can get, in time, any subcommittee assignment they want. Thus in the Senate the large number
of access points is likely to mean many opportunities for increasing
appropriations. Hence the structure itself promotes the sympathetic,
lenient treatment of agency budgets.

Chairman Carl Hayden (1955–1966) shared the strategic premises
of the group. And he provided another example of benign "live-and-
let-live" committee leadership.[34] Committee members and staff described him as "a very nonpartisan guy," "more respected and loved
than any other man," and "a very popular gent." He had legendary
success — during his forty-two years in the Senate — in exerting constituency-related influence. Members said: "Anything he wants on
this Committee, he gets — just like that." "Just let him intimate
that he wants something and thirteen guys will try to outrace each
other to give it to him." For a more general job description of the
Committee, Hayden commented:

> What's that old story about George Washington and cooling
> a cup of tea in a saucer? You have to make the tea before
> you can cool it. . . . We take the bill up like an appellate
> court.

In the decision-making process, Hayden operated (like his House
counterparts) within the subcommittee structure — as chairman of
the Interior subcommittee, a post of great importance for his state
of Arizona. He exercised even less control, however, over the rest of

---

[34] The characterization "live and let live" is from Horn, *op. cit.*, p. 34.

his Committee than did Cannon and Mahon. It was necessarily so, considering the wider distribution of influence inside the Senate group.

FOREIGN RELATIONS. "There is a minimum of partisan maneuvering on the *Foreign Relations Committee*," observed a senior Republican member, "less than on any other committee." None of the Committee's three strategic premises calls for partisanship. The first strategy of conditional support for the executive is explicitly bipartisan. A veteran of the Vandenberg era called the group "very unpartisan," noting that "the old saying that politics stops at the water's edge has a lot to it." And a restless newcomer explained why the Committee rarely had majority and minority reports by saying, "Fulbright has this tradition going back to Vandenberg and (Tom) Connally of nonpartisanship on Foreign Relations." Insofar as the Committee is responsive to executive branch expectations, therefore, nonpartisanship will prevail. The second strategy of policy individualism does not engender partisanship either. Indeed, policy individualism gets adopted as a decision rule precisely because policy partisanship is impossible or inappropriate. Like the members of the Finance Committee, Foreign Relations members describe internal alignments more in ideological or individualistic than in party terms. "We don't vote as Republicans or Democrats; we vote as reactionaries and liberals." Or, "It's more individuals than party . . . in foreign relations, you don't have to coax any Senator to express his views." On foreign aid, there has been some tendency for the party of the President to support him more strongly than do members of the other party. But Committee support has been, as with House Foreign Affairs, bipartisan.[35] The Committee's third decision rule, emphasizing Senate and Committee institutional prerogatives, also assumes cross-party cooperation. The only way for the Committee to assert its institutional independence in foreign policy making is to unite behind Committee-wide activities of some sort. Senate Committee strategies differ from House Committee strategies — but not in their common tendency to de-emphasize partisanship.

Member participation and specialization patterns resemble those on Foreign Affairs. All substantive legislative matters and all impor-

[35] Michael K. O'Leary, *The Politics of American Foreign Aid* (New York: Atherton Press, 1967), pp. 71–72.

tant hearings are handled in full committee, with everyone given the chance to participate. But in proportion to members' desires and expectations, their opportunities to contribute to the making of foreign policy are small. The resulting disappointment and frustration tend to drive down the rates of internal participation. A veteran Committee staffer described this pathology:

> When I first joined the staff, Bill Fulbright was the most junior member of the Committee. I remember one day when we were having trouble getting a quorum. (Chairman) Tom Connally said to (Staff Chief) Francis Wilcox, "Why are we having so much trouble getting a quorum? Call that damn Bill Fulbright and get him over here. I got him on the Committee and he never comes around. He's supposed to be here." Now a few years later, Fulbright was Chairman of the Committee and the following conversation took place in this room. He said to me, "Why are you having trouble getting a quorum? Call that damn Jack Kennedy. I got him on the Committee and now he never comes to meetings. Oh, I know, he comes once in a while and when he does, he sits at the end of the table autographing pictures of himself." That's how it has always been with the new members. They want individual responsibility immediately. And if they don't get it, they criticize the Committee and don't pay much attention to it.

The root problem is, of course, executive branch dominance of the environment. The Committee has a number of geographically related subcommittees, but, like those on Foreign Affairs, they are "consultative" and not legislative. They do not have their own staffs and they function largely as the consumers of executive branch information. They do not develop specialization and they, like their House counterparts, tend toward desuetude. "I'm on three of them," one member said, "and there hasn't been one meeting (of any one of them) — yeah, in eight months." In the 89th Congress, a time of rampant policy individualism, some members focused their frustration on an effort to invigorate the subcommittees. Some subcommittee chairmen wanted to hire their own staffs, develop expertise, and "if the President is wrong, correct him." But Chairman Fulbright's view prevailed. As he said:

> I do not think the nature or character of the Committee on Foreign Relations or responsibility lends itself to a breaking

down into (legislative) subcommittees. The Foreign Relations Committee is more of a committee to influence the
attitudes and policies of the State Department than it is to
legislate.[36]

Limited participation inside the Committee did not, of course, deter
the members from a great deal of external participation, i.e., speech
making, on the subject of foreign policy. And, in the context of the
Vietnam war, some of these extra-Committee exhibitions of policy
individualism did, indeed, influence the making of American foreign
policy.

Of all the Committee's policy individualists, the most influential
has been J. William Fulbright, Chairman from 1959 to 1966. And
the reasons are personal rather than institutional. He is described by
members and staffers as "the most intelligent," "the most brilliant,"
and "more savvy, more sophisticated, and more informed" than
other recent Foreign Relations Chairmen. Unlike most Senate chairmen, Fulbright devotes nearly all his energy (save in campaign
years) to the field of foreign policy. As much as any legislator can be
a specialist in that area, he is. His criticisms of American policy have
had an impact outside the Senate — on the public and on the executive branch. But his success has been an individual's success, not a
Committee result. Like-minded critics of American policy tended to
vent their frustrations on the Chairman, criticizing him for not concerning himself more with the Committee. For instance:

> Foreign Relations is the worst organized Committee of all.
> I have the greatest admiration for Fulbright, he has a bril-
> liant mind and the best understanding of these things in the
> Senate. But he hasn't organized the Committee. He doesn't
> try to get a majority behind him. . . . He does not let the
> subcommittees do anything.

> All the Committee does is talk. It doesn't act. It's the Chair-
> man's fault. Fulbright wants it that way. He's a loner and he
> controls the Committee. He's got a little clique that does the
> staff hiring. And they don't want subcommittees poking their
> noses into foreign policy. Bill Fulbright is a nice fellow, but
> as a committee chairman, he's lousy.

The temper of the criticism reminds us of those House Foreign Affairs members who vented their frustration on Chairman Morgan.

[36] *Congressional Record*, Daily Edition, January 14, 1969, p. 5147.

The cause of the frustration on both committees has been the great difficulty of achieving member goals amid monolithic environmental constraints. Senate Committee members find it easier to relieve their frustrations. For one thing it is easier and more rewarding for them to speak out individually. For another, they can trade on their institutional prerogatives to underpin a collective effort. It was the latter course that Chairman Fulbright took in response to members' grumbling when, in the 89th Congress, he attacked excessive executive power in foreign affairs and instituted some countervailing hearings in his Committee.

If it is true that House Committees differ from one another, it is also true that Senate Committees differ from one another. They differ for the same reasons. Their members seek different goals and inhabit different environments. Hence, they follow different decision-making strategies and develop different internal decision-making processes. This line of argument seems as valid for one set of committees as for the other. Furthermore, where members' goals and environmental constraints are similar for a pair of counterpart committees, their decision rules and decision processes look very similar. There is no point in retracing the lineaments of comparison, which, for every pair, show an admixture of like and unlike characteristics. But the two labor-education committees, the two Post Office committees, and — to a lesser extent — the two Interior committees show the greatest across-the-board similarity.

Our excursion into Senate committees has, however, produced a variation on our major theme, i.e., that committees differ from one another. It is, that Senate Committees, as a class, differ from House Committees as a class. Whatever the differences among the committees within a given chamber or whatever the similarities between a given pair of counterpart committees, there are fundamental cross-chamber differences that render all Senate committees different from all House committees. Since the House and Senate are different institutions, it should not be surprising that their committees are also different. Senate committees are less important as a source of chamber influence, less preoccupied with success on the chamber floor, less autonomous within the chamber, less personally expert, less strongly led, and more individualistic in decision making than are House committees. The more any given committee contributes to the overall influence of its parent institution, the greater is the difference between that committee and its counterpart in the other chamber. Institutional differences, that is, are magnified for institutionally important committees. Thus, the most marked differences we have observed are between the two taxing committees, the two appropriations committees, and the two foreign policy committees. Such, at least, is the line of speculation to which the bicameral focus of this chapter has led us.

CHAPTER SIX

Decisions

Having given our line of argument a comparative testing in the Senate, we return to the analysis of the six House committees. What remains for its completion, now, is an examination of the results of committee decision making. The first-order results are, of course, committee decisions. This chapter will describe the decisions of each committee and relate them to the variables previously discussed. We have argued that each committee adopts a set of strategic premises designed to achieve its members' goals within the constraints imposed by its environment. And we have argued that these strategic premises are made operative in terms of a set of decision rules. We have further argued that each committee's decision-making processes will be shaped by its members' efforts to implement those decision rules. Hence our description of each committee's decisions should have been pretty well prefigured in our earlier description of its decision rules. This chapter should not contain many substantive surprises.

The reader may be disappointed to find few, if any, across-the-board comparisons of committee "output" in this last installment of our analysis. In this study, committee "output" is defined as committee decisions. And we have not been able to describe the decisions of our six committees in ways that make broad comparisons possible. We have not, in other words, found any uniformly applicable and uniformly appropriate descriptive measures. So, as we did in dealing with decision-making processes, we shall treat each committee separately, making limited comparisons among two or more of them wherever possible. And we shall employ whatever standards of measurement seem applicable and appropriate to the committee or committees at hand. We shall be describing decisions directly and indirectly. That is, we shall examine the *substantive content of committee decisions* and we shall examine the *satisfaction or dissatisfaction of members and key environmental groups* with committee decisions. Admittedly more could have been done — even within the terms we have set. Those who question our analysis will at least find some leads to follow in doing further work. Those who are concerned with the much larger problem of measuring and comparing "policy" or "output" or "outcomes" may find some suggestions in this variegated description of committee decisions.

APPROPRIATIONS

The strategic premises of the Appropriations Committee reflect the members' desire for influence inside the House plus the members' attentiveness to constraints placed upon them by the special interests of the parent House and of executive-dominated policy coalitions. Substantively, the decision rules call for a balance between budget reduction and program support — with priority going to budget reduction, as most instrumental in the achievement of influence. The Committee's decisions, we would argue, reflect members' efforts to implement these decision rules. Insofar as this implementation is successful, individual goals and environmental expectations will be met reasonably well.

The discussion of Appropriations Committee decisions is aided by the availability of a unit of measurement — dollars. And while all of the Committee's decisions are certainly not amenable to this measure, enough of them are to give us a fairly adequate picture of Appropriations Committee decisions.[1] Table 6.1 reveals the frequency with which the Appropriations Committee reduced executive budget requests contained in the 130 appropriation bills passed from 1958 to 1965.[2] It also shows the frequency with which the Committee reduced budget requests from 36 selected bureaus between 1947 and 1962.[3] Table 6.1 makes it clear that for the vast majority of requests,

[1] Some decisions not so amenable are discussed in Michael Kirst, *Government Without Passing Laws* (Chapel Hill: University of North Carolina Press, 1969).

[2] The source for these figures is *Congressional Quarterly Almanac's* yearly summary listing.

[3] The source for all bureau-level figures in this section is Fenno, *The Power of The Purse*, *op. cit.* Chapters 8 and 11. A list of the bureaus will be found there on p. xxv. Studies confirming these summary findings for different depart-

Table 6.1
Appropriations Committee Decisions
on Executive Budget Requests

Committee Decisions	All Appropriation Bills: 1958–1965		36 Bureaus: 1947–1962	
	No.	%	No.	%
Decrease	119	91.5	423	73.6
No Change	8	6.2	106	18.4
Increase	3	2.3	46	8.0
Total	130	100	575	100

Table 6.2
Appropriations Committee Decisions
Relative to Previous Year's Appropriation

Committee Decisions	All Appropriations Bills: 1958–1965		36 Bureaus: 1947–1962	
	No.	%	No.	%
Decrease	17	19.8	155	27.0
Same	0	0	22	3.8
Increase	69	80.2	398	69.2
Total	86*	100	575	100

*Excludes supplementals and other non-comparable bills.

the Committee does act according to its budget-cutting decision rule.

At the same time, however, the Committee finds it possible to implement its decision rule calling for support for executive programs. And it does so by allowing the great majority of executive budgets to increase from one year to the next. In Committee parlance, "we give them less than they ask for," but "we give them more than they got last year." Table 6.2 describes Committee decisions from this perspective — again using whole appropriation bills (1958–1965) and selected bureau requests (1947–1962). Viewed from the two perspectives, appropriations decisions reflect an effort by the Committee's members to balance their two potentially conflicting strategic premises.

An influential committee, we have said, is one which can make

ments are Jonathan Knight, "The State Department Budget, 1933–1965," *Midwest Journal of Political Science* (November, 1968); Douglas M. Fox, "Congress and the U.S. Military Service Budgets in the Post–War Period: A Research Note," *Midwest Journal of Political Science* (May, 1971).

Table 6.3
Magnitude of Appropriations Committee
Decisions on Budget Requests

% Decrease	All Appropriations Bills: 1958–1965		36 Bureaus: 1947–1962	
	No.	%	*No.*	%
more than 20.0	33	25.4	57	8.2
15.1–20.0	9	6.9	26	4.5
10.1–15.0	13	10.0	50	8.7
5.1–10.0	22	16.9	80	13.9
0.1– 5.0	41	31.5	220	38.3
0	8	6.2	106	18.4
+0.1– 5.0	2	1.5	29	5.0
more than +5.0	2	1.5	17	2.9
Total	130	99.9	130	99.9

independent decisions and carry those decisions in the chamber. Appropriations Committee members believe that in order for them to be individually influential, their Committee must be influential. Is it? The problem of anticipated reactions, of course, makes it hard to assess the independence of Committee decisions. Do agencies "pad" their budget requests in anticipation of Committee budget cutting? And, if they do, can subsequent Committee budget cutting be viewed as implementing an independent judgment of the Committee? Despite executive protestations to the contrary, some "padding" doubtless occurs. But, as Aaron Wildavsky demonstrates, there are sound strategic reasons why executive officials would avoid excessive padding.[4] And, provided that padding represents a programmatic "extra" rather than waste, even a reduction in a padded budget will hurt the executive agency involved. If we look at the range of the Committee's budget reductions (and budget increases), the conclusion is inescapable that the Committee can and does make independent judgments concerning the course of executive program development — marginal in most cases, but substantial in some.

Table 6.3 displays the size and range of decisions relative to the budget estimate. The marginal character of most decisions is a crucial feature of Committee efforts to produce a balanced decision. And executives are not excessively unhappy with the marginal cuts. Still, even marginal ones do hurt. Of twenty-seven executive officials who were queried as to whether a five per cent reduction would be

[4] Aaron Wildavsky, *The Politics of the Budgetary Process* (Boston: Little, Brown, 1964).

"serious" and "harmful to the operation of your bureau (or department)," twenty-two responded with an unequivocal "yes," five gave
an equivocal "yes," and only one said "no." [5] Executive confessions
of trepidation in dealing with the Committee stem from the same
recognition of its proven capacity to affect them negatively. And as
we shall see, they do appeal many of their reductions to the Senate
Committee — an unnecessary step if reductions were inconsequential.
Relative to executive branch budgetary and program desires, Appropriations Committee decisions have an important element of independence.

By the same token, Committee decisions are independent relative
to House members' wishes. For nearly every item in the budget has
some supporters in the House; they will not want to see it reduced.
The Committee is anything but popular in the chamber. "There's a
latent hostility to the Committee," said one veteran House member.
"It's an obstructionist Committee with regard to the projects members want." Members of substantive legislative committees protest
that the Appropriations Committee's money decisions intrude on
their jurisdiction. "There is a complete bypassing of the Committee
on Foreign Affairs, and as a member of that Committee, I resent
it." [6] "I wish the powerful Appropriations Committee would quit
stepping on the toes of the Committee on Post Office and Civil
Service." [7] Appropriations Committee independence is viewed in
both procedural and substantive terms. The two top leaders of the
House commented:

> Sure there is resentment against the Committee. They have
> special privileges, let's face it, and the other members get
> jealous. They meet all the time when Congress is in session.
> Their bills are privileged and come to the floor without a
> rule. They get special treatment from the departments. Their
> colleagues have to reckon with them. They have a life-and-
> death power over things. You hear people say, "That's isn't
> fair." You hear that a lot.
>
> They work in secrecy. You can't find out anything until they
> get to the floor. And it's hard to lick 'em at that stage.
> They're a closed corporation. When they stick together, you

[5] Fenno, op. cit., pp. 268–269.
[6] Congressional Record, Daily Edition, June 17, 1960, pp. 12128–12129.
[7] 102 Congressional Record, p. 6995.

can't lick 'em on the floor. . . . The Committee likes to grasp for power. It's that tendency to concentrate. It's bad. They're a tremendously powerful committee, but sometimes they try to go a little too far.

These comments suggest that Appropriations Committee decisions are, to some degree, independent of House members' wishes. And they indicate, too, Committee success in carrying its decisions in the chamber.

Table 6.4 displays more solid evidence of Committee floor success. It shows that, over a sixteen-year period, ninety per cent of all its dollar recommendations for thirty-six bureaus were accepted in the parent chamber. Amendments to these Committee recommendations were passed at the rate of one amendment for every eight bureaus each year. Considering Committee recommendations on the budgets of eight whole departments plus the public works bill during the same period, amendments were passed on the floor at the rate of one for every departmental or public works bill submitted by the Committee. Furthermore, in these same bills the Committee was successful in defeating between seventy and eighty per cent of all amendments offered from the floor.[8] We do not have a firm standard by which to evaluate this evidence. But in view of the considerable unhappiness of members with Committee actions and in view of the large number of points at which an appropriations bill can be attacked and altered, we would argue that the Committee is very successful in getting its decisions ratified by the parent chamber.

Table 6.4
House Decisions on Appropriations Committee
Recommendations: 36 Bureaus, 1947–1962

House Decisions	No.	%
Increase	28	4.9
Accept	517	89.9
Decrease	30	5.2
Total	575	100

Floor success, we have said, is more than a matter of winning. It is also a matter of a committee's general reputation in the House. For

[8] Fenno, *op. cit.*, pp. 450–453.

it is by reputation that a committee gains the benefit of the doubt in close legislative situations. And it is by reputation that a committee stores up working capital for future legislative fights. Alongside House members' perceptions of Appropriations Committee independence and power, there exists a favorable view of the Committee. Three of the most prominent House leaders (two Democrats and a Republican) voiced it thus:

> They're a dedicated committee, a powerful committee, and a tireless committee. They are the hardest workers in the Congress. . . . They have a missionary spirit on that Committee. I admire them for it; and I respect them.

> The Committee has a very good reputation. I think the Committee is accepted as doing work of high standards. They present their bills well. They are very seldom amended on the floor. . . . You know they have gone through it with a fine-tooth comb.

> It's a dog's life. Nobody gives you any credit. You go down into the dugout the first of December and don't come out again until after adjournment. It's a hard committee. Everyone knows that. It's a labor of love and a devotion to duty that keeps you on that Committee. People have a lot of respect for them.

The Committee's favorable reputation is partly a self-fulfilling prophecy, since House members want their Appropriations Committee to be especially competent. But the Committee's own decision-making processes make an independent contribution to its reputation and, hence, to its floor success. Two central ingredients in its reputation — diligence and dedication — result from the distinctive subcommittee-based work ethic established by the members themselves. If "powerful" is the adjective most commonly applied to the group, "hard-working" comes close behind. And hard-working connotes a specialized command of detail that makes House members, by turns, respectful of the Committee and reluctant to challenge its decisions. By maintaining and trading upon the favorable aspects of its chamber reputation, Appropriations increases its likelihood of winning on the House floor.

The Appropriations Committee, we conclude, makes independent judgments and carries those judgments on the House floor. It is, therefore, an influential committee. And its members, too, are influential. Every comment of every committee member and House member in this book and in our interviews suggests that the pattern of Committee decisions we have described brings the individual members the influence they sought when they came to the Committee. They do not, as we know, leave Appropriations for other committees. When they do leave, it typically signals the end of their public careers. In support of this generalization, Table 6.5 indicates that for three-quarters of the members, Appropriations Committee membership is the climax of their political careers. If a committee's decisions can be described indirectly in terms of the level of satisfaction of the committee's members with those decisions, and if the degree to which a committee's members climax their public careers on the committee is a measure of that satisfaction, the level of member satisfaction with Appropriations Committee decisions would seem to be very high.

House members and executive officials, on the other hand, probably remain less satisfied with Committee decisions than Committee members themselves. Their lower level of satisfaction is guaranteed by the priority given to budget reduction in the Committee's decision rules. Prolonged, massive, concentrated dissatisfaction within these outside groups is mitigated, however, by the annual, fragmented, and marginal nature of Committee decisions. Environmental dissatisfaction is further dissipated by the countervailing decisions of the Senate Appropriations Committee. Agreed upon in pursuit of different personal goals and in response to different environmental constraints, the decision rules of the Senate Committee call for more emphasis on program support than on economy. Table 6.6 demonstrates that the Senate Committee does, indeed, act as a lenient appeals court. If most of the "same" decisions represent instances where no request for restoration was made, the Senate acts favorably toward executive-led coalitions in about nine out of ten cases. Senate decisions, too, are mostly marginal ones; but there is evidence that the largest Senate restorations go to those very items cut most heavily by the House group. Ninety per cent of Senate Committee decisions are upheld on the Senate floor. And when the two Committees meet in conference, the final dollar amounts are closer to the Senate's decision than to the House's decision in about two out of every three cases.[9] All these later outcomes of the process help

[9] *Ibid.*, pp. 661–670; Stephen Horn, *op. cit.*, pp. 160–161.

Table 6.5
Reasons for Leaving Committees: 1947–1967

	W.&M.		App.		F.A.		E.&L.		P.O.		Int.	
	No.	D/R	No.	D/R	No.	D/R	No.	D/R	No.	D/R	No.	D/R
1. Transferred to Other Committee	0	0/0	2	1/1	5	4/1	21	16/5	51	37/14	35	22/13
2. Ran for Senate	8	5/3	9	4/5	11	7/4	6	3/3	0	0/0	13	6/7
3. Ran or Appointed, Other Public Office	3	2/1	10	8/2	7	4/3	4	3/1	3	3/0	4	3/1
4. Defeated in Primary Election	3	2/1	7	3/4	8	6/2	7	4/3	4	2/2	3	2/1
5. Defeated in General Election	10	1/9	18	3/15	12	6/6	21	8/13	31	17/14	17	6/11
6. Retired from Public Life	10	7/3	21	7/14	9	2/7	11	2/9	6	4/2	11	7/4
7. Died	11	6/5	14	4/10	4	2/2	5	2/3	2	2/0	6	3/3
"End of Public Service" Reasons as Percentage of All Reasons, i.e. $\frac{4-7}{1-7}$	75%		74%		59%		59%		45%		42%	

Table 6.6
Senate Appropriations Committee Decisions
Compared to Final House Decisions

Committee Decisions	All Appropriations Bills: 1958–1965		36 Bureaus: 1947–1962	
	No.	%	*No.*	%
Increase	101	77.8	323	56.2
Same	14	11.5	193	33.6
Decrease	15	10.7	59	10.2
Total	130	100	575	100

"take the heat off" the House Appropriations Committee and allow it to continue producing the kinds of decisions we have described.

To assess the relative levels of satisfaction with a Committee's decision on the part of Committee members and environmental groups is to assess the stability of those decisions. Our very sketchy comments suggest that Appropriations decision patterns are quite stable. We should like to add one last factor that reinforces this overall assessment. Our interviews with Appropriations Committee members reveal an element of their satisfaction that rests upon, yet transcends, their satisfaction with Committee decisions and with the achievement of their individual goals. They express strong feelings of attachment to the Committee and to their fellow members. And they derive an added measure of emotional satisfaction simply from belonging to and identifying with the Committee.

As the members describe the Committee: "There's an *esprit de corps*, a comradeship." "I think it's more closely knit than any other Committee." "There's a tendency on this Committee for members to think of themselves as members of the Appropriations Committee first and members of the House second." These are the Committee members' own perspectives on what House leaders perceive unfavorably as "the club," "the clan," and "the closed corporation." As the focus for their attachment, Committee members often refer to their internal style of hard work and specialization. And, in a way designed not to exacerbate their potential conflict with House leaders, they affirm their *esprit* by making invidious comparisons with the Senate Appropriations Committee, maintaining: "All the work is done in the House." "In conference, the House is much better prepared than the Senate. We spend more time on it and have more information." "That's what gripes me. We do all the work . . . and then we have to bargain with them." These sentiments of group identification are not expressed by the members of all our committees.

It is unlikely that congressional politicians would gain any such psychic satisfaction from Committee membership were not their political goals (in this case internal influence) already being met. We are not, therefore, talking about a displacement or substitution of member goals. We are talking about increments of satisfaction that may come from pride of association, once original goals are being met. Indirectly, this extra level of satisfaction depends on the committee's decisions. More directly, we think, it is the result of the committee's internal decision-making processes. On Appropriations, members' pride centers on elements of decision making such as hard work, specialization, and unity. The satisfactions of group identification add to a committee's attractiveness and members' contentment with committee decisions during short-run intervals when political goals are not being met. Should there ever be a displacement of goals such that arrogant assertions of their group identity came to dominate committee members' discourse with their environment, the stability of that committee's decision patterns would surely be in jeopardy. In the Appropriations Committee, that does not appear to be in prospect. Overall, we think, the psychic satisfactions of Appropriations Committee members reinforce the stability of the Committee's pattern of decisions.

WAYS AND MEANS

The strategic premises of the Ways and Means Committee are intended to provide influence for its members while at the same time keeping them responsive to parent chamber and administration (party plus executive) desires. The Committee's decision rules call for writing a bill that will pass the House and for the prosecution of policy partisanship — with a priority for success on the House floor as most instrumental to the achievement of individual member influence. Though the environmental constraints of Ways and Means differ somewhat from those confronting the Appropriations Committee, the two money committees have very similar balancing problems. Both have to balance the goal of influence against the need for responsiveness to the parent chamber. Both have to balance attentiveness to the parent chamber against attentiveness to other external groups. Assessing the balance they achieve is difficult and tentative in any case. But, lacking a common dollar-and-cents measure, the assessment is more difficult and less satisfying with Ways and Means than with Appropriations.

On the crucial matter of writing bills that pass the House, there is little doubt as to the success of Ways and Means. Committee recommendations carry overwhelmingly on the chamber floor. In the period from 1953 to 1964, Committee decisions were tested on one hundred and nine roll calls. And the Committee won all but six — for an impressive winning margin of ninety-four per cent.[10] The Committee probably has the highest percentage of passed-and-unamended bills of all the committees in the Congress. A comparison of this sort is, however, quite inappropriate, since no other committee is so frequently protected from floor amendments by the use of the closed rule. Under this rule, there is but one chance to alter the committee's decision — on a recommittal motion taken just prior to the vote on final passage. The recommittal motion is usually written by the minority party and prescribes specific changes in the Committee's bill. It, too, comes to the chamber on a take-it-or-leave-it basis; it, too, cannot be amended. It will be written to capture the largest possible anti-Committee vote; but it cannot capture all of it. Often its minority party sponsorship drives away potential majority party support. No other congressional committee operates under such favorable procedural conditions as Ways and Means. And these special conditions help to account for its impressive record of floor victories.

Still, members of the parent chamber would not abide such extensive use of the closed rule unless they felt that the Committee normally reported out "a good bill" — substantively responsible and politically responsive to chamber sentiment. So the use of the closed rule must be read as the *result* of an underlying House confidence in its Ways and Means Committee. House members, as we have said, *want* the Committee to win on the floor, and they will help them to do so — as long as the substance of Committee decisions is believed to be responsive to House desires. And, by all accounts, Committee decisions are responsive to the parent chamber. John Manley concludes his extended analysis of Committee decisions from 1933 to 1968 by saying, "What is most impressive about House-Committee relations is the sensitivity of Ways and Means

10 Manley, *The Politics of Finance, op. cit.*, pp. 159, 161, Tables 5:1 and 5:2.

to widely held sentiments in the House." [11] Chairman Mills believes
that his search for consensus inside the Committee is the essential
guarantee of responsiveness to the parent chamber, "because our
committee is a cross-section of the membership of the House." A
top executive of Health, Education and Welfare summarized his
thirty years of experience with the Committee:

> The Ways and Means Committee is attuned to the temper
> of the House. They are sensitive to the feelings of House
> members — as sensitive as an adolescent girl. They don't rush
> into anything. They stop. They look around. You might
> think that with the closed rule, the Committee could be a
> dictator. But it isn't.

And, we might add, "it can't be." For the retention of the closed
rule is predicated on Committee sensitivity to the House. It is this
sensitivity, therefore, more than the closed rule that explains the
high percentage of Committee floor victories. And it is Committee
sensitivity, rather than its winning percentage, that makes Ways and
Means *sui generis* among congressional committees.

If an influential committee is one which, first, makes an independent policy judgment and, second, carries that judgment on the
House floor, Ways and Means clearly meets the second criterion.
But does it meet the first? Is the responsiveness of Ways and Means
to the House simply a rubber-stamp responsiveness and not independence at all? Manley considers this "independence-dependence
problem" (as he calls it) and concludes that many Committee judgments are made independently of the House. He says: "Committee
sensitivity to. . . what can or cannot pass the House is, however,
only part of the House-Committee relationship. Of equal significance is the Committee's decision to determine what does pass the
House by taking the lead. . . ." [12] So long as the Committee felt it
could not win on the floor, it refused to pass out the medicare bill;
when it finally did have the votes, the Committee passed the bill,
but wrote its own distinctive version of medicare in the process.
Similarly the Committee refused to report out the tax surcharge bill
in 1967 because of a judgment that it could not pass. A year later,
Committee members took the lead in convincing their deadlocked
conservative and liberal House colleagues of the need for some such

[11] *Ibid.*, p. 211.
[12] *Ibid.*, pp. 246–247.

bill and one passed. In the first case, the Committee made an independent contribution of substance; in the latter case, the committee made an independent contribution of energy.[13]

Committee independence is reflected, too, in House member protests against the closed rule. In debate over one rule, a party leader complained:

> The Ways and Means Committee must know and realize that it cannot continue to give the House ultimatums. Everything is up or down, yes or no. The House ends up, almost always, voting for a bill that is three-fourths decent, one-fourth lousy, without amendments. It is unfair. The Ways and Means Committee is a powerful Committee, but it should not rule the House on such important matters as taxation and social security.[14]

Nonetheless he voted in favor of the closed rule. By his words and his actions, he (like other House members) acknowledges and underwrites the independent influence of the Committee in the House. When House members follow the Committee either reluctantly or in the absence of any strong opinion of their own, they give evidence of Committee influence. We are inclined to believe, finally, that when a Committee is as successful as Ways and Means, some independent Committee influence must be present. No committee can make a perfect reading of member sentiment; some uncertainty always exists. Some support for the Committee, that is to say, must result from occasions when House members follow the Committee's lead rather than the other way around. Committee sensitivity is the prime necessity and the distinguishing characteristic of its relationship with the chamber. Committee leadership is secondary. But both help the Committee to implement its basic decision rule.

The Committee's policy independence is even more evident in relation to its Administration-led policy coalitions than it is relative to the parent chamber. House members' institutional interest in the Committee and the procedural prerogatives that underwrite its power — these are directed primarily at promoting Committee (and House) independence in relationship with the executive branch. The fact of Committee policy independence is recognized on both sides of this relationship. A Treasury official generalized: "Yes, the

13 *Ibid.*, pp. 214–219.
14 *Congressional Record,* Daily Edition, August 6, 1969, p. H6969.

Committee changes our proposals a lot. There are many things we never suggested that are in the tax law because the Committee decided they should be." And a top Committee leader summed up the view of the Committee:

> We legislate. They don't come here with a bill for me to introduce. We take their message; then, within the guidelines, write our own bill. . . . We have never rubber-stamped anything they have sent up. It is always a Committee bill. There are always amendments.

An example would be the revenue message of 1963 from which the Committee deleted nearly all the Administration's many tax reform proposals.[15] Two Treasury officials explained: "We take into account what is likely to get passed before we ever send a proposal. We'd be crazy not to." "Of course, we modify our proposals to meet what we think the Committee will accept — not entirely, of course." An example would be the 1962 trade bill, on which Chairman Mills consulted closely long before it was sent to the House.[16] Committee independence is greatest in the area of taxation and least in the field of trade. Executive officials attribute the difference in large part to a differential in Committee expertise. As one said, "Ways and Means has the staff on tax to write the bill themselves, but they don't on trade and social security." But the decision to employ the Joint Committee on Internal Revenue Taxation (JCIRT) is probably the result of a prior decision that tax matters are the heart of the Committee's jurisdiction and the core of its prerogative.

In any case, there is sufficient testimony, we think, to indicate that Ways and Means does exert an independent impact on policy. Thus it meets both criteria of an influential committee. And thus the Committee's decision patterns help its individual members to achieve the inside influence they seek.

The Committee's second decision rule calls for responsiveness to Administration-led policy coalitions — specifically the prosecution of policy partisanship. On the matter of responsiveness to the executive branch, we need to remember that the policy initiative, the policy agenda in revenue matters, comes from the executive branch. By working on that agenda — "within the guidelines" as just quoted —

---

[15] Philip M. Stern, "The Slow, Quiet Murder of Tax Reform," *Harpers* (December, 1963).
[16] Manley, *op. cit.*, p. 346.

Ways and Means indicates its basic responsiveness to executive demands. Coexisting with manifestations of independence is the feeling that, as one Democratic member put it, "On Ways and Means, you represent the Administration." On the matter of responsiveness to party concerns, we need to remember our earlier finding that final Ways and Means decisions are, indeed, markedly partisan. Chairman Mills, we also noted, has usually observed this pattern at the stage of decision.

Any discussion of policy partisanship in Ways and Means requires some discrimination among policies and among partisan alignments. Trade policy, once the very essence of partisan disagreement, has gradually lost its partisan character nationally. And this decline in environmental partisanship has been registered inside the Committee.[17] Table 6.7 is an adaptation and an extension of two tables from Manley's *The Politics of Finance*, displaying patterns of partisanship for three other policy areas — taxation, social security, and the debt limit — on "selected major bills." [18] Most important for our purposes, the Ways and Means Committee is consistently more partisan — across all policy areas — than is the House as a whole. Committee partisanship exceeds House partisanship in twenty-five of the thirty-three, or in seventy-five percent of the cases. This we interpret as indicating a distinctive Committee responsiveness to external partisan expectations and as showing some success, therefore, in implementing its second decision rule.

For each of the three policy areas, patterns of partisanship differ. Tax policy is the most consistently partisan, inside the Committee and out. And this record is evidence, we would argue, of Committee responsiveness to policy differences that are basic in distinguishing Republicans and Democrats — differences over the distribution of income.[19] Partisanship in social security matters now occurs only

[17] Richard A. Watson, "The Tariff Revolution: A Study of Shifting Party Attitudes," *Journal of Politics* (November, 1965); Manley, *op. cit.*, p. 210.

[18] Manley, *op. cit.*, pp. 201, 208. "Selected major bills," are those that are, in his judgment, major bills. His selection criteria are listed in *Ibid.*, Appendix II. Manley's selected major bills are not, therefore, the same as the *Congressional Quarterly* "Major Bills" being used throughout this book. In reproducing Manley's work, I have taken the converse of his Index of Likeness and called it the Index of Partisanship. Arithmetically, the Index of Partisanship is found by subtracting the percentage of the members of one party voting for a bill from the percentage of the members of the other party voting for the bill.

[19] See Aage Clausen and Richard B. Cheney, "A Comparative Analysis of Senate-House Voting on Economic and Welfare Policy, 1953–1964," *American Political Science Review* (March, 1970), pp. 138–152.

Table 6.7
Ways and Means Policy Partisanship: Index of Partisanship on
Selected Major Bills, 1955–1966

Revenue Bills				Social Security Bills				Debt Limit Bills			
Year	Subject	Comm. IP	House IP	Year	Subject	Comm. IP	House IP	Year	Subject	Comm. IP	House IP
1955	Corporation, Excise tax	93	90	1955	Social Security	33	8	1955	Increase Debt Limit	12	15
1956	Corporation, Excise tax	10	1	1958	Unemployment Compensation	87	61	1958	"	13	20
1959	Interest Rates on Gov't Bonds	93	96	1958	Social Security	12	1	1958	"	11	14
1961	Corporation, Excise tax	100	78	1960	Social Security	22	1	1959	"	30	6
1962	Investment Credit	100	89	1961	Social Security	40	10	1960	"	20	4
1963	Corporation, Excise tax	60	52	1961	Unemployment Compensation	33	15	1961	"	50	56
1963	Tax Reduction & Reform	100	89	1962	Social Security	100	84	1962	"	50	42
1964	Excise Tax	100	89	1964	Social Security	10	2	1962	"	89	86
1964	Foreign Securities Tax	72	91	1965	Medicare	88	71	1963	"	100	88
1966	Investment Credit	62	56					1963	"	90	81
								1963	"	100	86
								1964	"	100	86
								1965	"	75	80
								1966	"	100	81

when major policy departures (those of 1962 and 1965, for example) are at stake. Incremental adjustments in the core program, however, have become accepted national policy, commanding a bipartisan consensus. Policy on raising the debt limit has escalated from very low to very high partisanship. The opposition party in Congress (first the Democrats, then the Republicans) gradually came to view debt limit increases as an easy issue on which to get some leverage on the President — triggering a countervailing partisan responsiveness to the President's predicament by his own party.[20] In each of its various policy areas, the Ways and Means Committee acts as a responsive mechanism for the registration and prosecution of conflicting party expectations.

Forced to choose between a bill that will pass the House and the prosecution of policy partisanship, we have argued, the Committee will opt for the former. Some evidence to this effect can be found in the overall assessment of the Committee's performance given by party leaders. In a word, they find that performance too conservative — both in timing and in substance. Two House Democratic leaders summed up:

> Mills is conservative, careful, and cautious. He always takes three times longer bringing a bill out than we think he should. Nothing ever comes out of that Committee on time.

> I think they (House Democrats) feel Ways and Means is more conservative than the whole House and that they sometimes come out with things because of this. They have no problem with the mechanics of what Ways and Means does, but the policy — that's another matter. It's more conservative.

Presidents Kennedy and Johnson — in matters such as the tax bills of 1963–64 and 1967–68 — felt exactly the same way.[21] In these cases, as in others like medicare, the Committee's slowness to act was manifest. Manley's analysis of Ways and Means decisions led him to agree: "The Committee majority is more likely to come down on the conservative side of policy issues than on the liberal

---

[20] See M. A. Robinson, "Bumping Along the Dept Ceiling," *Reporter*, (October 1, 1959).

[21] Theodore Sorensen, *Kennedy* (New York: Bantam Books, 1965), p. 486; Lyndon B. Johnson, *Vantage Point* (New York: Holt, Rinehart, Winston, 1971), pp. 441–442, 453–454.

side"; and, one of the "constants" of its performance is "the conservative direction of the Committee's policy decisions." [22]

As shown in Table 3.1, however, the Committee is not in overall predisposition a conservative committee. The explanation for Committee conservatism lies in the preference its members display for writing a bill that will pass over prosecuting policy partisanship. They are slow to act because, as one complaining party leader acknowledged, "(Mills) won't risk losing the bill on the floor." They tilt their decisions in a conservative direction because that is their proven formula for floor passage — even if this means tempering some of their generally liberal predispositions. "Ways and Means has been successful in the House," says Manley, "because its conservative policy recommendations have been consistent with the voting composition of the House." [23] Committee members' desires for individual influence, we conclude, have kept them less responsive to Administration-led policy coalitions than party leaders — especially liberal Democratic ones — have desired.

Some of the lingering dissatisfaction of environmental groups can be alleviated by countervailing decisions on the part of the Senate Finance Committee. But such decisions do not occur as frequently or as regularly with these Committees as they do with the two Appropriations Committees. Relying, again, on Manley's assessment of the substantive decisions involved, Senate Finance appears to respond, in accordance with its distinctive decision rule, to the remedial appeals of clientele groups. "The Senate is generally more responsive to the demands of interest groups, lobbyists, and constituents than the House," concludes Manley, And "Senate decisions are more in line with the demands of interest groups, lobbyists, and constituents than the House." [24] Such piecemeal Senatorial products have been described, depending on the nearest gift-giving holiday, as "Christmas tree" bills or "Easter egg basket" bills. This is, of course, the pattern we would have expected.

Manley uses the difference in clientele impact to explain Senate dominance in conference decisions affecting tax and trade matters. The argument is that clientele appeals become more intense, more concentrated, and, hence, more controlling at the final decision stage. By the same logic, in that policy area where clientele demands

[22] Manley, *op. cit.*, p. 245.
[23] *Ibid.*, p. 246.
[24] *Ibid.*, pp. 288, 279.

are *least* influential, e.g., social security, it is the *House* and not the Senate which dominates conference committee proceedings.[25] The impact of the clientele-oriented Senate Committee (and Senate) on final decisions does not, however, necessarily bring compensation to those members of the Administration-led coalition that are unhappy with House Committee decisions. In the trade field, the combined clientele-Senate impact typically renders legislation more protectionist than it was in the House — not a result likely to please the executive branch. In the tax field, the results are as likely to displease as to please the executive branch. In eleven of twenty major tax bills since 1947, Senate decisions reflected either clientele-induced exceptions to tax increases approved by Ways and Means or clientele-induced additions to tax decreases approved by Ways and Means.[26] Sometimes, Senate decisions may withdraw the sting from those of Ways and Means. But things done on the Senate floor can be undone in conference. And liberal Democrats, especially, find their unhappiness with tax decisions compounded when conservative Finance conferees fail (as they often do) to fight in conference for "liberal" features of the Senate bill.[27] Until such time as Senate Finance acquires either a pro-Administration or a liberal majority or both, its behavior will not do much to assuage the occasional unhappiness of external elements with the performance of the House Ways and Means Committee. So long, however, as this dissatisfaction remains occasional, environmental constraints will not change, and Ways and Means decisions will continue pretty much as we have described them.

For the individual Ways and Means member, the present constellation of outcomes is highly satisfactory. His committee is influential collectively, and he is influential as an individual. Table 6.5 records his satisfaction. A smaller percentage of Ways and Means (and Appropriations) members leave their committee voluntarily than leave any of the other four. When asked whether they would consider changing committees, a Democrat and a Republican responded typically:

> Are you kidding! Why leave heaven to go to hell? There's no committee in Congress, including Appropriations, that's as

[25] *Ibid.*, pp. 280, 319.
[26] *Ibid.*, p. 277.
[27] *Ibid.*, pp. 294–307.

important as Ways and Means. Why step downward once
you have reached the top?

Being on Ways and Means gives me stature and respect. We
are a powerful committee and a prestigeful one. The House
is jealous of the Committee.

The original attraction and the subsequent attractiveness of the
Committee are the same — the opportunity to be more influential
than most other members of the House. The Committee's decision
patterns help to insure and explain this result.

Beyond the satisfaction they get from their influence, Ways and
Means members derive extra satisfaction from their membership in
the group and from their interaction with their fellow members.
Like the members of Appropriations, they express strong feelings of
group identification — positively in speaking of their Committee's
internal life and negatively in their invidious comparisons with Senate Finance. "It's like a fraternity. . . . There's a spirit of camaraderie that prevails." "You're a cut above them (other House
members) and it's a good feeling. It's a close-knit committee. Apart
from Appropriations, I'd say Ways and Means is the closest-knit
committee there is." Arguing from their responsible work style, they
assert their superiority over their Senate counterpart: "With all due
respect to the Senate, they don't know what the hell they're doing
over there. They're so damn irresponsible." "The Senators, Jesus
Christ! They put this in, take that out, spend three days — and we've
spent months on the bill. Someone has to be responsible." These
sentiments of solidarity and superiority bespeak an extra degree of
member attachment to the Ways and Means Committee. Such
sentiments derive most directly, we suggest, from the internal decision-making processes of the Committee. Once present, they may
reinforce the autonomy of those processes. Our overall assessment,
similar to that with Appropriations, is that the psychic satisfaction
of Ways and Means members further stabilizes the pattern of decisions we have described.

FOREIGN AFFAIRS

Foreign Affairs members come to their Committee seeking to help
make foreign policy, in an environment strongly dominated by the
President and the executive branch. So constraining is this environment, that Committee members have been hard put to develop any

strategic posture other than one calling for responsiveness to executive branch expectations. As a partial answer to their strategic problem, this posture commands agreement. But as a complete answer, it does not. Hence the malaise over strategic premises described earlier. The dilemma is not just a House matter, as the tergiversations of the Senate Foreign Relations Committee attest. But the Senate group. buttressed by its constitutional prerogatives, has more actively sought to gain leverage in dealing with the executive branch. On occasion, it has succeeded. In any case, its continual struggle to register some independent impact on policy has kept its members free of the kind of strategic lethargy characteristic of the House group.

Such decisions as House Foreign Affairs members do make show a distinctive responsiveness to Presidential-executive branch wishes. Table 6.8 presents some evidence in support of this generalization. It compares (in the manner of our earlier Tables 3.1 and 3.2) members of each of our six committees with committee nonmembers, using *Congressional Quarterly's* Presidential Foreign Policy Support Scores for all congressmen. Again, we have averaged these scores for each pairing of committee members and nonmembers for each of six Congresses and then combined these six averages into an overall twelve-year average. The rankings of Table 6.8 show members of Foreign Affairs to be more supportive of the President in foreign policy matters than the members of the other five committees. And by a substantial margin. The Republicans account for the largest part of that margin — they being the only Republican committee contingent to register more foreign policy support than the remainder of their party colleagues in the House. Foreign Affairs Democrats share that position with two other sets of committee Democrats — most notably with those on Ways and Means, whose administration loyalties pertain as much to foreign policy (viz. trade) as domestic. These figures do not record Foreign Affairs Committee decisions, as such, but they do indicate that the general posture of its members is highly supportive of the executive-led policy coalitions of their environment.

Foreign Affairs does not make a great many decisions. Its volume of output, ranging from twenty to thirty-five bills per Congress, is second lowest among the six committees.[28] The decisions it makes

---

[28] See Table 6.20.

Table 6.8
Committee Support for President's Foreign Policy
(Mean Presidential Foreign Policy Support Scores, 84th–89th Congresses)

	Democrats			Republicans			Total		
	Comm. Membs.	Other House Membs.	Diff.	Comm. Membs.	Other House Membs.	Diff.	Comm.	Other	Diff.
F.A.	73	66	+7	60	47	+13	68	58	+10
E.&L.	70	66	+4	46	48	−2	63	59	+4
W.&M.	76	66	+10	40	49	−9	61	59	+2
App.	66	66	0	43	49	−6	57	59	−2
P.O.	64	67	−3	46	48	−2	56	59	−3
Int.	62	67	−5	43	48	−5	54	59	−5

can be put into four categories: 1) The annual foreign aid bill. 2) Presidentially requested policy resolutions (i.e., Tonkin Gulf) and new programs (Peace Corps). 3) State Department regulations, reauthorization and amendment of old programs (Peace Corps, Disarmament Agency). 4) Minor resolutions, involving participation in international conferences, commissions, exhibitions, fairs, celebrations, memorials, and assorted projects. The categories are listed in descending order of perceived importance, time consumed, and numbers of decisions involved. In the Committee's annual *Survey of Activities* for the 88th Congress for example, two decisions fell in the first category, one in the second, eight in the third and twenty-two in the fourth. Sixteen pages were allotted to the description of the two bills in category one; three pages for the resolution in category two; thirteen pages for the items in category three; and nineteen pages for the twenty-two decisions in category four.[29]

The Committee's own judgment as to the relative importance of its various pieces of legislation is clear. The annual foreign aid authorization is the Committee's major bill. Indeed, it is the foreign aid program that brought the Committee to a new prominence and a new prestige after World War II. The Committee's one consensual decision rule is to approve and help pass the foreign aid bill. Committee decisions on foreign aid, therefore, give us the best positive indicator of its substantive performance.

Foreign Affairs support for foreign aid appears strong when the level of Committee members' support is compared with the level of House members' support. Figure 6.1 charts this comparison in terms of the percentage of pro-foreign aid votes cast by each group on final passage of the authorization bills, 1955–1966. The level of support among Committee members has stayed consistently fifteen to twenty percentage points higher than the level among House members generally. Figure 6.1 also indicates that changes in Committee and House support levels tend to occur at the same time and to move in the same direction. It is our view that this patterning of trends results from common responses in the two arenas to changing environmental constraints.

Figure 6.2 helps us to see what those constraints are. It breaks each of the trend lines in Figure 6.1 into its partisan components.

[29] Committee on Foreign Affairs, *Survey of Activities of the Committee on Foreign Affairs, House of Representatives* (Washington: U.S. Government Printing Office, 1964), pp. 14–69.

Figure 6-1
Committee and House Support for Foreign Aid,
Votes on Final Passage, 1955–1966

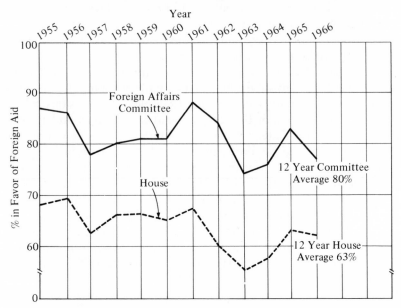

Committee Democrats and Committee Republicans give consistently higher support to the foreign aid program than do their respective party colleagues in the House. Indeed, a bipartisan consensus in favor of foreign aid has existed inside the Committee throughout the period.[30]

There has been, however, no durable bipartisan consensus on the House floor. A majority of House Democrats has consistently supported the program; but a majority of Republicans has not. So long as a Republican was President, House Republican support held steady at around sixty per cent and a supportive bipartisan consensus existed. But once the program came from a Democratic President, House Republican support slid far below fifty per cent. It dropped first in the House (in 1960 and 1961) and only later (in 1962 and 1963) inside the Committee, when Republican leaders moved to bring Committee support levels into closer alignment with House

[30] The distance between the two solid lines in Figure 6.2 is the Committee's index of partisanship, which is easily discernible as a good deal lower (see Table 6.7) than that for the Ways and Means Committee.

Figure 6-2
Committee and House Partisanship on Foreign Aid,
Votes on Final Passage, 1955-1966

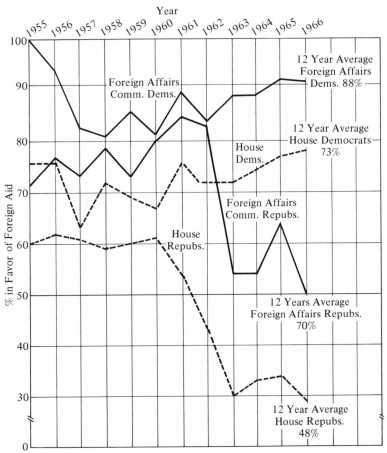

support levels by filling five vacancies left by program supporters
with five confirmed opponents of the program.[31] House Democratic
support remained solid regardless of which party occupied the

[31] One of the vacancies was that left by Walter Judd (Republican, Minne-
sota), who was by far the most influential pro-aid Republican — in the Committee and in the House. Several observers felt the Republicans packed the
Committee in retribution against a Democratic Administration which had campaigned to defeat Judd. His influence with his fellow Republicans is described
by Rep. William Avery, *Congressional Record*, Daily Edition, August 20, 1963,
p. 14620.

White House. Support levels were slightly higher, however, under Kennedy and Johnson than under Eisenhower. They were higher, we think, because some Southern Democrats who might indulge their doubts about the program under Eisenhower (e.g., the 1956–1957 decline) could be kept in the fold better by the rallying or disciplining force (e.g., the 1960–1961 increase) of a Democratic President. This explanation holds inside as well as outside the Committee. Both Committee members and House members, in sum, have been responsive to the President and the executive branch and to the partisan composition of the Administration. The Committee's response has been more bipartisan than partisan — as a result of the distinctively high degree of program support among Committee Republicans. A majority of House Democrats, it seems, support the foreign aid program as a matter of conviction. A majority of House Republicans support the foreign aid program *only* when it is a matter of conviction on the part of a Republican President.[32]

Another descriptive measure of the Committee's performance on foreign aid is the dollar amount it recommends relative to the executive's request — as compared with the dollar amount recommended by the other decision makers in the yearly authorization-appropriations sequence. We can put the Committee's money decisions in perspective by noting at the outset that the decision problem for all congressional decision makers has been: "How much of a reduction should we make in the executive request?" From 1955 to 1966, the two substantive legislative committees and the two appropriations committees made one hundred twenty separate decisions on the total dollar amount to be allocated to the foreign aid program. One hundred sixteen of the one hundred twenty, ninety-eight percent, were decisions to *reduce* the funds below the level requested by the executive branch. Two decisions gave the executive what it requested; two decisions increased the amount. Responsiveness to the executive on foreign aid must be judged, therefore, in terms of relative size of reductions. Foreign aid is not a strongly supported program in the Congress; its friends are those who seek to minimize — not elimi-

---

[32] Similar generalizations are found to hold for the entire field of foreign policy in Mark Kesselman, "Presidential Leadership in Congress on Foreign Policy: A Replication of a Hypothesis," *Midwest Journal of Political Science* (November, 1965). Similar conclusions for foreign aid are found in O'Leary, *op. cit.*, pp. 59–69.

nate — reductions in funds. In these terms, the House Foreign Affairs Committee should be numbered among the program's staunchest protectors.

Table 6.9 averages the yearly reductions made at each stage of the decision sequence for the period 1955–1966. Though these summary figures conceal fluctuations over time as well as the variations among reductions at each stage, they do indicate the relatively strong support of the House Foreign Affairs Committee for the program. The average reduction made by the Committee was smaller than that made at any of the other key decision points. The comparison in Table 6.11 between House Foreign Affairs Committee decisions and House Appropriations Committee decisions is especially dramatic. Given the marked difference in their decision rules — one calling for program support, the other calling for budget reduction — a commensurate difference in their substantive decisions was to be expected. We shall return to this comparison later.

Table 6.9
Foreign Aid Decisions: Percentage Reductions
in Executive Requests by Major Participants,
12-Year Averages, 1955–1966

	Average Reduction 1955–1966
1. House Foreign Affairs	−7.7%
2. House (authorization)	−10.0
3. Senate Foreign Relations	−8.0
4. Senate (authorization)	−10.5
5. Conference (authorization)	−10.3
6. House Appropriations	−22.3
7. House (appropriations)	−22.2
8. Senate Appropriations	−11.7
9. Senate (appropriations)	−13.7
10. Conference (appropriations)	−18.7

A comparison between House Foreign Affairs and Senate Foreign Relations presents still another perspective on the former group's support for foreign aid. In the first half of the period, the congressional bulwark of the program was the Senate Committee — whose members were still following the highly cooperative decision rule inaugurated in the Vandenberg period. Students who wrote in this period unanimously perceived the Senate and its Committee as

Table 6.10
Senate Committee and Senate Decisions on Foreign Aid:
Higher (+) or Lower (−) Funding Levels
1955–1966

	Senate Foreign Relations Decision Relative to House Foreign Affairs and House Decisions	Senate Decision Relative to Senate Foreign Relations Decisions
1955	+	+
1956	+	+
1957	+	+
1958	+	+
1959	−	+
1960	+	−
1961	−	−
1962	−	0
1963	+	−
1964	−	0
1965	−	−
1966	−	−

much more hospitable toward foreign aid than the House and its Committee.[33] By the later part of the period, however, the situation had become substantially reversed. The strong criticism of the foreign aid program was coming from the Senate Committee and from the Senate. The House Committee and the House were now positioned as the most reliable supporters of foreign aid and of the President's foreign policy generally. Table 6.10 charts the change in Senatorial attitudes in terms of their money decisions. Though we cannot pinpoint a time of change, Table 6.10 shows Senate performance in the last six years of the period to be very different from that in the first six years. From 1955 to 1960 (inclusive), the Foreign Relations Committee authorization figure was *higher* than that of the House Committee and that of the House in five of the six years. In the period from 1961 to 1966 (inclusive), the Senate Committee figure was *lower* than that of the House Committee and the House in five of the six years. A similar difference is shown for full Senate review of Senate Committee decisions. In the first six years, Committee recommendations were *increased* on the floor five times;

[33] For example, David N. Farnsworth, *The Senate Committee on Foreign Relations* (Urbana: University of Illinois Press, 1961), Chapter 5, pp. 89–90; H. Field Haviland, "Foreign Aid and the Policy Process: 1957," *American Political Science Review* (September, 1958), p. 703; Sidney Hyman, "Mr. Dillon and the Fight for Foreign Aid," *Reporter*, March 20, 1958, p. 12.

in the next six years, Committee recommendations (already reduced from House levels) were *decreased* four times and left untouched twice.

The Senate's growing disenchantment with foreign aid went beyond the dollars-and-cents decisions. In the early days, the Senate Committee supported the executive branch desire for new methods of funding — multiyear authorizations and Treasury borrowing — while the House Committee opposed it. But as the period came to an end, the House Committee and the Administration were often standing together against the Senate on such matters as multiyear authorization (1966), the separation of military and economic assistance into two bills (1965), and the channeling of foreign aid through multinational agencies (1965). In 1965, Senate Committee Chairman Fulbright flatly refused to introduce and floor-manage the military assistance segment of the Administration's program. And in that year the Senate Committee's bill called for the termination of foreign aid two years thereafter.[34]

A leader of the Agency for International Development described the Senate as he saw it in the period (1965) when it had abandoned its traditional "contingent support strategy" but had not agreed upon a satisfactory alternative.

> There is an antipathy toward the executive branch — not antipathy but a standoffishness. They want to be critics and advisers, too. They take the advise-and-consent business very seriously. They are very conscious that they were created that way by the Constitution. . . . Paradoxically, they have a growing feeling of impotence, that they aren't really influencing policy. . . . They could be constructive critics, but now all we have is a quiet desperation over there. That's dangerous.

The same AID official voiced executive branch satisfaction with the performance of Foreign Affairs:

> I can't think of any trouble we have with the (House) Committee in getting our bills passed. Most of them support the Administration on foreign aid. The only complaint I would have as an outsider would be that they don't act as critic as

[34] A good journalistic account is, Robert C. Albright, "Foreign Aid Storm is Brewing in the Senate," *Washington Post*, March 1, 1965, p. A13. The culmination of this trend occurred in November 1971, when the Senate voted to reject the foreign aid bill altogether. See *Congressional Quarterly* November 6, 1971, pp. 2259–2270.

much as they might. But that's good for us politically. The
Committee is — well, it is really a rubber stamp.

On the evidence, Foreign Affairs decisions do follow the Committee's one decision rule — they support and help pass the foreign aid
program. And, except for Senate authorization decisions in the first
half of the period, the executive branch has found Foreign Affairs
Committee decisions more satisfactory than those of any other decision-making unit in the Congress.

Committee members themselves are a good deal less happy about
Committee performance. Coming to the Committee to help make
good foreign policy, many of them end up feeling tightly constrained by their environment and a good deal less actively involved
than they had imagined they would be. "The subject matter, foreign
affairs, is important but not the Committee." "We don't have any-
where near the power we should have." "The Committee has been
called a eunuch. That's pretty accurate." The member goals of involvement and influence in foreign policy making remain partially
unmet.

Given this condition, it would be surprising to find Foreign Affairs
members, like those of Appropriations and Ways and Means, mani-
festing any emotional attachment to their Committee. They do not.
Nor do they exhibit any distinctive decision-making processes on
which to ground any such attachment. They express neither a special degree of internal friction nor a special degree of internal *esprit*.
Insofar as they have a sense of group identity, it is a diminished one,
thrust upon them by the presence of the Senate Foreign Relations
Committee. Frequently, the result of this comparison is a feeling of
inferiority — the very reverse of the sentiments expressed by members of Appropriations and Ways and Means. About half the members agreed with sentiments such as these: "I have the feeling
Senate Foreign Relations asserts itself more than we do." "Over the
years the Senate Committee has had men with greater knowledge,
experience, and ability." Some members were angry when William
White made this very inferiority a theme of his book *Home Place*.[35]
"White doesn't know what he's talking about. He's a victim of his
diet — Senators. He has no idea what the hell's going on over here."
But others spoke with resignation: "He pokes fun at us. I think he's
probably right. If I were a journalist, that's the way I'd write it."

[35] William S. White, *Home Place* (Boston: Houghton Mifflin, 1965) especially pp. 125–127. White's second thoughts are to be found in, William S.
White, "A Citadel Falls," *Washington Post* August 20, 1965, p. A18.

Table 6.11
Foreign Aid Decisions: Foreign Affairs and Appropriations
Percentage Reductions in Executive Requests, 1955-1966

Percentage Reductions

Year	Foreign Affairs	Appropriations	Difference
1955	-3.6%	-19.2%	-15.6%
1956	-23.7	-29.5	-5.8
1957	-16.1	-25.4	-9.3
1958	-9.7	-22.1	-12.4
1959	-6.8	-28.1	-21.3
1960	-4.2	-20.8	-16.6
1961	-7.9	-29.9	-22.0
1962	-4.0	-26.8	-22.8
1963	-9.0	-37.6	-28.6
1964	0	-14.4	-14.4
1965	-0.4	-5.0	-4.6
1966	-7.8	-9.2	-1.4
12-Year Average	-7.7%	-22.3%	-14.6%

Foreign Affairs members want to increase their institutional importance in foreign policy making — along with which would surely
come an increased sense of institutional pride. Until they achieve
the first, they will continue to lack the second.

Members of Foreign Affairs leave their Committee voluntarily
more often than members of Appropriations and Ways and Means
leave theirs. (See Table 6.5.) But they leave to pursue their careers
outside of the House. If they stay in the House, they stay on the
Committee — despite their disappointments and frustrations. And,
staying, they try to devise ways of fulfilling the original promise of
their Committee assignment.

It is one symptom of their dilemma that the Appropriations Committee exerts more influence over the foreign aid program than does
Foreign Affairs. Table 6.11 displays the contrasting decision patterns
of the two committees. While Foreign Affairs remains more responsive to executive branch wishes, Appropriations makes a greater
independent impact on the program.[36] And Appropriations sustains

[36] The one congressman who transferred from Foreign Affairs to Appropriations was asked why he did it. He said:

I've wondered a thousand times myself. If I had stayed on the
Foreign Affairs Committee, I would have been Chairman twice now
— with nothing to do but meet three or four times a year to rubber-

its deep reductions on the House floor — only three amendments (1960, 1961, 1966) to its money recommendations having carried in the twelve years. Furthermore, when Foreign Affairs and Appropriations clash on the House floor over nonmonetary kinds of influence — such as the length of foreign aid authorizations, the methods of foreign aid financing, and the propriety of substantive legislation on the foreign aid appropriation bill — Foreign Affairs regularly loses.[37] Its members could, of course, contest with Appropriations for influence by posing even greater threats to the foreign aid program. But this strategy would run directly counter to the policy goals of a majority of the committee. They want to make the program better, not kill it. As one member put it, "Foreign Affairs believes in the program; Appropriations does not."

Alternatively, Committee members might work to achieve success on the floor — carrying their recommendations intact and emerging as the authoritative foreign policy spokesmen for the President and the executive branch in the chamber. Members of the executive branch would applaud this achievement as well. But the Committee, as we have seen, lacks the political and institutional bases for establishing its authority in the House. Its members cannot establish themselves as experts. "The Committee has never developed any bite. We don't do any digging." "If you really pinned us down, I don't think you could find five or six of us who could answer such a general question as, 'Why are we giving aid to Africa?'" They cannot develop resources with which to bargain. "What can you offer a member? Do you say, 'If you vote for this, I'll give you a dam in Upper Volta'?" They cannot disguise the basic controversiality of the program. "If it's a controversial matter, members are going to

---

stamp the giveaways the administration sends up here — and then be a big shot the rest of the year. You asked me why I went on Appropriations. Well it's a committee with a lot of prestige. If you want a committee that gets you into the center of the workings of government, the Appropriations Committee is the best in the Congress . . . I sit behind closed doors four hours a day and nobody knows I'm in Congress. But I'd do it again.

[37] For these controversies, see Haviland, *op. cit.* (length of authorization); 107 *Congressional Record*, p. 16060 ff. ("Saund Amendment" re. financing methods); and *Congressional Record*, Daily Edition, November 16, 1967, pp. H15404–H15412 (waiver of points of order). Foreign Affairs members complain about their jurisdictional losses to other committees, too — especially, Agriculture and Armed Services. An example is the struggle over PL480 in *Congressional Record*, Daily Edition, August 25, 1967.

react and it doesn't make much difference if the Committee has done a good job or not." They cannot persuade the party leadership to bolster Committee prestige. "I don't think the leadership gives us the kind of support they give other committees." [38]

Some of the Committee's top leaders equate floor success with getting the aid bill passed — regardless of the number of restrictive amendments. And by this criterion, they perform well on the floor. The foreign aid bill has always passed.[39] But merely saving the principle of foreign aid is not enough for most. And the aid bill does provide a vulnerable floor target. From 1955 to 1966, the Committee confronted 286 proposed amendments of which 114 passed, thus altering the bill. The comparable figures for the appropriation bills were 75 amendments proposed and 31 passed. Without making too much of these figures, the aid authorization bill does appear to get altered by the House more often than the appropriations bill. "It's always a fight on the floor." "Everyone's shooting at you down there," said a Committee spokesman. "They're pulling amendments out of their pockets and out of their socks. . . . It's no picnic down there on the floor." The Committee does not have a bad reputation in the chamber, but neither do its recommendations carry any independent authority of the sort carried by Ways and Means or Appropriations. "Inside the House, we are thought of as a glamorous committee, but not a powerful one." "Foreign Affairs, I don't think, carries much weight in the House at all." Foreign Affairs probably can't be a highly successful Committee on the floor, saddled as it is with its attachments to the executive branch and to an embattled program.

In any case, influence in the chamber is *not* the members' most prominent goal, and the Committee's decision rules are *not* oriented toward floor success. We found Committee members, indeed, to be far more philosophical about their relative lack of influence in the House (and far less outraged, say, by Appropriations Committee dominance) than we had expected. Their dissatisfactions centered on their relationship with the executive branch and their relative inability to affect foreign aid policy as formulated and implemented

[38] An account of the Committee's greatest (1963) floor defeat, emphasizing leadership failure, is Paul Duke, "The Foreign Aid Fiasco," *Reporter*, January 16, 1964.

[39] Every one of the Committee's "major bills" in the period 1955–1966 passed the House — 65 in all. By this standard, the Committee enjoyed greater floor success than Ways and Means.

there. The problem is not easily solved, as the Senate Committee's search for a viable strategy indicates. And the Senate Committee has institutional resources unavailable to the House group. One consequence of the disparity in resources is that the Senate Committee has been less transfixed by the foreign aid program than the House Committee. It has pushed its quest for a share in policy making throughout the entire foreign policy area. And the thrust of Senate efforts in the mid-to-late 1960's was to educate the executive branch in policy alternatives and policy consequences. Neither the scope nor the pretentiousness of these Senatorial efforts comes naturally to the House group. It has an historical habit of playing second fiddle to the Senate; and it has been convinced that it is the foreign aid bill which has, at last, given it title to some parity. Paradoxically, it will probably have to enlarge its policy horizons before it can lay solid claim to that title.

During our period of study, the pattern of Foreign Affairs decisions seemed to be about as stable as those of Appropriations and Ways and Means. But the potential source of instability was very different. On Foreign Affairs, we would predict, change in the decision pattern would more likely result from member dissatisfaction than from environmental dissatisfaction. Whether internal sources of instability, however, are any more likely to generate change than external sources of instability is an across-the-board kind of predictive proposition beyond the competence of this study. Member goals and environmental expectations are the two key independent variables of the analysis. And, as far as we can tell, dissatisfaction in one case is as likely to produce change as dissatisfaction in the other.

EDUCATION AND LABOR

Education and Labor members come to their Committee to make good public policy. They inhabit a distinctively pluralistic and partisan environment; and they happily operate as integral elements of the party-led policy coalitions in that environment. Their key decision rules prescribe a blend of policy partisanship and policy individualism. And their internal decision-making processes bear the imprint of those two rules. If our analysis is correct, the Committee's decisions themselves should bear a similar imprint.

One way to look for the impact of policy partisanship on Committee decisions is to focus on internally expressed disagreements — as we did in Chapter Four. Another is to focus on Committee decisions as they are registered and reacted to on the House floor — as we did for Ways and Means decisions earlier in this chapter. If we examine Education and Labor decisions in different policy areas, we find, as with Ways and Means, a good deal of variation in the amount of partisanship they generate. But, by and large, the policies having the broadest impact on the society (and in that sense, the most important) have the greatest partisan content. Table 6.12 displays the number of "party votes" on all roll calls in what we think are the five most important policy areas within the Committee's jurisdiction.[40]

Table 6.12
Floor Partisanship on Education and
Labor Bills: Five Policy Areas, 1955–1966

Policy Area	Number of Bills	Number of Roll Calls	Number of Party Votes	Percentage Party Votes
Anti-Poverty	3	12	12	100%
Aid to Education (Elem. & Sec.)	6	20	17	85%
Labor Management (Excl. min. wage)	10	19	12	63%
Minimum Wage	4	13	8	62%
Aid to Education (College)	8	17	3	18%

Judging from the response they draw from Democrats and Republicans in the chamber, Committee decisions in four of its five key policy areas have a strong partisan content. This comes as no surprise. Committee members perceive these issues as partisan-ideological issues, deal with them in these terms internally, and package them accordingly for floor action. Decision making on issues of federal aid to education (elementary and secondary), minimum wage, labor management, and poverty gives to Committee activity

[40] By "party votes" we mean votes on which a majority of one party is opposed by a majority of the other party. These five policy areas were the only ones with a large enough number of bills and roll calls to make any analysis possible. The thirty-one bills used make up three-quarters of all the bills having roll calls; and the eighty-one roll calls used make up three-quarters of all roll calls involving the Committee.

its distinctive partisan flavor. The bipartisanship characteristic of decision making on aid to higher education provides the minor theme.

It is not the Committee's decisions, as such, that determine the partisan character of these issues. Committee Democrats and Republicans function within two much larger party-led policy coalitions, and they perceive the issues just about the same way their coalition partners perceive them. But if the Committee's members have any independent impact on partisanship, it is to *increase* rather than to decrease it. Such is the inference we draw from a comparison, in Table 6.13, of the partisanship of Committee members and House members on the set of roll calls used in Table 6.12. Our measure, introduced earlier, is the index of partisanship. In four of the five key policy areas and overall, Committee partisanship is substantially greater than House partisanship. Of the eighty-one roll calls involved, Committee floor partisanship exceeded House floor partisanship in sixty-three or in seventy-eight per cent of the votes. In acting on *their own* bills, therefore, Education and Labor members display the same distinctive degree of partisanship that they display on *all* bills — as shown in Table 3.2. Table 6.13 provides additional evidence that Committee members do prosecute policy partisanship. In so doing, they not only act within their respective policy coalitions, but they also impart an extra measure of partisanship to coalition decisions.

Committee partisanship, we argued in the earlier chapters, is not constant over periods of time, but is sensitive to changing external partisan alignments, i.e., to changes in party control of the presidency and party strength in the House. (See Table 2.5.) If we are

Table 6.13
Committee and House Indices of Partisanship:
Five Major Policy Areas, 1955–1966

	House Average IP	Committee Average IP	Difference
Labor-Management (Excl. Min. Wage)	30	58	+28
Anti-poverty	66	90	+24
Minimum Wage	44	62	+18
Federal Aid (College)	21	39	+18
Federal Aid (Elem. & Sec.)	47	48	+1

Table 6.14
Changes in Volume of Committee Decisions:
Major Legislation under Republican and
Democratic Presidents, 1955–1966

No. of Major Bills

Committee	Republican President 1955–1960	Democratic President 1961–1966	Increase in No. of Bills	Percentage Increase
Education & Labor	16	80	64	400%
Foreign Affairs	23	43	20	87%
Interior	31	51	20	65%
Ways and Means	50	64	14	28%
Post Office	19	23	4	21%
[Appropriations*	81	73	-8	-10%]

*Original appropriation bills only. These figures reflect the Committee's own reshuffling of its subcommittees and not Administration influence.

correct, such changes should alter the policy prescriptions emanating from the Committee's environment, which should, in turn, affect the content of Committee decisions. One very noticeable effect of this sort is the change that occurred in the sheer volume of policy prescriptions and, hence, the change in the *volume* of decisions by Education and Labor — both as the result of changing external partisan conditions. Table 6.14 compares, for our six committees, the number of "major bills" reported out under Republican President Eisenhower with the number reported out under Democratic Presidents Kennedy and Johnson.[41] Assuming that (for all committees) most major legislation results from a presidential-executive branch proposal (though not necessarily from executive initiative, which is more complex), it appears that in every policy area the Republican President was less of a legislative activist than were his Democratic successors. This is not surprising. What is surprising, perhaps, is the singularly huge disparity in presidential-executive branch activism and, hence, in number of committee decisions in the policy areas within the jurisdiction of Education and Labor.

The fourfold increase in the number of decisions is, we think, evidence of the special sensitivity of Education and Labor to changes in external partisanship. This change in volume could be attributed,

[41] "Major bills" are those listed in *Congressional Quarterly Almanac's* annual summary and which also have a House Report listed there. They are the same bills used in Table 4–2.

also, to the Barden-to-Powell switch in Committee leadership, which occurred at the very same time as the change in the White House. Indeed, it is impossible to determine for sure which of the two simultaneous changes contributed most to the increase. Since legislation coming to Education and Labor normally comes from the Administration, and since the Committee is unlikely to report out many bills over the objections of the Administration, we give greater weight to the change in presidential policy partisanship. We would then add to this the obstructive effects of Barden's leadership and the facilitative effects of Powell's leadership. As further evidence that presidential partisanship is the crucial variable, a similarly sizable increase in major bills was reported out of the Senate Labor and Public Welfare Committee at the same time and *without* a change in chairmen. Considering only bills within the jurisdiction of both Committees, the number of Education and Labor decisions for the two periods jumped 388 per cent (from 16 to 78 bills) while Labor and Public Welfare decisions increased 338 per cent. (from 16 to 70 bills).[42] Perhaps the difference between the two can be taken as a crude measure of the independent effect of the House Committee's leadership change. If so, it is strictly of secondary importance.

A third contributory factor was the change in party ratios, which, in 1959, gave Education and Labor the liberal, Democratic majority that it has had ever since. Without that change, no legislative explosion could have occurred. But the liberal majority, even though it controlled the Committee and reduced the Chairman's prerogatives, did not increase Committee output by a single bill between 1957 and 1958 (six bills) and 1959 and 1960 (six bills). The Senate Committee, moreover, had a liberal majority throughout the entire period, and its volume did not increase until the presidency changed party hands. Again, this argues for the central importance of presidential partisanship in the policy coalitions influencing Education andf Labor — at least where sheer volume of decisions is involved.

Gross changes in the size of the Democratic House majority do not appear to have any independent effect on the volume of Committee decisions. But, along with the changes in the White House, they do seem to have a perceptible effect on the *content* of Commit-

---

[42] Labor and Public Welfare, alone, had jurisdiction over health and some veterans' matters. Education and Labor, alone, had jurisdiction over the school-lunch program and some programs for the aging. These have been eliminated from the calculation.

tee decisions. Assuming that the content of the Committee's decisions always reflects something of what the President wants and something of what the Democratic House majority wants, different partisan combinations externally should result in different substantive decisions by the Committee.

Table 6.15 reiterates the four patterns of partisanship displayed earlier in Table 2.4. Since the greatest contrast is between the extreme or "pure" cases of 1955 to 1958 (Republican President, small Democratic majority) and 1965 and 1966 (Democratic President, large Democratic majority), we would expect the most marked difference in Committee decisions to occur across these two periods. Furthermore, we would expect to find the 1955-to-1958 decisions least favorable and the 1965 and 1966 most favorable to the Democratic-liberal policy coalition. For the two in-between or "mixed" patterns of 1959 and 1960 (Republican President, large Democratic majority) and 1961 to 1964 (Democratic President, small Democratic majority), we would expect to find Committee decisions less easily differentiated from one another than in the case of the "pure" patterns. And we would expect these decisions to be more favorable to the Democratic-liberal coalition than those of 1955 to 1958 while being less favorable than those of 1965 and 1966.

As a crude test of these propositions, we have listed a few salient and (more or less) comparable ingredients of Committee decisions on minimum wage and federal aid to elementary and secondary education. They are the only two categories of major legislation where any (however crude) comparability over time is possible. For minimum wage bills, we have listed the decision as to size of increase, length of time taken to achieve it, and number of new workers covered. We assume that the larger the increase, the shorter the wait, and the more new workers covered, the closer will be the decision to the desires of the Democratic-liberal policy coalition.[43] For federal aid to education bills, we include size of the authorization, type of grant, and the school construction/teachers' use of the money. We assume that the larger the authorization, the less the states are required to match the federal grant, and the more the money can be used for teachers' salaries as well as construction, the

[43] For confirmation of coalition positions, see Gus Tyler, *op. cit.*; Tom Wicker, *JFK and LBJ* (New York: Morrow, 1968), pp. 83–117; Lawrence O'Brien, *Federal Separation of Powers: Practice and Theory* (speech) as printed in *Congressional Record*, Daily Edition, October 10, 1966, pp. 24926 ff.

Table 6.15
Committee Decisions on Minimum Wage and
Federal Aid to Education
Under Four Patterns of Partisanship

Size of House
Democratic
Majority   Control of Presidency

            Democratic   *Republican*

	Democratic	*Republican*
	1965-1966	*1959-1960*
	Minimum Wage 1966	*Minimum Wage 1960*
	40 cent increase over 2 years, 7.2 million workers added	25 cent increase in one year, 3.4 million workers added
	Federal Aid 1965	*Federal Aid 1959*
Large	$1.3 billion for first of 3 years, nonmatching grants for school construction, teachers' salaries, and equipment	$1.1 billion per year for 4 year matching, two years non-matching grants for school construction
	Federal Aid 1966	*Federal Aid 1960*
	$2.1 billion for first of two years, (amendment to 1965 Act)	$325 million for 3 years, 1 year matching, two years non-matching grants for school construction
	1961-1964	*1955-1958*
	Minimun Wage 1961	*Minimum Wage 1955*
	25 cent increase in one year, 4.2 million workers added	25 cent increase in one year, no workers added
	Federal Aid 1961 (1)	*Federal Aid 1956*
Small	$850 million per year for 3 years, nonmatching grants, for school construction and teachers' salaries	$400 million per year for 4 years, matching grants for school construction
	Federal Aid 1961 (2)	*Federal Aid 1957*
	$325 million for 1 year, matching grants for school construction	$300 million per year for 5 years, matching grants for school construction

closer the Committee decision will be to the desires of the Demo-cratic-liberal policy coalition.[44]

To a considerable degree, the expected relationships do appear. The 1955 minimum wage bill (especially its lack of new coverage) was the least favorable to the Democratic-liberal coalition, and the 1966 bill, the most favorable. The 1960 and 1961 bills were very similar to one another (the 1960 bill died in conference and was refurbished for 1961); their provisions fell between the first two in terms of their appeal to the Democratic-liberal coalition.

Federal aid decisions do not present so neat a pattern. But the 1965 and 1966 bills were the most favorable to the Democratic-liberal coalition and the 1956 and 1957 bills were *among* the least favorable to that coalition. All four bills produced in the "in-between" periods, on the other hand, were less favorable than the 1965 and 1966 bills. Two of them, 1959 and 1961(1), and probably three, to include 1960, were more favorable than the 1956 and 1957 bills. The two bills that conform least well to our expectations are the extremely liberal bill of 1959 and the extremely conservative bill of 1961(2). Both bills, however, were more the products of strategy than of policy decisions. The 1959 measure was an early-ditch effort to prod a reluctant Administration into support for *some other* compromise bill later in the session. The 1961 bill was a last-ditch effort to salvage *something* when the major 1961 measure became mired in the Rules Committee. In sum, there is a good deal of evidence in Table 6.15 to indicate that external partisan constraints have a substantive effect on the output of the Education and Labor Committee. As environmental patterns of partisanship change, so do the contents of Committee decisions.

According to our reading of Table 6.15, Committee members (and their coalition partners) sometimes temper their policy decisions to fit existing partisan alignments. At the same time, however, Committee members remain strongly partisan and ideological; these characteristics limit the extent to which they can make strategic policy accommodations. Committee members, that is, do want to

[44] Excluded from this analysis are the crucial aid-to-segregated-schools and aid-to-private-schools issues, which played such a prominent part in federal aid controversies. Positions on these issues cannot be identified with party-led coalitions. For confirmation of the coalition positions that are used, see Frank Munger and Richard Fenno, *National Politics and Federal Aid to Education* (Syracuse: Syracuse University Press, 1962); Eugene Eidenberg and Roy Morey, *An Act of Congress* (New York: W. W. Norton, 1969).

achieve "some" change in public policy, but they simultaneously insist on a "good" change in policy. And, when forced to choose, many of them will often opt for "good" policy — even if this choice is highly likely to net them no change at all. More often than our other five Committees, Education and Labor members will be reluctant to choose "something" over "nothing." More often than the other five, they will prefer a live political issue to a passed compromise bill. A case in point was the last-minute willingness of Committee members to forego a minimum wage bill and a federal aid to education bill in 1960 in order to agitate both issues in the 1960 presidential election. When they adopt this stance, Committee members are reinforced by a similar attitude on the part of their coalition allies. In the 1960 minimum wage example, the AFL-CIO supported the breakup of the efforts at compromise in conference committee. In the federal aid case, the National Education Association lost all interest in the possibility of a conference committee compromise, thereby making a conference impossible. Whether Education and Labor members eschew compromise in pursuit of policy partisanship or policy individualism, external allies will be found in the Committee's pluralistic environment to match their devotion (flexible or inflexible) to a policy goal.

More general evidence for the Committee's distinctive aversion to compromise decisions can be found in the relative lack of success that Education and Labor decisions enjoy once they leave the Committee. Of the twelve bills listed in Table 6.15, for instance, only seven passed the House. And of the seven, two were completely rewritten on the floor. This record of floor success is surely not one to rival that of Ways and Means. Table 6.16 compares the floor record of Education and Labor with that of Ways and Means. It lists the number of bills (again using the *Congressional Quarterly's* "major legislation") reported out by each committee and the percentage of those bills that subsequently passed the House. From 1955 to 1966, fifty-nine per cent of Education and Labor's major bills, compared with ninety-four per cent of those from Ways and Means, passed the House. Given the similarly controversial nature of the policy subjects handled by the two groups and given the similarly partisan constraints emanating from their policy environments, the comparison is an intriguing one. The explanation, of course, lies in the difference in members' goals, in their institutional environments, and

Table 6.16
House Passage of Major Bills: Education
and Labor, Ways and Means, 1955-1966

Congress	Education and Labor			Ways and Means		
	Bills Reported	*Bills Passed*	*% Bills Passed*	*Bills Reported*	*Bills Passed*	*% Bills Passed*
84th (1955-56)	4	3	75%	14	12	86%
85th (1957-58)	6	5	83%	18	17	94%
86th (1959-60)	6	4	67%	18	17	94%
87th (1961-62)	29	9	31%	27	26	96%
88th (1963-64)	19	12	63%	18	17	94%
89th (1965-66)	32	24	75%	19	18	95%
Totals	96	57	59%	114	107	94%

in the decision-making processes that flow from them. Education
and Labor members' policy goals do not lead them to place a special
value on floor success; they do not feel constrained by the institutional prescriptions of the House; and they do not adopt consensus-
building, influence-preserving internal processes. Their relative lack
of floor success should *not* be viewed invidiously. If it is a price they
must pay for the long-range pursuit of good public policy, they (and
their coalition allies) will deliberately pay it.

In further reference to Table 6.16, committee bills may fail to
pass in two ways. They may be held up in the Committee on Rules.
Or they may be defeated on the floor. We shall discuss the success of
Education and Labor at both stages.

The Rules Committee will stop a bill for one of two reasons —
because its members do not think the bill is good public policy or
because, in the judgment of the party leadership, the bill stands no
chance of passing on the floor.[45] For much of the period studied,
Rules Committee judgments on good public policy were much more
conservative than those espoused by the majority on Education and
Labor. Furthermore, Rules Committee responsiveness to the leadership made its members a good deal more sensitive to problems of
floor success than the members of Education and Labor. On both

[45] See Robert Peabody, "The Enlarged Rules Committee" in R. Peabody and
N. Polsby (eds.) *New Perspectives on the U.S. House of Representatives* (Chicago: Rand McNally, 1963, pp. 129-164; Robert Pratt, "The Taming of the
Shrew: Myth and Politics in the House Committee on Rules," Unpublished
manuscript, Wesleyan University (Middletown, 1969).

counts, the two committees were natural antagonists. The Rules Committee became the graveyard of many Education and Labor bills — more so than for those of any other House committee.[46] And the liberal Democrats on Education and Labor helped lead two successful efforts to reform the Rules Committee — by packing it in 1961 and by passing the 21-day rule in 1965.[47]

Two analyses by Walter Kravitz illuminate this conflict.[48] The first, of the 87th Congress (1961–62), shows that of the twenty-five bills that eventually died in the Rules Committee, nineteen were the products of the Education and Labor Committee. Among them were sixteen of the twenty major bills that Table 6.16 shows failed to pass the House in that Congress. The Rules Committee recorded adverse votes on four of the sixteen; they stopped the other twelve by doing nothing. Since the Rules Committee had just been packed with party regulars, we attribute a good deal of its inaction to leadership doubts concerning likely House passage. The second study, of the first session of the 89th Congress (1965), shows that of all the committees taking advantage of the new twenty-one day rule for bypassing the Rules Committee, far and away the heaviest user was Education and Labor. Of twenty-one resolutions introduced under the rule, fourteen came from Education and Labor. The Committee's running battle with Rules tells us something about the content of Education and Labor decisions. They give distinctively more weight to what the Committee's members and their coalition partners consider to be good public policy; they give distinctively less weight to considerations of success at subsequent stages of the legislative process in the House. The problem is, of course, one of balance. But Ways and Means, which tilts its decisions to the conservative side and which worries about success at later stages, strikes a very different balance from that of Education and Labor. And

---

[46] See Douglas M. Fox and Charles H. Clapp, "The House Rules Committee and the Programs of the Kennedy and Johnson Administration," *Journal of Politics* (November, 1970) pp. 670–671.

[47] Exhibit A in the case against the Rules Committee in 1961 was its action in preventing the House-and-Senate-passed federal aid to education bill of 1960 from going to conference.

[48] Walter Kravitz, "The Influence of the House Rules Committee on Legislation in the 87th Congress," in Joseph S. Clark (ed.) *Congressional Reform: Problems and Prospects* (New York: Crowell, 1965), pp. 127–137; Walter Kravitz, "The Twenty-One Day Rule in the first session of the 89th Congress," Unpublished manuscript, *Legislative Reference Service*, Library of Congress, October 28, 1965.

Ways and Means bills have, therefore, little difficulty getting through the Rules Committee.

As one would expect, Education and Labor decisions may also run into extra difficulty on the House floor. Three federal aid bills (1956, 1957, 1961) were defeated there. Two minimum wage bills (1960, 1961) and the most important labor management bill (1959) were completely emasculated there. None of our other five committees experienced any such difficulty in the chamber. One can, of course, attribute this record to the inherent controversiality of the policy subject, upon which Committee members have no effect. "The subjects are so controversial, you know there's going to be a fight when you get to the floor. There isn't a bill that comes out of this committee — oh, maybe a few — that doesn't touch a difference in philosophy." But we attribute much of the Committee's difficulty to actions taken by Committee members which maintain rather than minimize this inherent controversiality. Such member actions are deliberate — taken in pursuit of decision rules calling for policy partisanship and/or policy individualism. Insofar as they are shaped by strong Democratic-liberal policy partisanship, Committee decisions may activate the blocking, conservative coalition in the chamber — as they did when the minimum wage bills were rewritten *via* the (Paul) Kitchen (Democrat, North Carolina)-(William) Ayres (Republican, Ohio) substitute bills of 1960 and 1961, or as they did when the labor/management bill was rewritten by the (Phil) Landrum (Democrat, Georgia)-(Robert) Griffin (Republican, Michigan) substitute bill of 1959.[49] These floor defeats are often the product of the Committee's policy partisanship plus its unrepresentativeness. One of the two Republicans and one of the two Democrats just mentioned commented: "Everything that comes out of this committee is changed, altered, or killed on the floor. It's not like other committees where the committee bill goes right through. That's because this is a stacked committee." "The Committee is suspect. That's because so many Southern members feel that it is a stacked committee on the Democratic side." In 1972, the Committee Chairman, Carl Perkins (Democrat, Kentucky), opined that he would like "to

[49] For this and other generalizations on the Landrum-Griffin Bill, see Alan K. McAdams, *Power and Politics in Labor Legislation* (New York: Columbia University Press, 1964); Samuel Patterson, *Labor Lobbying and Labor Reform: The Passage of the Landrum-Griffin Act*, Inter-University Case Program (Indianapolis: Bobbs-Merrill, 1966).

see us have a more moderate Southerner or two. It would be helpful in the long run; we could iron out more differences in Committee, with less chance of an upset on the floor." [50]

The policy individualism so prominent in our description of internal Committee process also causes difficulty on the floor, as individual members continue their quest for good public policy. Committee members may upset previously constructed coalitions by introducing issues disruptive of those coalitions — as with the Powell and Wainright antisegregation amendments to the education bills of 1956 and 1957. In such cases, the members' attitude is:

> I tried (my amendment) in the Committee . . . and I'll try it again on the floor. . . . They (the party leadership) tried to talk me out of it before, but they haven't talked to me recently. I just believe in it, that's all.

> Lots of the time . . . if a person has an amendment, he'll hold it back just so we can get the damn bill out of Committee. Then he'll propose it on the floor. We have a lot of amendments. It's not like the Appropriations Committee. There, you don't get a member of the majority proposing an amendment against the bill. They're more disciplined.

This propensity for policy individualism on amendments introduces a great deal of uncertainty into Committee floor performance. "It has been traditional . . . ," said one member, "that when we consider minimum wage legislation, we end up in a great deal of confusion on the floor, often in fact, in seething, swirling, agitated controversy and confusion." [51] Even when the Committee carries a bill without apparent difficulty, those managing the bill remain ever fearful that at any moment some errant Committee member may unexpectedly rise on the floor and threaten the outcome.[52]

[50] Judy Gardner, "Carl D. Perkins: The Poor Are Always With Him," *National Journal*, January 8, 1972, p. 74.

[51] *Congressional Record*, Daily Edition, May 26, 1966, p. 11049. See also the "sneak punch" amendment by one Democrat to a Democratic bill that triggered the comment.

[52] A fine example is the crucial Elementary and Secondary Education Act of 1965 as described in Eidenberg and Morey, *op. cit.* In that case, the errant member was Representative Edith Green. See also the Green Amendment to the Elementary and Secondary Education Act amendments in 1967, which none of her fellow Committee Democrats could understand, and the Green Amendment to the Elementary and Secondary Education Act amendments in 1969, which threatened that bill. *Congressional Record*, Daily Edition, May 23, 1967, pp. H5932–5956, and April 23, 1969, pp. H2972–2983.

It does not diminish committee difficulty on the floor that its individual members are especially talented. "This Committee is the brightest committee in the House," exclaimed one veteran member. "What an array of talent!" Committee talent seems to be expressed as much individually as collectively. A man who sits on both Education and Labor and Interior commented:

> The overall quality of the Education and Labor members is higher than Interior. Its intellectual level is a cut above Interior. Even so, even with this, there's a greater tendency to trust Interior on the floor. The guys on the floor don't have the confidence in Education and Labor.

A top executive official, experienced in dealing with Ways and Means and Education and Labor discussed them in a similar vein saying:

> I have never thought . . . that the level of intelligence was as high on Ways and Means as it was on some of the other committees. IQ-wise, I don't think they are very outstanding; yet they report excellent bills. Adam Powell, for example, is much smarter than ninety-five per cent of those on Ways and Means. . . . He and Edith Green are two of the smartest people in Congress. Yet they don't bring out particularly good legislation. I don't mean Wilbur Mills isn't smart — he is. . . . But I'd say Ways and Means averages out to about C+. So you have a C+ committee that reports out A legislation.

He then went on to compare the floor performance of the two committees in such a way as to highlight the policy individualism of Education and Labor:

> When congressmen see Wilbur Mills bringing out a bill, they know certain things. They know Wilbur Mills has done his homework. They know the Ways and Means Committee has worked on the bill. And with the closed rule and all, they can be sure the Committee has the situation well in hand. . . . When an Education and Labor bill is on the floor, things are so confused that the Members don't even know who is in charge of the bill. There are amendments coming out of your ears. . . . From the beginning every bill is accompanied by bickering. Powell, Mrs. (Edith) Green, (Carl)

Perkins, and (John) Brademas are all talking at once, vying to see who will get what. And it shakes the confidence of the Members of the House.

Everything we have previously said about the two Committees inclines us to believe the thrust of this description. A set of decisions coming from an influence-seeking, House-oriented, corporate Committee will be packaged for the floor more carefully than will a set of decisions emerging from a policy-seeking, non-House-oriented, individualistic committee.

Education and Labor decisions, we conclude, give plenty of evidence of having been shaped by the Committee's decision rules — rules calling for policy partisanship and policy individualism. At the same time, it is also clear that these particular rules help produce a pattern of decisions far less stable and far less predictable than the ones made by the first three (and the next two) committees. Obviously, most Committee decisions will leave *some* Committee members and *some* environmental groups deeply dissatisfied. But as for the overall pattern of decisions, there appears to be a good deal of acceptance and, hence, less dissatisfaction. Everyone involved knows that he operates within constraints — particularly, electoral results — over which he has little control. Committee members know, in particular, that they operate as cogs within much larger policy coalitions. Win or lose, they accept Committee decision patterns, with all their unpredictability, as coalition-produced — as decisions to which they make, and to which they are *content* to make, a very limited contribution. Political scientists writing case studies involving Education and Labor typically comment on the singular lack of Committee influence on decision making. And they are inclined to view this fact as somewhat abnormal. Thus Eugene Eidenberg and Roy Morey, writing about the Elementary and Secondary Education Act of 1965, stress "this peculiar 'surrender' of congressional autonomy over a vital phase in the decision-making." [53] As Education and Labor members view their participation in the process, their limited contribution is neither peculiar nor a surrender. It is the normal operation of a highly permeable committee.

Education and Labor members express none of the dissatisfactions and frustrations with their Committee's performance that Foreign Affairs members do. They appear to be well satisfied, therefore, with

[53] Eidenberg and Morey, *op. cit.*, p. 77.

the achievement of their goal of policy involvement and policy influence. But, again, their involvement and their influence are achieved *within policy coalitions.* Education and Labor members do not normally assess their Committee's performance at all. They relate their satisfactions and dissatisfactions, instead, to their coalition's performance. They express less of a sense of institutional identity than the members of any of our six committees. And because their environment is so penetrable, they do not express that desire for an institutional identity that Foreign Affairs members, faced with a less penetrable environment, do express. The psychic attachments of Education and Labor members run to their coalition allies and not to their fellow committee members. They have no pride-producing internal processes and none which they would not willingly alter, if they could, on behalf of their coalition allies. Education and Labor members, for example, affect neither superiority (as do Appropriations and Ways and Means members) nor inferiority (as do Foreign Affairs members) toward their counterpart Senate Committee. They view the members of Labor and Public Welfare simply as fellow policy coalition members, pursuing the same goals, in the same environment, with the same decision rules. Conference committee bargaining between them, we suspect, is almost always policy bargaining and almost never institutional bargaining. That is to say, Education and Labor conferees do not go to conference feeling any special obligation to uphold the position of the House. "Nine times out of ten, they go there already committed to sell out the position of the House," claimed a Republican Committee member.[54] The percentages may be exaggerated, but the position it describes — relative, say, to that of Appropriations or Ways and Means Conferees — is accurate. Certainly the members of neither the House nor the Senate Committee offered any systematic differentiation between their respective policy products; the question of "who wins" in conference seemed a meaningless one for both groups. So long as the coalitions to which they belong are working for good public policy and so long as they can participate fully in those coalitions, most Education and Labor members will be reasonably well satisfied with the pattern of decisions we have observed. This is particularly so with the option of policy individualism always present as a safety valve for individual members' frustrations.

[54] *Congressional Record*, Daily Edition, March 8, 1972, p. H1844.

In terms of satisfaction with the pattern of Committee decisions, interested outsiders are probably somewhat less satisfied than the members themselves. We say this because their expectations call for greater predictability of results than do the expectations of committee members — many of whom are content simply to be "where the action is." Executive officials, who prescribe a legitimating function for congressional committees, complain, as we have seen, about the uncertainties of Committee members and of Committee decision making. For party leaders, who believe that winning on the House floor is the way to win elections (and keep themselves influential), the Committee probably presents more ambiguous cases than they wish. For clientele groups, who want sympathetic spokesmen on congressional committees, the Education and Labor Committee's distinctive permeability is probably most satisfactory. But its policy individualism may produce greater volatility (as in the Landrum-Griffin case) than clientele groups would prefer.

These various problems arise, however, precisely because Committee members are so easily swayed by their coalition allies and have so little decision-making autonomy. Paradoxically, so long as their various coalition partners want the members of the Education and Labor Committee to function within policy coalitions, for that long will those same partners have to endure the unpredictability of the Committee's performance. It seems likely, therefore, that the instability of Education and Labor decision patterns will continue despite the mixed satisfactions of the various participants.

POST OFFICE AND CIVIL SERVICE

Post Office members see their committee assignment as helpful to them in serving their constituents and in achieving re-election. The dominant environmental influences are two clusters of clientele groups, whose policy expectations usually combine to generate a conflict-free set of constraints. Secondarily, Committee members are subject to the influence of the executive branch, whose policy expectations tend to be diametrically opposed to those held by the clientele groups. Since the clientele groups — especially the postal employees — are most helpful to them in meeting their electoral goals, the Committee members' first decision rule calls for responsiveness to clientele expectations — for larger pay increases and lower postal rates. The Committee's second, fallback rule calls for a compromise responsiveness to presidential-executive branch expectations — for smaller pay increases and higher postal rates. When their internal processes seemed to be impeding their full responsiveness to clientele interests and limiting their influence with the executive branch, committee members established a new set of decision processes. We would expect the pattern of their decisions to be prefigured in the push and pull of their two decision rules.

Table 6.17 displays Post Office Committee decisions on the nine postal employee pay increase bills passed by Congress from 1955 to 1966. And it compares House Committee decisions with the policy expectations of the two key environmental groups, the President and executive branch and the clientele group leader, the National Association of Letter Carriers.[55] Table 6.17 also compares House Committee decisions with those of the Senate Committee, the conference committee, and final presidential action. The standard of comparison used is the average pay increase allowed postal employees as a result of each proposal or decision. While, admittedly, this is not all there is to a pay bill — which is a very complex piece of legislation involving, among other things, classification, fringe benefits, timing — the pay increase is the heart of the bill, and the average percentage increase is an evaluative measure commonly used by the participants.[56] The nine bills listed in Table 6.17 make up the largest — and, we think, the most important — single set of decisions made by the Post Office Committee in the period studied.

Table 6.17 makes strikingly clear the pattern of environmental conflict to which the Post Office Committee ordinarily responds. On every bill (save the negotiated settlement of 1955) the sharpest controversy in pay policy is that between the executive branch and the National Association of Letter Carriers. Invariably, Committee decisions are made in this contxet of basic antagonism. Said one Committee veteran:

> Year after year since 1945, instead of the Bureau of the Budget, the Committee and the representatives of the employees getting together and negotiating and trying to find out

[55] In all cases where the position of the National Federation of Post Office Clerks was readily available, it was the same as that of the National Association of Letter Carriers.

[56] The main sources of these figures are the relevant *Congressional Quarterly Almanacs*. To fill in the blanks, Committee hearings, floor debates, and newspaper accounts were also used.

Table 6.17
Average Postal Pay Increases 1955-1966:
House Committee and Other Participants' Decisions

Year	Congress	Executive	NALC	House Committee	Senate Committee	Final Bill	Presidential Action
1955 #1	84th	6.5%	10%	7.6%[1]	10%	8.6%	vetoed
1955 #2	84th	8%	8%	8%	8%	8%	signed
1957	85th	0	12.5%	12.5%	11.5%[5]	12.5%	vetoed
1958	85th	6%	12.5%	12.5%[2]	12.5%	10%	signed
1960	86th	0	12%	8.4%	8.4%	8.4%	vetoed and overriden
1962	87th	8.2 (3 steps)	14% (2 steps)	13.9% (2 steps)	11.2% (2 steps)	11.2% (2 steps)	signed
1964	88th	3%	6%	5.6%	5.6%	5.6%	signed
1965	89th	3%	7%	4.5%[3]	3.6%	3.6%	signed
1966	89th	2.4%	2.9%[4]	2.9%[4]	2.9%[4]	2.9%[4]	signed

[1] Raised to 8.2% on floor by Committee Democrats.
[2] From 1957 bill; Committee did not consider pay raise until conference in 1958.
[3] Dropped to 4% on floor by Committee Democrats.
[4] To take effect 6 months earlier than Administration proposed.
[5] House bill taken to floor instead of Committee bill.

the right thing to do, we have had to have these tests of strength. Instead of getting the right answers, we are getting answers that come out of conflict.[57]

The Administration and the clientele groups do not ordinarily consult one another prior to initiating action on pay increases. As a Post Office Department executive said: "That would be an exercise in futility. . . . They are never satisfied. . . . They want everything." And in their adversary "tests of strength," they frequently employ some of the harshest weapons of legislative combat — the discharge petition by clientele groups and the presidential veto by the executive.

Post Office decision rules tell us that Committee members will give primary allegiance to the clientele groups. Table 6.17 furnishes confirming evidence. In seven of the eight clientele-Administration conflicts, the Committee decision on pay increases is closer to the desires of the clientele groups than it is to those of the Administration.

On the evidence of Table 6.17, the Senate Post Office Committee has also followed a decision rule highly supportive of clientele demands. In every instance, their pay decisions were closer to clientele than to executive branch requests. Earlier we suggested (on the basis of interview assertions) that Senate Committee members would be slightly less attached than House Committee members to this prime decision rule. Table 6.17 cannot settle the matter either way. But the evidence does lean in the suggested direction. The House Committee bill was closer to clientele expectations than the Senate Committee bill was, three times — 1957, 1962, 1965. The Senate Committee bill was closer to clientele expectations once — in 1955. Also the House Committee appears more often as the prime mover in Congress, for it initiated clientele demands (see underlined entries) in six of the nine years and in five of the six Congresses. House Committee leadership was the strongest in the years when the executive opposed all pay increases — 1957 and 1960. Furthermore, the presidential veto of 1955 (1957 was a pocket veto) was upheld by the Senate. The larger view of Table 6.17 is, however, one of House and Senate Committees pursuing the identical decision rule and working cooperatively with clientele groups to secure the largest possible pay increases.

[57] 103 *Congressional Record*, p. 12334.

Postal employee groups want and get sympathetic Committee members to recommend favorable legislation. But they also want something more. They want their Committee spokesmen — and we speak now about the House Committee — to pave their path at each and every subsequent stage in the legislative process. In addition, that is, to favorable substantive decisions, they want favorable procedural decisions as well. Some members of the House Committee must superintend the movement of each bill through formal legislative channels and must legitimate combat at each juncture. House members are not likely to join a legislative battle unless it has been staged and structured by some members of the duly authorized committee. Since clientele groups in the field of postal legislation are typically working counter to executive branch wishes, their legislative path is especially difficult. And they are in particular need of Committee members who will run legitimating, procedural interference for them. Their staunchest Committee allies — a minority of the group — gladly meet this need.

When, for example, pro-Administration Chairman Murray refused to act in 1957 and 1960, strong clientele supporters blasted a bill out of their own Committee via the difficult (218 member signatures) discharge petition. With the threat of a presidential veto hanging over their heads — in 1955, 1957, 1960, 1965 — Committee allies of the clientele groups nonetheless brought a clientele-backed pay bill to the floor and pushed it through the House. In 1960, the Committee's efficient minority led the successful fight to override the President's veto — one of only two overrides in the eight Eisenhower years.

The clientele-Committee member alliance has won some spectacular victories in the House. Indeed, only one postal pay bill was defeated on any kind of vote in the House in twelve years. And that loss had nothing whatever to do with the postal segment of the bill.[58] Strictly in terms of winning, the Post Office Committee has as excellent a record of floor success as any of our six Committees — certainly it does on postal pay. It does not, however, command the other ingredient of floor success — the esteem of the House. "I don't think they respect the Post Office Committee," say Committee members. "They laugh at us." The Committee's contribution to its floor

---

[58] The first version of the 1964 pay bill was defeated in the House because Congressmen were unwilling to vote themselves a large pay raise in an election year. A second bill, with the same postal benefits and a lower congressional pay increase, passed later in the year.

record is primarily procedural. Its members provide the clientele groups with legitimate transportation to each successive battlefield; the clientele groups do the serious fighting. On the floor, Committee spokesmen (or mouthpieces) certify as to clientele approval or disapproval of each item before the House. Floor victories are not the direct result of Post Office Committee advocacy. They are the result of prodigious, effective lobbying efforts by the postal employee unions in face-to-face contact with individual members of the House.

A high-ranking Post Office Department executive summarized:

> The pressure from the postal employee groups is terrific — just terrific. They are the best-organized union in the world. . . . When they want to turn on the heat, they are almost unbeatable. They pass bills over the President's veto. They get discharge petitions out like no other group can do. . . . The Post Office employees have carried every pay bill in the Congress for the last fifteen years.[59]

It is acknowledged by all participants that the postal workers "carry the ball" and that all other federal employees "ride on their backs" in getting pay raises. And it is an indicator of postal employee influence that whenever there was any disparity between the average pay increase given to the postal employees and that given to all the other Civil Service employees (i.e., those in the "classified" schedule) the disparity was in favor of the postal employees. As Table 6.18 shows, such was the case in five of the eight years.

Table 6.18
Average Percentage of Pay Increases for Postal Employees
and Classified Federal Employees: 1955–1966

Year	1955	1957	1958	1960	1962	1964	1965	1966
Postal Employees	8%	12.5%	10%	8.4%	11.2%	5.6%	3.6%	2.9%
Classified Employees	7.5%	11.0%	10%	7.5%	9.6%	4.3%	3.6%	2.9%

House Committee member Joel Broyhill, representing a nearby Virginia district mainly populated by civil servants, lauded clientele power, in this vein:

> I represent probably the largest number of classified employees of any member of Congress, and I certainly recognize that without the leadership, drive, and organization on the

---

[59] See also President Eisenhower's less admiring account of employee "pressure" in his veto message of 1960, in 106 *Congressional Record*, p. 15184.

part of postal employees, and *letter carriers particularly*, we would not have had as many pay adjustments in my eleven years in Congress as we have had. So I commend the postal employees for supporting other employees coming into the bill and riding their backs, so to speak, in getting these pay raises.[60]

A member of the Senate Committee spoke similarly to the National Association of Letter Carriers, saying:

You letter carriers are the organization and muscle of the postal workers and federal employees of this country. You have personally been responsible for 90 per cent of the pay raises and other beneficial legislation for federal employees approved in recent years.[61]

The letter carriers' officials concur in these estimates of their prowess. Publicly they speak of themselves as "the most aggressive and most influential of all postal organizations," with "a position of dominance and respect unequaled by any other voluntary labor organization in or out of the government," and as a group which "as a matter of survival . . . has had to develop to a very fine point the gentle art of lobbying." [62] Privately they say:

This organization is the most powerful one in the field. We are the bell cow. Most of the legislation is written right here. We carry the load for the rest of the federal government. . . . We have the most powerful lobby of any group, labor or management, in Washington.

This string of encomiums to the postal employees contains neither hint nor mention of their Committee allies.

On the House (and Senate) floor, as elsewhere, the Post Office Committee remains clientele-dominated. Its members make a necessary but very insufficient contribution to the success of the alliance. The proportion of Committee to environmental contributions to floor victory is the reverse of what it is with the Ways and Means and Appropriations Committees. Post Office is, paradoxically, a winning but not an influential committee. It does not make indepen-

---

[60] Committee on Post Office and Civil Service, *Hearings on Federal Employees Salary Act of 1963, U.S. House of Representatives*, 88th Congress, 1st Session (Washington: U.S. Government Printing Office, 1963), p. 117.

[61] *Congressional Quarterly Almanac*, 1965, p. 649.

[62] William C. Doherty, *Mailman USA* (New York: David McKay, 1960), pp. 189, 21–22.

dent decisions and *it* does not carry its decisions in the chamber. Clientele groups make the weightiest contribution to floor victories, by acting directly to influence House members — many of whom, incidentally, are alumni of the Post Office Committee and have retained their clientele contacts.

To this point, we have described Committee member adherence to their primary decision rule. But on occasion, they repair strategically to the second rule. The occasion comes when they and their clientele allies deem it prudent to compromise with the President, for fear that a test of strength may cause them to lose everything. These compromises come in two varieties. In one kind, Committee spokesmen and employee groups decide to scale down the level of the pay raise to avoid a certain presidential veto, which they are convinced they cannot override. In the other kind, Committee members agree to accept a minimal postal rate increase in exchange for executive support for a pay bill.

The best examples of the straight pay raise compromise are the bills of 1955, 1965, and 1966. In 1955, as Table 6.17 shows, the Senate Committee-House Committee-clientele alliance bargained to an 8 per cent increase after President Eisenhower had demonstrated, on an earlier bill, the will and the capacity to block any pay legislation he did not like.[63] In 1965, despite President Johnson's strongly voiced opposition, the Committee voted twenty to three, in favor of a 4.5 per cent increase. But, when the President brandished his veto, Committee spokesmen introduced an amendment to their bill on the floor, dropping the figure to 4 per cent. Urging its House passage, its Committee sponsor gave voice to the group's second decision rule: "In view of the realities . . . we are either going to reduce HR10281 to 4 per cent and get a bill this year or we are going to stand pat and get no bill." [64] When presidential opposition persisted, Senate Committee leaders invoked the same rule in scaling the increase down to 3.6 per cent. The Senate Chairman said, "We've got to come up with a bill that is acceptable to the President." [65] In 1966, rather than fight, Committee and clientele groups agreed early on a 2.9 per cent pay increase that would meet President Johnson's guidelines — despite the organized letter carriers' position that a 7 per cent increase was "fully justified." [66] Afterward, the House Com-

---

[63] Eisenhower had also successfully vetoed a pay raise bill in 1954.
[64] *Congressional Quarterly Almanac, 1965*, p. 2026.
[65] *Washington Star*, October 6, 1965, p. A2.
[66] Committee on Post Office and Civil Service, *Hearings on Federal Salaries*

mittee's effective chairman, James Morrison, spoke to the National
Association of Letter Carriers' convention and described their strategic fallback to the second decision rule. He said:

> You didn't want the bill you got. I didn't want it. Jerome
> Keating (NALC President) didn't want it. But you realized
> that it was this or nothing at all. . . . You had the wisdom
> to take all you could possibly get this year . . . and next
> year we're going to go back and take the rest! [67]

In that "next year," 1967, it might be added, a familiar scenario was
enacted — a pay raise bill followed by a presidential veto, then a
combination reduced-pay-raise and postal-rate-increase bill followed
by a presidential signature.

On the record of Table 6.17, it appears that Committee members
were somewhat more likely to invoke their second decision rule in
dealing with a Democratic than with a Republican President. They
calculated that a Democratic veto was more likely than a Republican
veto to be upheld by the Democratic majority in Congress. Besides
this, since a majority of the Committee and most of the letter carriers'
leaders were Democrats, they were more cross-pressured in fighting
with a Johnson than with an Eisenhower. Though not the controlling factor in the Committee's strategic decisions, partisanship
was contributory.

The two best examples of the postal pay/postal rate kind of compromise are the combination bills of 1958 and 1962. As noted earlier,
the executive branch consistently advocates increased postal rates to
offset increased postal pay. And it sometimes takes the position: no
rate increase, no pay increase. This is the position the Eisenhower
Administration took in the 85th Congress and the Kennedy Administration took in the 87th. Both backed their stand by first vetoing
a postal pay increase bill — Eisenhower a major one, Kennedy a
minor one.[68] These policy expectations of the executive branch run
counter to those of the postal employees, who do not want their pay
increases to be dependent on a rate increase and who do not accept
the idea that their working conditions should be governed by the

---

and Fringe Benefits, House of Representatives, 89th Congress, 2nd Session
(Washington: U.S. Government Printing Office, 1966), p. 58.

[67] *Postal Record* (September, 1966), p. 25.

[68] Kennedy vetoed a 1961 bill that increased pay by changing provisions for
longevity in the postal service. Since it was not comparable with the other pay
bills in Table 6.17, it was omitted.

Table 6.19
Postal Rate Decisions 1962: Additional Revenue
and Public Service Write-off (in millions)

	Executive	House Committee #1	#2	Senate Committee	Final
First Class	437.8	437.8	437.8	437.8	437.8
Airmail	17.3	17.3	17.3	21.2	21.2
Second Class	90.6	17.4	53.4	26.6	27.3
Third Class	181.6	71.8	93.0[1]	97.2	93.7
Total New Revenue	727.3	544.3	601.5	582.8	580.0
Public Service Write-off	74.0	235.0	247.8	373.0	373.0

[1] Raised to 161.9 on House floor.

financial status of the postal service. But, even more, these expectations are opposed by the second cluster of postal clientele groups —
the postal users. These groups, too — especially the third class mailers — also have their House Committee spokesmen. These spokesmen
will do their best to avoid the raising of postal rates altogether. As
Chairman Murray lamented: "It's the easiest thing in the world to
get a salary bill approved by Congress, but the most difficult task to
get approval of a postal rate bill." [69] "Ever since I have been a member
of the Post Office Committee, I have endeavored to raise the postal
rates. Since my membership in 1943, we have been able to increase
the postal rates only once in 1949 and once in 1951." [70] Once the
executive convincingly frames the problem as "no rate increase, no
pay increase," Committee members will enact a rate increase.[71] But,
faithful to their first decision rule, they will be as responsive as possible to the expectations of their postal user allies by minimizing
rate increases.

Table 6.19 displays the postal rate decisions of the House Committee and other participants in the combined federal salary/postal
rate bill of 1962. In explanation, the original Kennedy Administration proposals, shown in the first column of the table, were made
in 1961 — to which the House Committee responded with its bill
#1. The Committee brought the bill to the floor under a closed rule;
when the rule lost, the party leadership, fearing defeat, withdrew the

[69] 102 *Congressional Record*, p. 11946.
[70] 103 *Congressional Record*, p. 14599.
[71] The bargains are described in *Congressional Quarterly Almanac*, 1958,
p. 208; *Congressional Quarterly Almanac*, 1962, p. 363.

bill entirely. After consultation with the Administration, the Committee reported out bill #2 in 1962. By that time, the Senate Committee, which had been balking for a year at the idea of any rate increases, agreed to recommend a rate increase — which it did. The key elements in the rate decision (a few minor ones have been omitted) are: first class and airmail rates, second class rates (for magazines and periodicals), and third class rates (for advertising, i.e., "junk mail," and nonprofit group mailings). The public service write-off is the amount of the postal deficit which can be charged against the general treasury (on the grounds that the postal system performs certain public services), thus reducing the operating deficit of the system. In effect, this write-off is a government subsidy of those postal users who are not paying their own way. And these users are the second class and third class mailers, who traditionally have not paid rates sufficient to cover the cost of handling their mail. The higher the public service allocation, the better these postal users like it. The terms of the argument here revolve around whether the postal system should be regarded as a business (in which case it should not run at a deficit) or as a public service operation (in which case a deficit is acceptable). On this matter, the executive branch has opted for the first position while the subsidized user groups have opted for the second.

Table 6.19 does not describe clientele expectations; since they are on the defensive, they do not usually set a figure. Users naturally do not want any increase and they typically argue that any increase constitutes a threatening burden to their business. The implication of their testimony is that any increase should be kept to a minimum. House Committee support for the clientele position can be read into its consistent reduction in executive proposals for additional revenue. Since first class and airmail users are totally unorganized (and more than pay their own way), both Committees are likely to assent to executive proposals here.[72] In the face of the pleas of the large magazine publishing firms, direct mail advertisers, and nonprofit organizations, both Committees reduce executive proposals for higher postal rates on second class and third class mail. And, in further support of clientele group expectations, both Committees increase executive proposals for the amount of the public service write-off. Both

---

[72] In 1958, the House Committee refused to enact the Administration's request for a special five-cent nonlocal, first class rate. The Senate agreed, but the House position prevailed in conference.

House and Senate Committees in 1962, anyway, appeared to respond equally favorably to clientele groups in making these decisions. In conference their compromises were most favorable to the postal users — on the low side regarding postal rates and on the high side regarding the public service write-off. Within the context, then, of their fallback, compromise-with-the-executive decision rule, both Committees followed their preferred, support-the-clientele-groups decision rule.

House (and Senate) Post Office Committee decisions follow a stable, predictable pattern. Each year, in the words of a House Committee veteran: "The situation is somewhat like an old movie shown on television. You watch it thinking you have never seen it; but, nonetheless, you have a strong feeling it has all happened before." [73] Given the consistent, clientele-inclined nature of the pattern, clientele groups have every reason to be satisfied — overall, if not in each case. And so far as we could tell, they were. Officials of the executive branch, on the other hand, have less reason to be satisfied overall. And so far as we could tell, they were not. It was from the executive branch that demands for a wholesale reorganization of the postal service and a whole new pattern of decisions would, eventually, come.[74]

As for the members, the Committee's efficient minority of staunch clientele spokesmen seem satisfied that these decisions help them to achieve their individual constituency-service, re-election goals. "The postal workers in my district will do anything," said one member. "They're restricted, of course, by the Hatch Act — but their wives aren't. They have been good to me . . . and are they ever powerful." Another said he would advise each new Committee member "to look around and see what he has in his district and see if he can't forge a union with the letter carriers." He added, "They've been awfully important to me." Another called Post Office "a darn good political committee — not the government workers so much as the letter carriers. . . ." The following 1965 newspaper account reported:

> (Senate Committee member Ralph Yarborough) who was
> re-elected to the Senate last November after a bitter battle,

[73] 106 *Congressional Record*, p. 12694.

[74] For an end-of-the-period summary, see Meg Greenfield, "What's the Matter With the Mails?" *Reporter*, February 11, 1965. For a brief discussion of the postal reorganization of 1970, see the Epilogue.

credits the 10,000 letter carriers in Texas with being the deciding factor in his victory. Addressing the pay raise rally of the National Association of Letter Carriers . . . Yarborough said his re-election resulted primarily from the help "of my good wife and the 10,000 letter carriers who were walking and talking. . . ." [75]

In 1966 the entire cluster of clientele groups sponsored an "appreciation lunch" (suggested contribution, $50) in Helena, Montana to assist a key Committee spokesman, Arnold Olsen, in a difficult re-election fight. Washington cosponsors of the fund-raising event were the National Association of Letter Carriers and of the Association of Third Class Mailers. Said the latter:

> I'm helping out on this thing for a very simple reason. All the lobbyists interested in mail rates are interested in having friends in Washington. Whether they're Democrats or Republicans, we want to keep them there. So we sit down and ask for personal donations. Arnold Olsen . . . he's a pal. If he wins, he's going to hold hearings on these new zip code regulations.[76]

The National Association of Letter Carriers donated one of its top staff members to run Olsen's campaign. He won.

In that same year, the postal organizations sponsored a number of fund-raising efforts to re-elect Representative James Morrison, regarded by the letter carriers' organization as "the Postal Worker's greatest champion" and slated to become the Committee's new chairman come 1967. One such dinner alone raised $80,000. He lost — thereby indicating there were limits to postal clientele electoral power, in this case their inability to overcome the impact of Morrison's votes for the 1965 Civil Rights Bill on his Louisiana constituents.[77] After his defeat, Speaker McCormack extolled Morrison's Committee-based constituency service, saying, "If anyone in Congress knew how to go about obtaining improvements in a congressional district's postal facilities, it was Jimmy Morrison" — to

[75] *Washington Star*, June 22, 1965, p. A2.
[76] *Washington Post*, September 26, 1966, pp. 1, 14A.
[77] See Postal Record, *op. cit.*, p. 24; *Washington Post, op. cit.*; *Washington Star*, May 5, 1965, p. A2; *Washington Post*, August 21, 1967, pp. A15; A16. A full account of the testimonial dinner will be found in *The Register*, Baton Rouge, Louisiana, May 15, 1965.

the tune of more than 1.6 million dollars in the four years preceding his defeat.[78] Committee-derived constituency service clearly cannot insure continuous re-election. But it is hard to see how it can do anything but help. And that is all the interested individual member wants from his Committee membership.

Constituency-re-election payoffs to Committee members help stabilize Committee decision patterns. At the same time, however, members' satisfaction is neither so deep nor so widespread as to provide a strong guarantee of that stability. Table 6.5, which records the reasons for leaving each committee, confirms the frailty of member satisfactions. For one thing, a great many members (the largest number of the six committees) transfer to other committees. What they want most from the Committee, it seems, is to get off it. While on it, many of them are likely to remain markedly disinterested. Another large group (again the largest of the six committees) loses at the polls. This may seem an ironic result for a re-election-oriented committee. In partial explanation, the Committee is probably used by party leaders as a dumping ground for new members whose re-election chances (and, perhaps, talents) already appear dim. But insofar as this high casualty rate accurately reflects the limitations of clientele group help, many committee members will be reluctant to marry their fate to the work of the clientele groups. Lack of interest and high turnover combine to kill the growth of that institutional pride that can reinforce members' satisfaction and, hence, stabilize decision patterns. Postal committee members have a sense of group identity — but it is the identity of a low-energy, low-influence, low-prestige committee. Some of that self-image began to be dissipated by the internal changes of 1965. But a positive sense of self-esteem would only come after an accumulated record of performance.

As the period ended, therefore, allegiance to Committee decision patterns was probably strong among that minority of the members who had made a big investment in their clientele group relations. But allegiance was probably weak among that majority of members who had not yet made or did not plan to make any such investment. So long as environmental influences held constant, this minority/ majority equipoise would underwrite the stability of Committee decisions. But only, as we shall see, for that long.

[78] *Congressional Record*, Daily Edition, October 25, 1966, p. A5577.

INTERIOR AND INSULAR AFFAIRS

Congressmen are attracted to the Interior Committee, as they are to Post Office, for constituency service-re-election reasons. But they come to Interior with a great deal more positive enthusiasm — as self-starters, not (like Post Office) as assignees. And more of them participate actively as policy entrepreneurs. Interior, again like Post Office, operates within a clientele-dominated environment. But the clientele expectations directed toward Interior are more plural in origin, more discrete in content, and more district-bound in impact. Interior Committee decision rules reflect these differences. The primary decision rule calls for the equitable processing of all constituency-related bills, from Committee member and House member, from Democrat and Republican alike. The second one calls, in controversial cases, for a balancing of conflicting clientele interests — with a tilt in favor of the commercial users of natural resources. These rules help explain the Committee's decision-making process. They also help explain the pattern of Committee decisions.

In the eyes of Interior members, the distinctive feature of their Committee activity is the large volume of bills they process. "Interior handles more pieces of legislation than any other committee in the House. If you include all the private bills, Judiciary does, but . . . you can't count them." Table 6.20 compares the volume of bills, referred and reported, public and private, for our six committees in the 89th Congress.[79] Ways and Means confronts the largest number of initial legislative proposals. Interior, however, reports out the highest percentage of the proposals referred to it for action.[80] And, in absolute terms, it reports out the greatest number of bills. Assuming that the number of bills reported out of a committee is a reasonably accurate indicator of the number of bills formally acted upon by that committee, Interior does "process" or "handle" the largest number of bills of our six committees. Given the Committee's key decision rule, this is just about what one would expect. The volume of individual bills turned out by the Committee is the distinctive result of a prior strategic decision to process all constituency-related bills.

[79] Each committee is its own source. I assume the criteria are the same and I assume the figures include both public and private bills.

[80] The disparity in "bills reported" between Interior and Ways and Means would be even greater — 120 bills to 81 bills — if private bills were excluded.

Table 6.20
Volume of Bills Referred and Reported:
Six Committees, 89th Congress

	Bills and Resolutions Referred to Committee	*Bills and Resolutions Reported by Committee*
Interior	1057	130
Ways and Means	3161	109
Education and Labor	950	51
Post Office	870	48
Foreign Affairs	364	34
Appropriations	*	32

*Does not entertain bills and resolutions from outside sources.

Obviously, these figures concerning volume bear no relation whatever to the substantive importance of the decisions. Indeed, that is precisely the distinction Interior members draw by emphasizing sheer volume. The vast number of bills handled by Interior are noncontroversial in substance and minor in scope. But they are constituency-related bills perceived to be of considerable value to the individual member — the very kind of legislative product that attracted members to the Committee in the first place. As Chairman Aspinall put it once, on the floor:

> These bills which the Committee on Interior and Insular Affairs of the House bring to you today may not be the most important bills nationally or internationally that could be brought before this body, but nevertheless I wish to say that they are important bills as far as certain areas of our Nation are concerned and as far as certain members of this body are concerned.[81]

A majority of these "little bills" that "don't amount to much" come to the House floor under special procedures designed to move noncontroversial matters along as quickly as possible. A member explains, "I'd say about sixty per cent of our bills or more are put on (the) consent calendar or (come up under) suspension (of the rules)." In the first case, unanimous consent is expected; in the second case, objections by less than one-third of the House are expected.

[81] *Congressional Record*, Daily Edition, February 16, 1966, p. 3052.

A nonpartisan distribution of bills is a further concomitant of quick passage. A subcommittee chairman summed it up:

> I'll bring to the floor sometimes as many as seven bills and they'll all pass by unanimous consent. One day I brought up nine, and they all passed by unanimous consent. . . . If I have six bills, I let the member from the state introduce it. If he's a Democrat, fine; if he's a Republican, I'll offer it to him and let him put his name on it.

From 1957 to 1966, eight hundred and thirty-four Interior bills passed the House. Only forty-two of those bills, or about one in twenty, produced as much as *one* roll call vote.

Table 6.21 describes, for five Congresses, the stable pattern of the many minor Interior Committee decisions. Using *Congressional Quarterly's* designation of "major bills," it appears that an average of less than ten per cent of Interior Committee legislation is of "major" or national significance. The sharp increase of "major" matters from Interior in the 89th Congress may presage the ecological awareness of the later 1960's and 1970's. But even there, the Committee's eighteen per cent of "major bills" is still far below the one hundred per cent for Appropriations, the sixty-two per cent for Education and Labor, and the fifty per cent for Foreign Affairs, in that same Congress. The final column of Table 6.21 lists the number of original proposals having content that has been treated in one or more of the bills reported out of Committee. Many policy demands, that is, duplicate one another. The figure is one regularly prepared by the Committee itself as evidence, presumably, of the large percentage of policy expectations actually met by the Committee. Summing up the yearly totals in the column, it appears that the Interior Committee met nearly two thousand separate House policy demands in a ten-year period. This suggests that members had an even greater degree of success in implementing their first decision rule than one could infer simply from the number of bills reported.

Both of the Committee's decision rules and its decision-making processes emphasize success on the House floor. Interior members must get their bills passed if they are to reap electoral benefits. But their regional unrepresentativeness threatens such passage. Therefore they cultivate House confidence by the careful, orderly processing of bills, the minimization of partisanship, the emphasis on special-

Table 6.21
Some Characteristics of Interior Committee
Decisions: 85th–89th Congresses

Congress	Year	Bills and Resolutions Referred	Bills and Resolutions Reported	No. of "Major Bills" Reported	% of "Major Bills" Reported	No. of Bills Referred "Dealt With" in Bills Reported
85th	(1957–58)	865	218	8	4%	450
86th	(1959–60)	926	177	9	5%	375
87th	(1961–62)	909	181	14	7%	365
88th	(1963–64)	862	164	13	4%	357
89th	(1965–66)	1057	130	23	18%	392

ized expertise, the stress on Committee independence of the executive, the internal effort to conciliate non-Western members of the Committee, and the external effort to portray subsequent Committee decisions as national in outlook. Floor success is evidence, therefore, of success in implementing Committee decision rules. And from everything we can discern, the Committee *is* markedly successful on the House floor. In 1965, Wayne Aspinall said that since he had become Chairman (in 1959), he had "only lost two bills — two inconsequential bills." Since, by Congressional Quarterly's generous classification, no major Committee bill was defeated during that period, the two losses must, indeed, have been minor. As for the rest of the Committee's minor bills, we assume they pass without difficulty. Of the Committee's major bills, only *three* were lost on the floor during the 1955–1966 period — one in 1955, one in 1956, and one in 1958. And each of the three subsequently passed. Eleven major bills were held up on their way to the floor by the Committee leadership and/or the Rules Committee and/or the House leadership. Typically, the delay lasted for only one year. Seven of the eleven passed in the succeeding Congress.[82]

Interior members are unanimously agreed on the fact of their floor success — both in terms of carrying their bills and of holding the esteem of their colleagues. "Everything the Committee reports goes through without a snag. I think the House knows the Committee does a careful job." "The members over there (have) confidence in the Committee. They know we aren't trying to hide things or sneak things or pull the wool over their eyes." Members emphasize that the success of their Committee depends a great deal on the reputation of their chairman. For instance: "Aspinall has the reputation of being the best Committee chairman in the House. You never see an Interior bill defeated on the floor, do you? That should give you some indication of what the House thinks of Wayne Aspinall." And:

> There are some committees that start with anywhere from a 20- to 50-vote edge. There are three committees that, when they come to the floor, the House knows they have probably done their work. Ways and Means, first of all. Mills. . . .

[82] Of the remaining four: Sleeping Bear Dunes Lakeshore (1966) passed two Congresses later; Hells Canyon Dam (1955) never reached the floor; Pennsylvania Avenue Historical Site (1966) and Gold Mining Industry Aid (1966) have not yet passed.

Then, in order, Interstate. Oren Harris. . . . Then Aspinall.
He has the respect of the House and they know once a bill
has gone through our process, chances are it's okay. Wayne's
a master of the subject.

From the members' perspective, they need, they want, and they
achieve success on the House floor.

The three Committee floor defeats on major bills occurred on the
Hawaii Alaska Statehood Bill of 1955, the Fryingpan-Arkansas Rec-
lamation Project in 1956, and the Domestic Minerals Stabilization
Bill in 1958. The latter two bills are the more typical of Interior
Committee decisions. The conditions under which they lost are in-
structive as to the conditions under which they normally win.

The Fryingpan-Arkansas Project was designed to irrigate land in
the Arkansas River basin in eastern Colorado, with some of the
water being taken from the Fryingpan River, which is located on
the western slope of the Rockies — the transfer to be made via a
transmountain tunnel.[83] It was the major constituency project of
Interior Committee Republican J. Edgar Chenoweth of eastern Colorado. The bill came to the floor first in 1954, again in 1956, and,
finally, in 1962. On the first two occasions, it failed to get a rule, by
the close margins of 188 to 195 and 179 to 194. On the third try, it
passed by voice vote. It had presidential and executive branch support every time. But it failed primarily because of the inability of
the Committee's Westerners to convince the non-Westerners on the
Committee and in the House that it was, beyond question, a sound
and feasible project. From a purely physical standpoint, the project
was vulnerable to opposition leader John Saylor's charges that it was
"the Rube Goldberg of the Rockies," the "unsound" product of
"bright schemers in the Bureau of Reclamation," lacking in proof
that enough water even existed to make it work. Opposition to the
project from Colorado's western slope and from Southern California,
both of which stood to lose water to the project, added to the feeling that neither the merits nor the politics of the project had been
settled. Congressman Aspinall, who represented western Colorado,
voted for the project, but his failure to speak for it on the floor
caused further uncertainty. And, finally, on each of the first two

---

[83] Material on the three Fryingpan-Arkansas bills can be found in: 100 *Congressional Record* 1954, pp. 12445–12454; 102 *Congressional Record* 1956, pp.
14796–14802; 108 *Congressional Record* 1962, pp. 10148 ff, 10388 ff, 14823.

occasions, the bill was brought to the floor within a week of adjournment — the least propitious time to push through a bill about which substantial doubts could be generated.

In 1962, Wayne Aspinall (now Committee Chairman) floor-managed a revised version of the bill. He assured the non-Western members that the project was no longer controversial. He testified: "Never has a project been as thoroughly studied by federal and state agencies and by Congress as the Fryingpan-Arkansas Project. Its physical feasibility is satisfactory, its economic feasibility is satisfactory, its financial feasibility is satisfactory. If you can find any more unanimity in a state (Colorado), I would like to know about it." His view of the matter was accepted by his colleagues. John Saylor offered five amendments. The two that Aspinall approved were accepted; the three that Aspinall opposed were rejected. When Saylor tried to force a roll call vote on final passage, only twenty-eight other members stood up with him.

Two years later Aspinall lectured the proponents of the Central Arizona Project on the lessons of Fryingpan-Arkansas:

> The House of Representatives is a stickler and has been since I went to Congress in 1949, it is a stickler on considering reclamation projects. . . . The first thing that is necessary in the House of Representatives, as you know, is to secure the approval of the nonreclamation state representatives, is to show the physical feasibility of a project . . . . and that means that those of us who are from reclamation states have to show the three facets of feasibility for these projects. . . . We would have been stopped in our tracks if we had authorized this project (before we knew sufficient water was available). This is the same thing that happened . . . on the Fryingpan-Arkansas in Colorado. It twice passed the U.S. Senate, but we were never in a position to get it out of the House. This is the difference between the two bodies.[84]

The lesson of the Fryingpan-Arkansas defeats was that the House Committee needs to take — and normally does take — precautions to win the approval of the non-Western House members. The related "difference between the two bodies" is that the Senate floor pro-

[84] Committee on Interior and Insular Affairs, *Hearings on the Central Arizona Project, Subcommittee on Irrigation and Reclamation, U.S. House of Representatives,* 88th Congress, 2nd Session (Washington: U.S. Government Printing Office, 1964), pp. 38, 47–48.

vides a more hospitable climate. A Bureau of Reclamation official concluded:

> Reclamation is a Western problem and most of the House is from the East. The Committee has to sell every reclamation project to the House. . . . We don't have many votes in the House. But in the Senate, we have nineteen states (seventeen reclamation plus Alaska and Hawaii) and friends in other states. It's much, much easier.

This House/Senate difference accords with our earlier observations about the permeability of Senate Committees and the greater "Westernness" of the Senate institution.

The same lesson can be drawn from the defeat of the Domestic Minerals Stabilization Bill of 1958, to subsidize the lead, zinc, fluorspar, and tungsten industries.[85] Floor-manager Aspinall characterized these industries as "sick and just about ready to collapse *in toto*." But the opposition encountered on the floor was indicative, again, of the difficulty that Western-oriented legislation may confront there. The Committee's most powerful non-Westerner, John Saylor, once more had not been mollified; and he led the opposition, speaking for the non-Western (and his district's) coal industry. He argued:

> Can you go home and say that you took care of the people in the lead and zinc mines; can you go home and say that you took care of the folks that happen to be in the fluorspar and tungsten mining areas, but you did not take care of the miners in your own district? How are you going to explain that to the people in your home towns? . . . This bill is not to relieve the distressed conditions in the entire mining industry — no — just the chosen few.

Committee member Walter Baring (Democrat, Nevada), on behalf of the people whose districts needed the subsidy, asked non-Westerners to reciprocate for past favors.

> There are many members here from farming communities who have asked us for their support. There are many city representatives who have received our support for rivers and harbors and other pieces of legislation directly affecting them. This is your chance to pay back to the mining people for the benefits you have received.

[85] Material on the Domestic Minerals bills will be found in: 104 *Congressional Record* 1958; pp. 18565 ff; 106 *Congressional Record* 1960, pp. 14336 ff; 107 *Congressional Record* 1961, pp. 16905 ff.

But Saylor's argument proved more persuasive to the House majority. It found receptive ears among many big city Democrats — the most influential and active of whom was Mike Kirwan from industrial Youngstown, Ohio, and the chairman of the Appropriations subcommittee on the Interior Department. Noting that the bill had already passed the Senate, he said:

> In the other body, there is not one Senator east of the Rocky Mountains on that Committee on Interior and Insular Affairs, not one. Everyone on that Committee on the Democratic and Republican side alike comes from west of the Rockies. That is the section that is chiefly getting the good out of this. . . . Let me ask you what they are going to do over there in Michigan where they paid billions in taxes and where they have a couple of hundred thousand people out of work and idle? There is nothing in here for them — just $650 million to subsidize four minerals to help 10,000 miners, chiefly in the West.

After being riddled with amendments, the bill failed by vote of 159 to 182. A scaled-down bill to subsidize only lead and zinc was passed and vetoed in 1960 and was passed into law in 1961. These two later Committee victories were by small margins, 197 to 192 and 196 to 172, providing further indication of the Committee's difficulty on the House floor once controversy has been aroused. The secret of its normal floor success is the prevention or minimization of controversy prior to the floor stage.

Not only must the Committee keep down regional controversy. It must also keep down partisan controversy. On the bills just discussed, floor voting broke along both regional and party lines. Among Committee members, the regional split was greater than the party split. Among all House members, however, the party split seems to have been at least as great as the regional split. A regional controversy inside the Committee, it appears, can very easily become overlaid with a partisan controversy, once it hits the floor. Table 6.22 displays the relationship between regional and party voting on the two Fryingpan-Arkansas votes combined and on the minerals bill. The percentages are those in favor of the bill. The Interior Committee's problem with non-Westerners in the House is evident in the lower right-hand corner. But they will have difficulty, it appears, wooing more non-Westerners unless, at the same time, they can defuse

Table 6.22
Party and Regional Voting:
Fryingpan-Arkansas, 1954, 1956;
Domestic Minerals Stabilization, 1958

	Committee Members:		Percent in Favor of Bill	
	Rep.	*Dem.*	*West.*	*Non-West.*
Fryingpan-Ark. (2 votes) N = 46	72%	52%	84%	20%
Domestic Min. (1 vote) N = 27	54%	71%	85%	29%

	All House Members:		Percent in Favor of Bill	
	Rep.	*Dem.*	*West.*	*Non-West.*
Fryingpan-Ark. (2 votes) N = 756	69%	27%	58%	46%
Domestic Min. (1 vote) N = 341	30%	60%	71%	39%

the equally obvious partisanship on the House floor — as displayed in the lower left-hand corner.

One partial explanation for floor partisanship is that House members follow the lead of their fellow partisans on the Committee — when those fellow partisans give a strong lead. On Fryingpan-Arkansas, the Committee Republicans strongly supported their fellow Republicans' project and House Republicans followed suit. Committee Democrats, on the other hand, gave no clear lead, and House Democrats had no stimulus to support a dubious project. With the minerals bill, party enthusiasms were reversed. Committee Democrats gave a strong lead and House Democrats followed in support. Committee Republicans gave no clear signal, and House Republicans were left to cast philosophical votes against federal subsidies.[86] This partial explanation leads to an even more basic explanation for floor partisanship. Apparently natural resource issues *are* partisan issues. Herbert McClosky and others have found this to be so — primarily in public power but with a possible spillover into other resource questions.[87] If natural resource issues are partisan, it may mean that a

[86] The minerals bill supports David Mayhew's generalization that Democrats help their fellow partisans in pushing their policy interests whereas Republicans do not. But the Fryingpan-Arkansas bill runs counter to it. See David Mayhew, *op. cit.*

[87] See Herbert McClosky, Paul J. Hoffman, Rosemary O'Hara, "Issue Conflict and Consensus Among Party Leaders and Followers," *American Political Science Review* (June, 1960).

latent partisanship always awaits the Committee's bills on the House floor. From 1955 to 1966, the House had fifty-nine roll calls on Committee bills; forty-five of them (seventy-five per cent) were "party votes." At the same time Committee members cast "party votes" on only fourteen (twenty-four per cent) of these roll calls. The comparison indicates the presence of floor partisanship and the Committee's considerable effort to dampen it.[88] Part of an effort to minimize floor partisanship, of course, is the avoidance of roll calls altogether. In this and other floor stratagems, the Committee will lean on the party leadership.[89] Committee floor success may be as much due to its success in minimizing partisanship as to its success in minimizing regional friction. To a considerable degree (as with the mollification of John Saylor) the two efforts overlap.

The record suggests that in addition to implementing its first decision rule, the Committee also implements its second one. That is, if strong clientele conflict occurs, the Committee does seem to arrive at decisions amenable to the chamber. But the second decision rule also calls for special concern, in cases of conflict, for the commercial users. Does the content of Committee decisions suggest the implementation of this part of the rule? We think it does. But we shall not offer conclusive evidence — only the hints that come from case studies. We shall discuss three in particular, the three we think produced the sharpest conservation/user controversy of the period. The first is the Upper Colorado River Storage Bill; the second is the Wilderness Bill; the third is the Lower Colorado River Bill.

The Upper Colorado River Storage Project called for a series of dams in Colorado and Utah to be built for the purpose of storing water to be used for irrigation, power, and future development of

[88] In every policy area on "major bills," the average Index of Partisanship for Committee members is lower than it is for House members. On all reclamation votes from 1955 to 1965 (twenty-three in all) the average Committee IP was twenty-eight; the average House IP was forty-two. On fifteen Parks and Public Lands votes, average Committee IP was twenty-six, average House IP was thirty-four. On eight mining votes the figures were forty-two and forty-seven. Other votes were scattered. For a comparison with the more partisan Education and Labor Committee — both as to absolute levels of IP and Committee/House comparisons, see Table 6.13.

[89] Leadership help in avoiding roll calls was alluded to on the third Frying-pan-Arkansas vote. See 108 *Congressional Record* 1962, p. 14823. For the same thing on the Navaho-San Juan Chama Project, see 108 *Congressional Record* 1962, pp. 10167. Another example of leadership assistance can be found in the case of late vote switching on the San Angelo Project. See 103 *Congressional Record* 1957, pp. 13191–2.

the Upper Colorado River basin area (roughly, the area north of Arizona plus New Mexico).[90] It was of great importance to the districts of several Committee members, especially that of Wayne Aspinall. Strong clientele support came from the Colorado River Association — an *ad hoc* amalgamation of user interests. Conservationist groups, however, objected strongly to one of these dams, Echo Park, on the grounds that the storage reservoir would flood the Dinosaur National Monument and set a precedent for despoiling the national parks. "Recognizing that there are values and benefits on both sides," the Committee reported out a bill in 1954 that was "based upon a determination as to which course of action would be of greatest benefit to the local area and to the nation as a whole." The bill included the Echo Park dam, thus delivering values and benefits primarily to the users of the water. In the face of intense lobbying by conservationist groups such as the Sierra Club and the National Parks Association, House leaders determined that the bill could not pass and decided not to take it to the floor. In 1955, the Interior Committee reported out a revised bill that removed the Echo Park dam from the project. Irrigation and Reclamation Subcommittee Chairman Aspinall did not claim it was a better bill, just that "it is all we possibly can hope to get through the House." Conservationists, however, pushed further — for a statement of congressional intent that no dam was ever to be built within the park system. House leaders, again, held up the bill. In 1956, the Committee amended its second bill, adding the declaration of intent demanded by the conservationists. The bill went to the floor, supported by both sets of party leaders. During the floor debate that followed, Aspinall found it necessary to go up into the House gallery to confer with Executive Director David Brower of the Sierra Club so that he could assure Eastern House members that the club had, indeed, withdrawn all objections to the bill. It had; and the bill passed, 256 to 136. The Interior Committee had been pushed from its preferred position to a less preferred one, to an even less preferred one — each one more desirable to the conservationists and less desirable to the

[90] A detailed study focusing particularly inside the executive branch is Owen Stratton and Philip Sirotkin, *The Echo Park Controversy*, Inter-University Case Program (Indianapolis: Bobbs Merrill, 1959). Other materials used in this discussion will be found in: Committee on Interior and Insular Affairs, *House Report 1774*, 83rd Congress, 2nd Session (Washington: U.S. Government Printing Office, 1954); *Congressional Quarterly*, June 17, 1955, p. 706; 102 *Congressional Record*, pp. 3474 ff.

users. The Committee's own preferences and efforts were, in accordance with its second decision rule, especially solicitous of the commercial users.

The idea of a National Wilderness Preservation system was to give permanent statutory protection to certain public lands already classified by executive order as "wilderness," "wild," "canoe," or "primitive" areas, to restrict the use of these lands, and to provide for additions.[91] As noted earlier (see page 38) conservationist (or preservationist) and user groups clashed over the idea, with the users fearing that the land would be "locked up" and unavailable for the "multiple use" prescribed by federal land policy. The Interior Committee began holding hearings on the matter in 1957 and produced its first bill in 1962. By that time, opposing forces had come to disagree on two main points. Preservationists wanted all commercial use of the land stopped; users, mining interests particularly, wanted "multiple use" of the land. Preservationists wanted additions and reclassification to be done by the executive branch; users wanted this done by affirmative act of Congress — an indication, in itself, of users' preferred access to the House Interior Committee.

The 1962 Committee bill, was designed, in the words of Chairman Aspinall:

> to accomplish my objectives of fair and equitable treatment for all: those who enjoy isolated wilderness as well as those whose livelihoods depend on such areas, while safeguarding the overall national interest.

In its balancing, the bill favored the user side of both disputes. It called for "multiple use" of the land, provided for prospecting and mining for twenty-five years with a review at the end of twenty-five years, and left any change in the system dependent on affirmative congressional action. The decision was denounced by preservationist groups as designed "to preserve for a minority of commercial interests an opportunity to exploit any area of the public's land that may attract them." In order to protect its bill, the Committee voted to send it to the floor under suspension of the rules — permitting no

[91] Materials used in this discussion are: *Congressional Quarterly* November 23, 1962, pp. 2197–8; *Congressional Quarterly* May 22, 1964, pp. 1008–1010; Committee on Interior and Insular Affairs, *Hearings on Wilderness Preservation System*, 88th Congress, 2nd Session (Washington: U.S. Government Printing Office, 1964), pp. 1291 ff; 110 *Congressional Record*, pp. 17427–17458.

amendments and requiring a two-thirds vote. House leaders refused to grant this restrictive request; Aspinall, backed by his Committee, refused amid charge and countercharge to bring the bill to the floor in any other way. In 1964, the Committee reported out another bill (which passed) — compromising with the preservationists but still protecting user interests. Prospecting would continue, but no new mineral leases could be granted after 1989. Reclassification of lands could be accomplished by executive action, but additions to the system (including reclassification from "primitive" to "wilderness") could only be made by act of Congress. The chairman of the Subcommittee on Public Lands stated the Committee's position thus:

> I am strictly for multiple use of the public lands but do realize the need for the preservation of some primitive areas; however, not at the cost of the local economy such as the cattle business, lumber and mining industries.

It was a perfect statement of the Committee's second decision rule — the one it had followed throughout the Wilderness Bill controversy.

A third dispute, the Lower Colorado River Bill (or the Central Arizona Project) followed a script similar to the Upper Colorado bill.[92] Part of this vast reclamation and power project involved the building of two hydroelectric dams in the Grand Canyon area, which conservationist groups felt would destroy the scenic beauty of the Canyon. Private users of hydroelectric power favored the two dams. In 1966, the Interior Committee, despite strenuous conservationist opposition, reported out a Colorado River Bill including the two dams. The protests, led by a national advertising campaign of the Sierra Club, produced what *Congressional Quarterly* called "the most intensive conservation campaign in more than a decade." The Committee bill was not moved to the floor, for fear it could not pass over aroused non-Western opposition. In 1967, the Committee reported a bill (which passed) without either dam — thus capitulating to conservationist demands. Again, the Committee's clear preference was to assist the Western-oriented private users of water; and it held out until the conservationist lobbying in the House had put it in an all-or-nothing position.

[92] Material for this discussion was taken from *Congressional Quarterly* November 1, 1968, pp. 3019–3031.

As the period ended, conservationists were angry at the Interior
Committee for not acting on two cherished projects, the Scenic and
Wild Rivers Bill and the National Redwoods Park Bill.[93] In both
cases, the Senate had already passed such a bill, but the House Committee had not yet reported one. This Senate/House situation was,
we think, both typical and instructive. The Senate Committee is, as
we suggested it would be — for both ideological and constituency
reasons — more responsive to conservationist groups. And this fact
further highlights the user-orientation of the House Committee. A
useful indicator of greater Senate responsiveness is suggested by the
Wild Rivers and Redwoods bills. The Senate Committee acts more
quickly on conservationist-sponsored measures than does the House
group. Assuming that users' interests favor the status quo whereas
conservationists are pressing for change, the House Committee is
slow to act, thus taking a generally pro-user posture. Then, when the
Committee does act, it can — in a reversal of the Appropriations and
tax sequence — sit as an appeals court to hear the pleas of the commercial interests. The pattern fits the Wilderness Bill, the Wild
Rivers Bill, the Redwoods Park Bill, the Indiana Dunes Lakeshore
Bill and, we would guess, others.

Of the thirteen parks and lands "major bills" reported by the
House Committee from 1955 to 1966, the Senate had reported the
bill first in ten instances, and sometimes more than once before the
House acted.[94] Of the three House-initiated bills, the Land and
Water Conservation measure was partially a revenue-raising measure
(hence, appropriate for House initiation) and another was the user-

[93] Marjorie Hunter, "Wild Rivers Bill Faces House Snag," *New York Times*
January 23, 1966, p. 57; Drew Pearson, "Lumber Lobby Irks Governor Brown,"
Washington Post, March 23, 1966, p. E11. (Both eventually passed.)

[94] The reader should be reminded again that "major bills" are those bills reported by each House Committee which *Congressional Quarterly Almanac* called
"major" and for which CQ listed a House Committee report. A fair number
of national parks, recreation areas, lakeshores, etc., are passed through the House
without an Interior Committee report, as amendments to a Senate bill. In a
few other cases CQ has simply not listed House report numbers. The cases
reported in the following listing represent a somewhat arbitrary and incomplete
inventory of parks and lands bills. The ten were: Outdoor Recreation, 1958;
Cape Cod Seashore, 1961; Grand Canyon Park, 1962; Padre Island Seashore,
1962; Point Reyes Seashore, 1962; Wilderness, 1964; Sleeping Bear Dunes Lakeshore, 1966; Bighorn Canyon Park, 1966; Indiana Dunes Lakeshore, 1966; His-
toric Properties, 1966. The three passed first by the House were Public Land
Law Commission, 1963; Land and Water Conservation Fund, 1964; Guadelupe
Mountains Park, 1966.

backed Public Land Law Commission (subsequently chaired by Aspinall) to recommend a long-range land-use policy.[95] In general, House Committee members believe their deliberateness in decision making is essential to their floor success; they explain it, therefore, in those terms — acknowledging that "you can't keep up with the Senate" if you want to do a thorough job. This rationale, however, is most persuasive when it is the Westerners who are on the legislative offensive (as with reclamation projects like Fryingpan-Arkansas). Here, Committee deliberateness helps win non-Western support and promotes Western user interests in the bargain. When, however, non-Westerners have joined the legislative offensive (as in conservation issues), it is less persuasive for the Committee to argue that its deliberateness is a condition of floor success. In these latter cases, the Committee's lengthy consideration entails a distinct pro-user bias. Besides, when it wants to, the House Committee can act faster than the Senate group. On major bills involving mining and minerals, desired (we assume) by commercial groups, this appears to be the case. Of eight of twelve such bills from 1955 to 1966, the House Committee acted *first* and the Senate Committee second.[96] One generalization consistent with the patterns of both the lands and mining bills is that the Committee is following its second decision rule — in balancing conservation and user interests it normally tips the balance in favor of the users.

Clientele reaction to Committee performance follows logically from the observance of the second decision rule. As we would expect, commercial user groups are more satisfied than conservationist groups. An official of the American Mining Congress summarized:

> We have no trouble with the Interior Committee. By that I mean the men on the Committee are knowledgeable, they do their homework, and they know the subject. So we get along well.

[95] The Commission was set up as part of the bargain which produced the Wilderness Bill. It's user-oriented report can be found in *New York Times* June 24, 1970, pp. 1, 22.

[96] The eight were: Minerals Stockpiling, 1955; Mineral Subsidies, 1956; Mining Industry, 1959; Lead Zinc Subsidy, 1959; Helium Conservation, 1960; Lead Zinc Subsidy, 1961; Lead Zinc, 1963 (two bills). The Senate first passed: Domestic Minerals Stabilization, 1958; Office of Mineral Exploration, 1958; Coal Research, 1960; Mining Industry, 1962.

An official of the Citizens Committee for Natural Resources took a very different view. He said:

> Our problem is not with men or with personalities. It's with the philosophies of the Western congressmen on the Committee. They are too responsive to the commercial interests of the areas they represent. I don't blame them. But they are our problem.

And a Sierra Club official voiced a similar feeling about the Committee staff. "When we call over to the Committee for information, they are very uncooperative. They are hostile to us and our relationship is very bad." These reactions constitute further evidence of Committee observance of its second decision rule.

Committee members themselves appear well satisfied with the benefits of their membership. Those who joined the group to help meet constituency needs find success. "I am probably the only freshman who has gotten a bill through the House already." "I was able to save a project after five months (on the Committee) — a $1,600,000 project, which is awfully important to my district." Major projects take longer — Edgar Chenoweth's Fryingpan-Arkansas, Wayne Aspinall's Upper Colorado Storage Project, Morris Udall's Central Arizona Project, for example.[97] As one of the three men put it: "It's all personal friendship — write letters, talk to members, have dinner with them — it's all personal. It takes a few years to build these friendships." Most of the Committee's members, newcomers and veterans, Westerners and non-Westerners, can point with pride to some specific Committee-based accomplishments in aid of their constituencies. Congressmen believe that the ability to point with pride helps them electorally. And, believing it, they gain satisfaction from their membership.

Objectively, it might be noted, there is no clear evidence that Interior membership has any "appreciable impact" on a Westerner's re-election chances. Charles Bullock's statistical comparison of narrowly elected, freshmen Western congressmen on and off the Interior Committee shows that the two groups — the "on"s and the "off"'s — are not re-elected to second terms at a significantly different rate. His results, however, do suggest some Interior Committee-re-election relationship — with one in twenty (five per cent) Committee West-

---

[97] A good description of former Chairman Clair Engle's accomplishments is: *Congressional Record*, Daily Edition, March 1, 1965, pp. 3734–3736.

erners being defeated at the polls and nine in twenty-nine (thirty-one per cent) non-Committee Westerners being defeated from 1947 to 1967.[98] The Committee's own primary decision rule contributes to this result, for it provides that the legislation of *all* congressmen should be processed for House approval. A study of all first and second term Westerners on and off the Interior Committee for the 89th Congress shows that Committee Westerners got more of their *own* bills reported out of Interior than non-Committee Westerners. But, including equivalent bills (i.e., those with someone else's name on them but covering the same problem, as per Table 6.20), legislation desired by non-Committee Westerners was reported out of Interior at the same rate as legislation desired by Committee Westerners.[99] Interior Committee processes make it possible for congressmen off as well as on the Committee to point with pride to their constituency service — and to reap whatever re-election benefits may accrue. In any objective accounting, Interior Committee membership probably does not make much of an independent contribution to a congressman's re-election. Post Office Committee members — even the staunchest allies of the postal unions — also suffer a high rate of electoral attrition. Continued membership on a clientele-oriented Committee tells us something about the strong orientation of a congressman to his constituency. But those congressmen with stronger orientations to House influence or public policy can transfer away from clientele-oriented committees without, thereby, significantly damaging their re-election chances. And, of course, they do.

Interior, like Post Office, is a high-turnover Committee. Electoral defeat contributes less to turnover on Interior; but on both committees (Table 6.5), turnover is primarily the result of transfers to other committees. The important difference, however, is that transfers and high turnover on Interior are not accompanied by the member dissatisfaction that characterizes Post Office. Interior members

[98] Charles Bullock, "Freshman Committee Assignments and Re-election in the United States House of Representatives," Unpublished manuscript, 1970, esp. pp. 16–22.
[99] The results are reported in Roger Handy, "Comparative Success of the House Interior Committee Member in Securing Legislative Output," Unpublished manuscript, University of Rochester, 1971. For getting one's own bill out of Committee, success rates are nineteen per cent for members and seven per cent for nonmembers. For getting one's own bill *or* an equivalent out of Committee, success rates are thirty-six per cent for members and thirty-seven per cent for nonmembers.

feel their individual goals have been met. But there is more to it than
that. Interior Committee members draw a great deal of extra psychic
satisfaction from belonging to this particular group. And they display
strong feelings of group identity. The result is a fascinating disparity
between objective and subjective measures of Committee prestige.
By every objective standard (turnover, transfers, freshmen, length of
prior service) utilized in this study, Interior is a distinctively low-
status Committee. Yet its members overwhelmingly perceive it to be
"one of the most important." It is a situation exactly the reverse of
Foreign Affairs, which ranks high according to objective measures of
prestige, but whose members regard it as a good deal less important.
For them, the disparity nourishes dissatisfaction. On Interior, the
disparity produces satisfaction.

Using their own home-grown standards (especially the huge volume of bills they handle), Committee members unabashedly rank
Interior close to Ways and Means and Appropriations in the hierarchy of House committees:

> Some people say Appropriations is first, and I think I'd
> agree. Second, probably Ways and Means. I'd put Interior
> third. Yes, I think right behind Ways and Means — third.

> I think it's ridiculous it's not treated as a major committee.
> . . . Omitting the exclusive committees, Ways and Means
> and Appropriations, where you have to have years and years
> of service to get on, it's one of the most important.

And, as we have said, Interior is more like Appropriations and Ways
and Means than it is like any of the other three in the House-
orientation of its decision rules, in its decision-making autonomy,
and, now, in its expressions of corporate identity and corporate pride.
Less than the two money committees, but more than the other three,
Interior members describe the "camaraderie" and the "warm feeling" of the Committee. And a top leader asserted their superiority
over the Senate group in terms of their more heterogeneous membership and the consequent thoroughness of deliberation. He declared:

> Ours is a national committee. It's not like the Senate Com-
> mittee which is a provincial Committee. . . . Hell, they're
> completely parochial. . . . They can do anything when they
> get thirteen members together and they usually do anything
> they want.

Again we would argue that these group-related satisfactions add to the gratifications the members derive from achieving their personal goals. Together, they give greater stability to Committee decision patterns than the achievement of individual goals produces by itself.

Interior Committee turnover should *not* be interpreted as a sign of dissatisfaction. Rather, for a sizable minority of members, a committee assignment that meets objectives of constituency service and re-election is a short-term goal. They want the assignment to Interior. They profit from it and enjoy it while they are there. But they do not want it permanently. Westerners want it, perhaps, while they find their way around the natural resources bureaucracy and while they consolidate their electoral base at home with at least one re-election success. Non-Westerners do not normally want it; but once there, they value it as an excellent legislative apprenticeship. It is, indeed, a source of group pride that Interior is in the view of its members "a training ground for other committees" and "the best training ground for floor participation in the House." Committee veterans expect a large turnover, and their internal processes make a virtue out of that necessity, as they perceive the Committee to be a "school" for freshmen congressmen, with Chairman Aspinall as a "schoolmaster" devoted to teaching parliamentary procedure, and an orientation to the House.

For members whose ultimate goals involve House influence or public policy, it is considered perfectly natural that their careers eventually take them to another committee or to the Senate. More go to Appropriations than to any other — a committee whose work style (hard work, subcommittee specialization, low partisanship, concern for floor success) is very similar to that of Interior, and for which Interior is an especially appropriate apprenticeship. On Appropriations, certainly, former Interior members will be able to exert a broader House influence without giving up any of their opportunity to service their constituency. An Interior member who transferred to Appropriations explained:

> It's common sense that when you get the chance, you go to a higher committee in the House. In my state legislature I was Chairman of Education. Then later I had a chance to move up to Highways and I did. I could run the education program of the state through the highway program. There was that much power. The same in Congress. The authoriz-

ing committee on the Interior was fine and good. But it didn't have the power.

On Appropriations, the implication is, the Congressman can get funds for his constituency (possibly for projects he had gotten authorized while on Interior) while at the same time wielding a broader influence in the chamber.[100] This view of Interior as a desirable steppingstone for many of its members indicates that the idea of a hierarchy of committees can be misleading in its implications for some low-status committees. The similarly low status of Post Office and Interior masks a universe of difference between them.

In this chapter, we have presented evidence to demonstrate that committee decisions do, indeed, follow those decision rules that each committee's members have devised to accommodate their personal goals to the constraints of their environment. That is, a committee's decisions are explainable in terms of its members' goals, the constraints of its environment, its decision strategies, and — to a lesser, refining degree, perhaps — by its decision-making processes. Enough evidence has been mustered, we hope, to lend strength to the line of argument we have pursued. We have not, of course, *proven* anything, for we have not tried very determinedly to muster a contrary body of evidence. Those who find themselves resisting our selective use of evidence are invited to provide counterexamples and to fashion another line of argument. We hope that what we have presented will seem worth that kind of further development and testing.

To the degree that a committee's decisions follow its decision rules, committee members and the most interested outside groups should be reasonably satisfied with committee performance. For those rules are, after all, an effort to accommodate the views of each. We have not found a measure of satisfaction that would allow us to describe and compare amounts of internal and/or external satisfac-

---

[100] A similar line of reasoning can be found in Charles Bullock, "Correlates of Committee Transfers in the U.S. House of Representatives," Paper Delivered at Annual Meeting of Midwest Political Science Association, April 29, 1971.

tion. But we have detected varying degrees of it. For member satisfaction, a necessary condition would seem to be committee *activity*. No member goal can be achieved without some minimal level of activity. Post Office members' dissatisfaction arose because that Committee slipped below an acceptable level of activity; it "wasn't doing anything." Foreign Affairs has simmered with dissatisfaction because its members have felt they "weren't doing enough." Both would have been satisfied with increased activity. The other committees have been active. For Education and Labor members, indeed, their increased activity was the basis for their newly found satisfaction in the Powell years.

Members of our other three committees require an additional condition for their satisfaction. They feel the need to make an *independent* contribution to decision making. Especially, they want to feel a measure of independence relative to the executive branch — in both an institutional and a policy sense. They want to preserve autonomous decision-making processes and they want to develop substantive expertise. When they do achieve such independence, they develop a psychological feeling of group identity, which further strengthens their independence. Ways and Means, Appropriations, and Interior members' satisfaction, then, seems to be based on both their *activity* and their *independence*. During the period studied, these three committees maintained a higher and steadier level of satisfaction with their own performance than did the three other committees.

It is hard to generalize about the conditions of satisfaction for the groups comprising the environment. Perhaps it is enough to remind ourselves, again, that individual committees face quite varied sets of environmental constraints. For two of our committees, the institutional constraints of the parent chamber are most important. House expectations call for a balance between autonomous and responsive decision making. And, so far, Ways and Means and Appropriations seem to have maintained a balance satisfactory to House leaders and House majorities. For the other four, the policy coalitions of their environments are more important. But dominance in those policy coalitions varies, so that the expectations confronting the four committees also vary. The executive-led coalition confronting Foreign Affairs wants legitimation plus assessments of political feasibility. The clientele-led coalitions facing Interior and Post Office want access to members plus sympathetic committee member spokesmen.

The party-led coalitions facing Education and Labor want all these things plus a partisanship that will abet victory at the polls. How can we compare levels of satisfaction across such diverse expectations? Is the executive branch more satisfied with the legitimation it gets than clientele groups are with the spokesmanship they get? All we can say is that the leaders of each coalition do seem pretty well satisfied with the committees that interest them — the executive with Foreign Affairs, the postal employees with Post Office, all but the preservationist groups with Interior, the Democrats and Republicans with Education and Labor.

Looking across the six committees, some of the gross similarities and differences noted earlier do appear to carry through to their decisions. That is, Ways and Means, Appropriations, and Interior remain strikingly similar to one another and strikingly different from Education and Labor, Foreign Affairs, and Post Office. The three committees with a consensus on House-oriented decision rules do seem to be more successful on the House floor than the three committees whose decision rules are not House-oriented. Members of the same three, more autonomous committees express a greater overall satisfaction with their committee's decision processes and decisions than do the members of the three less autonomous committees with theirs. And from the autonomy and satisfaction of the first three flows a sense of corporate identity and corporate pride that is missing in the three less autonomous, less satisfied committees. On the other hand, the decisions of our three less autonomous committees seem to bring relatively greater satisfaction to interested and influential environmental groups than do the decisions of our three more autonomous committees. Education and Labor, Foreign Affairs, and Post Office are more permeable and, hence, relatively more responsive to the wishes of people outside the Congress than are Ways and Means, Appropriations, and Interior.

Utilizing these *relative* distinctions, we find two types of House committees. One type is identified by the House orientation of its decision rules, the autonomy of its decision-making processes, its emphasis on committee expertise, its success on the House floor, its members' sense of group identity, and the relatively higher ratio of member to nonmember satisfaction with its performance. The other type is identified by its extra-House-oriented decision rules, the permeability of its decision-making processes, the de-emphasis on committee expertise, its lack of success on the House floor, the absence of any feeling of group identification, and the relatively higher ratio of nonmember to member satisfaction with its performance.

Since no committee falls completely into one category or the other, we probably should think of these as "ideal types" toward which committees tend — a *corporate* type, on the one hand, and a *permeable* type, on the other. Committees of the corporate type tend to be more influential but less responsive than permeable committees. Permeable committees tend to be more responsive but less influential than corporate committees. Ways and Means, Appropriations and Interior come closest to the corporate type of committee. Education and Labor, Foreign Affairs, and Post Office come closest to the permeable type of committee. And, we might add, all Senate committees tend toward the permeable category. There are no corporate committees in the Senate.

Epilogue

Congressional committees differ from one another. And House committees differ from Senate Committees. That much, at least, our description has made clear. We hope that we have also clarified the ways in which they differ. If we have, it is our further hope that the variables and the categories of this study may help to orient further discussions of congressional committees — both academic and civic.

On the *academic* side, it it tempting to press for a premature verdict by purporting to show, here and now, that our scheme is useful for understanding committees other than those we have studied. But that judgment will have to come from political scientists with a working knowledge of such other committees. We do not know enough to speak confidently of committees whose members we have not interviewed and whose performance we have not examined. Descriptive studies of congressional committees seem destined to continue. And for good reason. The bulk of congressional decisions will continue to be made by committees. We dare to hope that political scientists interested in other committees will find in this study an invitation to take its variables and categories and try them on for size.

In fact, it is our ambition to develop here not just a set of descriptive categories but a scheme with some explanatory value. We have argued that committee decision processes and committee decisions (assuming these are what one wishes to explain) differ *because* member goals, environmental constraints, and, hence, strategic premises, differ. Since these variables are presently lacking in precision, the scheme defies any very precise test. One way to explore the explanatory usefulness of the scheme would be to test it over time to see whether change in the independent variables does produce change in the dependent variables. Our attempt to offer general descriptions of each committee that would hold for an entire twelve-year period has placed special emphasis on continuities rather than changes. Some changes, of course, have been discussed at length. But the description in the preceding chapters can best be viewed as providing *a base-line description* of each committee — one that holds more or less well for the period 1955–1966, with its Democratic majorities — and against which comparisons can be made at later (and, perhaps, earlier) points in time. We look forward to such longitudinal tests as can be made.

Informed readers will have noted, nonetheless, that changes in the patterns described here *have* occurred in the period since the main body of interviewing was completed — that is, between 1967 and 1972. Such changes have not been dealt with thus far in the book. And they cannot be treated in any detail here. But they do provide, perhaps, material for a very sketchy "pre-test" of our scheme's usefulness. If not, they will at least help update the analysis. The Post Office, Interior, Foreign Affairs, and Education and Labor Committees are the four cases in point. Subtle changes may have affected our other two committees, but they have not turned up in the published sources on which we have largely relied.

The most drastic change occurred when the Postal Reorganization Act of 1970 removed authority over postal employee salaries and postal rates from the jurisdiction of the *Post Office and Civil Service Committee* and gave it to the United States Postal Service.[1] A more complete alteration in the content of a committee's decisions could hardly be imagined. This alteration, we would argue, resulted from prior changes in the Committee's policy environment that its members were powerless to alter and that they had no strong incentives to resist. And they acted despite the resultant diminution in their ability to pursue their goals of constituency service and re-election, on the Committee.

A single event — the 1966 pre-Christmas mail breakdown in Chicago — triggered a public concern over postal issues that eventually

---

[1] Published sources for this discussion are: *Congressional Quarterly*, December 5, 1969, pp. 2507–2512, March 27, 1970, pp. 839–844; Mike Causey, "The Federal Diary," *Washington Post*, March 23, 1970; Post Office and Civil Service Committee, Hearings on Post Office Reorganization, Part II, 91st Congress, 1st Session (Washington: U.S. Government Printing Office, 1969), pp. 732–771.

shattered the monolithic, clientele-dominated environment of the Committee. Postal-reform advocates seized upon the event to wrest the policy initiative from the clientele-Committee alliance, and the results were the formation of the Kappel Commission in 1967, the Commission's postal corporation proposal of 1968, President Nixon's appointment of a Postmaster General dedicated to the Kappel proposal, Nixon's subsequent reorganization bill of 1969, and the concomitant formation of a prestigious lobbying group, the Citizen's Committee for Postal Reform. The climactic environmental event was the ten-day postal strike in March 1970. The effect of all this activity was to increase the salience of postal issues nationally and to bring the executive branch to leadership of the policy coalition confronting the Post Office Committee.

The first reaction of the Committee-clientele alliance to new environmental stimuli was a traditional one. The members pushed a pay increase bill through the House (and the Senate) in 1969. And they wrote their own postal-reform bill — introduced by the new Chairman Thaddeus Dulski — which retained the existing structure but added some congressional influence over salaries and rates. The National Association of Letter Carriers, in the words of its president, "campaigned very hard" against the Administration's postal corporation bill. And it triumphed in a thirteen-to-thirteen tie vote, in October 1969, whereby the Committee refused to substitute the corporation bill for the Dulski bill. In a new version of the standard executive branch riposte, the Administration threatened to veto the pay bill unless the Committee also accepted its postal corporation proposal. Clientele group counterreaction, however, was only partially standard. Deciding that they had no opportunity of overriding a presidential veto, the letter carriers moved to compromise, characteristically, with the executive. This time, however, they were compromising on all the rules of the game to which they had traditionally been attached.

In January 1969, the president of the National Association of Letter Carriers, James Rademacher, opposed the corporation idea on the familiar grounds that "we would be denied access to the Congress and Congress would be virtually unable to come to our aid." But in December of 1969, Rademacher was bargaining on a pay-raise–postal corporation compromise with the President. The compromise was consummated without the participation of his Post

Office Committee allies; its terms radically weakened the long-standing clientele-Committee alliance. The drastic step was taken, said Rademacher, because it was "the only way to get a pay raise." But, we would argue, the context had changed to the point where the letter carriers' organization perceived direct bargaining with the President as the only way to salvage something out of a situation which it no longer controlled. The Post Office Committee — deadlocked at thirteen-to-thirteen and with Chairman Dulski unable to lead any more members to his view — was seen as a tottering reed on which to depend in the face of increased Administration pressure. The tight clientele-Committee alliance had relied heavily on the low salience of its subject matter; under inconspicuous circumstances the minority of Committee members devoted to the alliance could act in the name of the majority, whose only interest in the Committee was to leave it. But in a time of high salience and under pressure from an executive-led policy coalition, a Committee majority would be perfectly willing to relinquish the constituency-re-election benefits of Committee membership. Doubtless the National Association of Letter Carriers could see that just such a time was at hand. It was — as proved by the subsequent fifteen-to-eleven vote whereby the Committee voted out a corporation bill. Strictly speaking, the Committee was following its second decision rule. But the members followed it, as never before, to their permanent personal detriment.

Committee action did not stem from a change in members' Committee-related goals. Members acted on the basis of a weak commitment to those goals and in response to a qualitative change in environmental expectations. Always a nonautonomous, environment-dominated committee, it had no internal resources with which to resist dominance by a new environmental element. As of 1970, Committee members could still exercise a general oversight of the U.S. Postal Service and could still make decisions affecting the working conditions of most federal employees. But they could extract fewer constituency benefits from these kinds of decisions. In sum, the history of the Post Office Committee from 1966 to 1972 shows how changes in the *environmental constraints* affecting Committee members seem to explain a subsequent change in the entire pattern of Committee *decisions*.

On the Foreign Affairs Committee, changes in *environmental constraints*, starting in 1967, seem to explain a subsequent change in the

Committee's *decision-making process*.[2] In this instance, external
policy and institutional changes were involved. Domestic controversy over the Vietnam War cracked the Committee's monolithic
policy environment. As policies of the executive branch came under
increasing public attack, and as war critics asked them "where the
hell were you guys?" Committee members saw an opportunity and
a necessity to become more assertive and critical in pursuing their
policy-oriented goals. Their vehicle has been increased subcommittee
activity. It began with an inquiry into the President's war powers
in 1970. But a qualitative change occurred in 1971. In that year, the
House Democratic caucus resolved that no member of that party
could serve as chairman of more than one subcommittee. It further
resolved that each subcommittee chairman could hire at least one
member of his subcommittee staff. This change in institutional constraints had its greatest effect (among our six committees) on the
internal operation of the Foreign Affairs Committee.

Several senior Committee members, forced to choose between a
subcommittee chairmanship on Foreign Affairs and one on their other
committee, chose to give up their Foreign Affairs subcommittee. Thus,
three of the younger, restless Committee members inherited subcommittee chairmanships they could not yet have had under previous party rules. And each hired his own staff director. Consequently,
in the 92nd Congress, Foreign Affairs subcommittees became distinctly more active than they ever had been in the period we have
described.

It is too early to say whether these changes in decision-making
processes will be accompanied by changes in Committee decisions.
On the basis of extensive subcommittee hearings, the Committee
denied all executive requests for foreign aid to Greece and to Paki-
stan in 1971. Such decisions may or may not continue — as, indeed,
they have arisen off and on in the past. The important possibility is
that, over time, a revivified set of subcommittees could develop some
policy specialization and sufficient expertise to increase Committee
influence with the executive branch. Chairman Morgan — anxious,

---

[2] Published sources for this discussion are: Neal Gregory, "House Democrats
Seek to Limit Powers of Chairmen, Senior Members," *National Journal*, January
2, 1971, pp. 16 ff; John Maffre, "New Leaders, Staff Changes Stimulate House
Foreign Affairs Committee," *National Journal*, June 19, 1971, pp. 1314–1322;
Congressional Quarterly, "Senate, House Committees Differ on Foreign Affairs,"
November 20, 1970, pp. 2825–2828.

as always, to maintain harmonious working relationships inside the group — has given his approval to the new internal arrangements. He seems willing, if not anxious, for his Committee to be both active and independent to a greater degree than previously. The long-run question is whether or not these internal changes will help the Committee's members to develop agreement on a new activist set of strategic premises — above and beyond (or in place of) support for the foreign aid bill. In view of their traditional frustrations (and the similar ones of their Senate counterparts) in coping with an environment that is still executive-dominated, it would be foolhardy to hazard a firm prediction, much less a positive one, concerning such a development.

On the Interior Committee, a change in *members' goals* between 1967 and 1972 seems to explain a change in internal *decision-making processes*.[3] There is a slowly increasing number of Interior members whose goals emphasize making good public policy more than achieving re-election through constituency service. These members have came to the Committee favoring a strongly preservationist natural resources policy. Commercial users are weak or nonexistent in many of their constituencies. Most of them are Easterners, some are liberal Westerners; most are Democratic, some are Republicans. They do not constitute a Committee majority. Indeed, their Committee strength is closer to about twenty per cent. But they are a growing, leavening force. And in 1971, they secured majority support for some changes in Committee rules.

The rules changes were designed to loosen Chairman Aspinall's control over internal decision making by increasing subcommittee independence in scheduling hearings, holding meetings, drawing up a budget, and hiring staff. The changes also included, as the price of support from junior Republicans, an increase in minority staffing and control over such appointments by the entire minority. The changes increased internal democracy on an already markedly democratic Committee. The proximate targets were the Committee's processes; for only such targets could draw the fire of a majority. But the impetus for the change came from liberal Democratic members

[3] Published sources for this discussion are: Interviews in 1968 and 1972; Dennis Farney, "Ruler of the Land," *Wall Street Journal,* January 21, 1972, pp. 1 ff; Joint Committee on Congressional Operations, *Rules Adopted by the Committees of Congress,* 92nd Congress, 1st Session (Washington: U.S. Government Printing Office, 1971), pp. 38–47.

who saw those processes thwarting their preservationist policy goals. The addition of three such policy-oriented members in 1967 was the first augury of change. A year later, a liberal Democrat painted this perspective of the future:

> Aspinall runs a tight ship. He works with the conservative Democrats and the Republicans. Wayne's a conservative guy. And the committee is very centralized. He watches the sub-committees closely. Oh, it's good training; but the liberals get shafted on this Committee. I don't kid myself. I don't have any influence on Interior. I'm a Sierra Club vote. I've urged other liberals — Kastenmeier and Ryan — to come on the Committee, using the Redwoods Bill as bait, saying the Committee has held up the bill. Also, the oil shale thing that's coming up. The oil lobby must be worried about what the makeup of the Committee will be someday. Up to now, the Committee has been a rotten borough of the Western Congressman. . . . I'm working with the younger Republicans laying the ground work for the rebellion I hope will come next year.

The "rebellion" came in 1971; and the man just quoted was a prime mover.

A 1972 appraisal would be that the Committee's decision processes have been altered slightly, but without any concomitant alteration in Committee decisions. Chairman Aspinall, surprised by the changes but devoted to the idea of Committee rules, rode with the punch and is as much the Committee's leader as he ever was. His own appraisal of the rules changes is simply that they have brought "a slowdown in the work." An official of Friends of the Earth, a strongly preservationist group, saw even less change. He said:

> I think we got better legislation out of the last couple of congresses than this one. So the rules changes haven't helped us at all as far as we can see. Actually it's worse.

As for why policy-oriented members have not, as yet, made a big imprint on Interior Committee decision-making or decisions, this same official mused:

> They are usually preoccupied with their other committee assignment. So they don't provide any leadership. They vote with us, but they don't take the time to learn about the subject matter. They don't have a real interest. On the Sawtooth Recreation Bill, we couldn't even get one of them to

make our motion for us. So what good are they if you can't
even get them to make a motion?

The Committee members who *do* know the subject matter and *do*
take a real interest are those with goals of constituency service and
re-election. Mostly Westerners, the stakes are, for them, more immediate and the incentives to participate greater. They are still a
solid majority. And, in the 1972 assessment of one preservationist
group leader, "They look upon Aspinall as their guardian and savior,
not the enemy." That is, of course, because Chairman Aspinall
shares their strategic premises. But winds of change are blowing
through the Committee to a degree not present in the period from
1955 to 1966. Already, said one observer, "it's just not as happy a
world as it was." Should more policy-oriented members come to the
Committee, we would expect to see Interior — the most fragile of
our "corporate" committees — move from the "corporate" toward
the "permeable" end of the committee spectrum.*

In 1967, Education and Labor acquired a new Chairman, Carl
Perkins of Kentucky.[4] In this case, what might seem from the outside to be a major change was *not* — because none of the explanatory variables of our analysis changed and because the new Chairman shared the strategic premises of the members. Carl Perkins was a
veteran cog in the Committee's liberal-Democratic majority; he had
always been responsive to labor and educational clientele groups and
to Democratic administrations. He willingly accepted the institutionally feeble chairmanship forced on his predecessor and ran the
Committee in accordance with its tenets. In his view, "The job of
the chairman is to keep the Committee running smoothly, to move
the legislation along in as expeditious and orderly a manner as possible." Some Committee members were pleased. A leader of the revolt against Powell commented, in 1968:

> Carl Perkins is running the Committee the way a chairman
> should. He's working for the Committee and trying to move

---

* Chairman Aspinall was defeated in a primary election in September, 1972.
As of January 1973, James Haley of Florida became Chairman. Haley gives his
views in: Paul Leventhal, "Outlook 73," *National Journal*, November 11, 1972,
pp. 1755–1757.

[4] Published sources for this discussion are: Jean M. White, "Marking Up of
Poverty Bill Provides Rare Public Spectacle," *Washington Post*, October 20,
1967, pp. A1 ff; Judy Gardner, "Carl D. Perkins: The Poor Are Always With
Him," *National Journal*, January 8, 1972, pp. 73–74.

things along. He's not throwing a log jam in your way all the
time. I believe that the Chairman should be an executive
officer working for the Committee, expediting the Committee's business and not acting like lord and master.

This managerial view of the chairmanship gave — as the members
intended it should — free rein to policy partisanship and policy individualism.

By all accounts, Education and Labor's decision-making processes
and its decisions have remained exactly as we have described them.
When, for example, Chairman Perkins countered Republican delay-
ing tactics on the 1967 poverty bill by holding public markup sessions, the Committee's internal processes were put on public view.
The *Washington Post* described this "spectacle" as a combination
of "silly semantics, parliamentary tangles, good humor, bad tempers,
honest doubts, parochial politics, bipartisan emotions, sincere bill
drafting efforts, and unabashed grandstanding" — to produce a bill
that emerged "tattered and torn" after a week of "bickering, bluster-
ing, and maneuvering." An institutionally weak chairman can rely
only on personal force to influence this very typical Committee performance. And Perkins is not a man of commanding personal force.
Some members seem a little unhappy about that fact. Said one:

> Carl Perkins doesn't control the Committee as tightly as he
> should. It's very loose. . . . The members don't respect his
> expertise or his political power. And they may put things in
> the bill that Perkins doesn't want. They like him but they
> won't follow him. Maybe that's good. Maybe that's the way
> a committee should be run, with the members in control.

Indeed, that is exactly what the members have wanted — to control
the Committee free from a forceful chairman. For they believe this
arrangement provides them with the optimal opportunity to pursue
"good" public policy in a partisan, pluralistic environment. They
have revolted against two chairmen who failed to share that view.
Now that they have one who does, to expect him to exert a special
degree of influence is to expect to have their cake and eat it too. The
case of Education and Labor, 1967–1972, provides more supporting
evidence for our contention that *every chairman* must be studied
and evaluated *only* in terms of the member goals, environmental
constraints, and strategic premises of *his* committee.

Turning, finally, to *citizen* interest in congressional committees, such interest seems certain to continue — especially in the context of efforts at congressional reform. If the legislative reorganization acts of 1946 and 1970 are any indication, citizen reform advocates will still devote most of their time, energy, and discussion to committee practices. To them, this book commends a somewhat different strategy from the one they normally employ. It is, we think, poor description and wishful prescription for them to operate on the assumption that all committees are alike, should be reformed alike, and can be reformed alike. Since committees differ, reformers might be well advised to adopt a selective strategy, one which operates on a committee-by-committee basis rather than one which seeks blanket changes for all committees. Whatever the presumed target of committee reform, it seems clear from this study that diagnoses will have to differ from committee to committee. And, we would contend, prescriptions should vary accordingly.

To take only the gross distinction between corporate and permeable committees, it seems unlikely that the same kinds of changes will be equally appropriate to both clusters. In the first place, there would seem to be a necessary trade-off between the degree of influence and the degree of responsiveness that a committee can exhibit. And the reformer will have to be clear just how much of the influence of corporate committees or how much of the responsiveness of permeable committees he wishes to give up in order to introduce more of the weaker characteristic. This kind of assessment must be made both within the House and between the House and the Senate.

In the second place, within the corporate cluster there are differences between those committees whose members' goals stress influence in the chamber and those whose members' goals do not. The first type is likely to be more resistant and less fragile in coping with reforms than the second. Similarly, within the permeable cluster, committee responsiveness runs to different outside groups — to political parties, to the executive branch, and to clientele groups. And reforms applicable to one may not be applicable to another.

In the third place, if we look beyond the corporate/permeable distinction at all the dimensions conventionally used to discuss committees — their autonomy, their representativeness, their expertise, their domination by the chairman, their partisanship, their success on the floor, their subservience to the executive, their policy performance, etc. — it is obvious that for each separate dimension, committees must be arrayed along a spectrum. And a change that is appropriate to a committee at one end of a spectrum may be grossly inappropriate to a committee at the other.

One cannot know whether a selective reform strategy would be any more successful than the more global strategy to which interested citizens have for so long been addicted. Perhaps a combination of strategies would be most promising. But it can be noted that individual committees have, by themselves, changed their own practices in ways far more significant than the reorganization acts of 1946 and 1970. Some of these changes have fallen within the purview of our analysis. Others are mentioned in this Epilogue. The point is that important changes have been brought about by particular committees in response to the goals of their particular members and in response to expectations generated in their particular environments. The logic is retail, not wholesale. And citizen reform advocates could do worse than attune themselves to the logic of repeated success instead of the logic of repeated failure.

The seniority rule is only the most visible of such failures. Generations of reform advocates have inveighed against the method of selecting committee chairmen, have made it the focal point of their effort, and have failed to change it. At the same time, piecemeal changes within individual committees have been rendering that target increasingly irrelevant and symbolic. Committee majorities have been taking control of their committees — in their own way and in their own time — to eliminate many of the substantive consequences of the seniority rule. And they have done it without altering the rule. Reforms are coming about, but by a logic foreign to many reformers. The mass media have not helped. They have fed the citizenry altogether too many facile commentaries on the seniority rule in terms of the age, region, and philosophy of committee chairmen.[5] And they have attempted altogether too few analyses of the degree of agreement between committee chairmen and their committee members on strategic premises or decision rules. The demographic kind of analysis can, and is, done in wholesale, summary fashion. The contextual kind of analysis must be done on a retail, committee-by-committee basis. And we will learn far more about committee problems, processes, and prospects for reform from the

---

[5] One excellent scholarly analysis of the seniority rule and the committee chairmen it produces is: Barbara Hinckley, *The Seniority System in Congress* (Bloomington: University of Indiana Press, 1971). From another angle, her findings, too, diminish the importance of the seniority rule.

second kind of analysis than from the first. Contextual analysis will, moreover, direct our attention away from the seniority rule and toward the more important determinants of each committees performance. Much more consequential for changing congressional committee practices than a change in the seniority rule would be changes in the personal goals of a committee's members or a change in the configuration of environmental constraints within which a committee's members work. Citizen reformers might profitably try to effect these kinds of changes — on a committee-by-committee, chamber-by-chamber basis. Such is the redirection of discussion and effort commended to them by this book.

The subject of the Epilogue has been committee change. Whether one wishes to understand change or to engineer change, a capacity to differentiate among committees is essential. Whether the descriptive and explanatory devices offered in this study are equally essential remains, of course, an open question.

Appendix A

Number of Individuals Interviewed*

	House Committees							Senate Committees				
	App.	E.&L.	F.A.	Int.	P.O.	W.&M.	App.	Fin.	F.R.	Int.	L.&P.W.	P.O.
Committee Members	43(1959) 5(1960) 2(1961) 2(1963) 24(1964) 1(1965) 1(1968)	21(1961) 7(1965) 13(1968)	30(1965)	2(1964) 28(1965) 1(1968)	15(1965) 1(1968)	15(1964) 12(1965)	15(1960) 3(1961)	8(1965)	8(1965)	11(1965)	1(1961) 6(1965)	5(1965)
Committee Staff	5(1959) 3(1961) 2(1963) 2(1968)	2(1961) 3(1965) 1(1968)	1(1965)	1(1965)	1(1965)	3(1964) 1(1965)	4(1960) 2(1961)	1(1965)	1(1965)	1(1965)	1(1961) 2(1965)	—
Executive Officials	41(1960)	3(1968)	2(1968)	3(1968)	1(1968)	3(1964) 1(1968)		Same as for House Committee				
Clientele Group Officials	—	4(1968)	—	4(1968)	3(1968)	2(1968)		Same as for House Committee				
House Leaders	12 (scattered)											

*No interviewee listed more than once in any one year.

292

Index